Providing for the Older Adult

A GERONTOLOGICAL HANDBOOK

Sandra Cutler Lewis, MFA, OTR

About the Author

S andra Cutler Lewis, MFA, OTR received her bachelor's and master's degrees from the University of Pennsylvania. Articles pertaining to geriatrics have been published in journals such as: *The Gerontologist*, the *American Journal of Occupational Therapy, Hospital and Community Psychiatry, Osteopathic Annals*, the *Activity Director's Guide*, and the *Journal of the American Geriatrics Society*. Most recently she has completed a book entitled, *The Mature Years: A Geriatric Occupational Therapy Text*. She is also listed in *Who's Who of American Women*.

Past work experience in adult care has included: community evening arts programs in a settlement house; psychiatric occupational therapy in a private mental hospital; occupational therapy in a rehabilitation center, and acute care occupational therapy in a general hospital. Since 1972 she has worked solely in geriatrics in a large state mental hospital. During this time Ms. Lewis has been a member of a multidisciplinary, community-based program that focused upon preventing institutionalization as well as serving patients within the institution. Her services as a consultant to nursing homes have been frequently requested. She was also responsible for developing a field work curriculum for occupational therapy students in geropsychiatry.

Ms. Lewis has lectured on topics pertaining to gerontology at a number of universities and colleges and has coordinated and presented a variety of workshops and seminars to employees at institutions and community centers. Her audience has included physicians, psychologists, physical therapists, recreational therapists, social workers, occupational therapists, nurses, gerontologists, student nurses, residents, architects, lawyers, nursing home administrators, nurses' aides, and activities workers. Her most recent involvement, in the area of gerontological education, includes occupational therapy consulting to a home care training center. As part of a multidisciplinary team she has shared the responsibility for the development and presentation of an intense 15 week curriculum for home health aides.

She has been a speaker at a number of multidisciplinary conferences and has initiated several educationally-oriented community projects that relate to the elderly.

Sandra Cutler Lewis, MFA, OTR

Supervisor of Geriatric and Physical Restoration Services
Occupational Therapy Department
Norristown State Hospital
Norristown, PA

Occupational Therapy Consultant
Long Term Care Service
Norristown State Hospital
Norristown, PA

Occupational Therapy Consultant
St. Mary's Manor
Lansdale, PA

Consultant and Instructor
Temple University Health Management Training Center
Temple University
Philadelphia, PA

Foreword

In an increasingly complex world, problems become more complex. Fortunately, resources for dealing with these problems increase apace. This increase in resource options, however, creates a problem in that new resources may not be widely known or may be a new part of a known resource system not traditionally associated with the specific problem. This text provides needed information for service providers, and those who train service providers, in the care of the elderly with that vital linkage between diagnosed problems and available treatment resources.

Its format is clear, concise and thorough, providing the reader with ready access to the major issues on aging. Among the topics covered are:

— Theories of aging
— Biological, physical and socioeconomic changes relating to the older person
— Advocacy
— Methods for combating ageist attitudes
— Case histories
— Problem-solving techniques
— Problems of the adult child as caretaker
— The roles of a variety of disciplines in caring for the elderly client

Probably the most generally useful aspect of this text is the detailed exposition of the numerous gerontological and therapeutic programs that provide caregivers with a rich array of useful treatment modalities.

I would expect this text to quickly become a well-worn addition to the library of the trainer of service providers for the elderly.

Toby Friedman, M.A.
Executive Director
Temple University Health Management Training Center

I would expect this text to quickly become a well-worn addition to the library of the trainer of service providers for the elderly.

Toby Friedman, M.A.
Executive Director
Temple University Health Management Training Center

Preface

T he purpose of this book is to provide a comprehensive examination of aging, and a pragmatic guide for gerontological practitioners. Included within this concept is a compilation of communication techniques and programs that can readily be utilized by caregivers. Resources and references regarding jobs relating to gerontology and empathetic programs concerning the elderly are also explored.

Discussion and interviews with the well elderly and service providers in the field (eg, nursing, social work, psychology) present a stimulating forum concerning some older people's views about successful aging, and individual caregiver's reflections about their functions and responsibilities. Within the context of the professional interviews there are discussions of case histories and how specific intervention methods were helpful to the well-being of a particular client. The problems facing the adult child in caring for frail elderly parents are also frankly discussed.

This book, built upon the foundations of *The Mature Years: A Geriatric Occupational Therapy Text,* is in response to a number of persons from a variety of disciplines, who approached me and asked if a second book, similar to the first but targeted at a wider and more general audience, could be written. Because of the rapid growth of, and the many developments in, the field of aging at this time, preparing a gerontological handbook has been especially challenging and exciting.

I would specifically like to express my gratitude to Doris Kaplan, Director of Occupational Therapy, for her encouragement of this project, and to the staff of the Occupational Therapy Department at the Norristown State Hospital for their support and interest.

One of the most helpful services in this undertaking has been the library, and I wish to acknowledge my appreciation to the librarians at the Norristown State Hospital and the Montgomery County (PA) Public Library for their efficient and professional assistance.

Special thanks are also extended to all the caring people who generously gave their time and energy in being interviewed.

To my husband, Paul Lewis, and my children, Ethan, Judy, and Sharon, I would like to express my love and deep appreciation for their stalwart support and encouragement.

I would like to conclude with the thought that age prejudice concerns us all. Each one of us bears the responsibility of trying to eliminate ageist attitudes. How and where do we start to develop positive images, in terms of aging? It is my frank opinion that attitudes about the older adult begin in the home. In this respect, everyone can help to change negative attitudes about the old. If we teach our children to value the continuum of life, then quite possibly the ageist stereotypes of the elderly will not be present in future generations.

Sandra Cutler Lewis, MFA, OTR

Contents

Providing
for the
Older Adult

A GERONTOLOGICAL
HANDBOOK

1
Shaping Attitudes About Elders

G rowing old in a society that worships at the altar of youth and the latest technological advances often means that the older person is devaluated within the social, intellectual, and economic hierarchy of his own community. Attitudes—how we feel about something—direct the quality and manner in which we perceive ourselves and others. Attitudes can be used as a compelling and powerful force. For example, in *Anatomy of an Illness: As Perceived by the Patient,* Norman Cousins relates how positive attitudes, including laughter and a general uplifting approach to life, were used as weapons in his personal war against disease.[1] Our attitudes and fear of growing old are an interwoven part of the plastic world we live in. Our society is in need of a healthier view of aging.

Christopher Lasch takes a sobering view of American society and its relationship towards aging. He proposes that two approaches to the problem of aging have emerged. One focuses upon improving the quality of life, and the other deals with aging in terms of advancing the life span through medical and scientific discoveries. Both rest upon an aversion to the prospect of bodily decay. Although people have always feared death, an almost irrational panic concerning aging seems to have developed. What lies behind this fear?

Lasch feels that our society views older persons as useless. Retirement means the right to enjoy life. Older people are expected to have nothing better to do with their time than relax.

By devaluating wisdom and experience, and emphasizing physical strength, dexterity, and the ability to constantly develop new ideas, society defines productive life in terms that automatically exclude older adults.

Lasch firmly believes that the terror of old age and death is associated with the emergence of narcissism as a contemporary way of life. In past times, work and love were united in a concern for posterity. It was the older generation's responsibility to hand down knowledge and wisdom to the younger. Because knowledge is now considered in terms of technological change, traditional wisdom and knowledge have become old-fashioned and, consequently, non-transferable. It is as though the older generation has little or nothing to teach their children. This superfluity of old age has its origin in the severance of a sense of historical continuity. It is Lasch's contention that the prolongevity movement is not born from a natural response to medical improvements but rather from changing social relationships and attitudes which cause a loss of interest in posterity. People desperately cling to their own youth and seek every means possible to prolong their lives. Thus, it is hoped that old age can be abolished completely. Lasch holds that the fear of age is not based upon a cult of youth, but rather upon a cult of the self.[2]

With these concepts bombarding our consciousness, is it any wonder, in the age of the plastic society, that plastic surgery to remove signs of aging has become so popular? If one cannot be young, he might as well look young. Why should a person be made to feel ashamed of aging skin spots, wrinkles, or graying hair? If one's life experience has value, then perhaps earning these characteristics would shed a new meaning to one's existence. These physical aspects of aging, no longer a badge of shame to be hidden by make-up or dye, could be valued as a badge of respect and a sign of a beautiful person.

Society, Literature and Aging

How a culture views itself can be manifested through its literature, its heritage, its work ethic, and its social practices. Our attitudes towards human beauty are based upon the ancient Greek tradition that idealized youth as beautiful.

Elizabethan England was no exception in sharing man's dread of the aging process. The closing lines of Jacques' speech in William Shakespeare's *As You Like It* describe the seventh and last stage of man's life..."Last scene of all, that ends this strange eventful history, is second childishness, and mere oblivion, sans teeth, sans eyes, sans taste, sans everything."[3] The concept that the aged are primarily senile and helpless is thus perpetuated for posterity.

Although we cannot say that it is only in this century that man has become critical of his aging peers, certain changes wrought by the full development of the Industrial Revolution and the machine age (eg, forced retirement) have only added a deeper message to Shakespeare's lines. Formerly, a person could work at his profession or trade until he felt it was time to reduce his own work load. However, with today's mandatory retirement age, many people experience a loss of identity at a premature age.

An examination of contemporary artistic and literary endeavors reveals how our society perceives aging today. Sharon Curtin's quest to understand what it is like to be old in today's America took her across the United States. Her brief statement: "We dote on youth. We shelve the old, and what does this say about the whole of life?"[4] We should pause to think about our priorities concerning life's values. Today there is more than a generation gap. There is a true separation of the ages.

Excerpts from Simon and Garfunkel's *Bookends* album, written when they were in their 20s, testifies to the significance of the separation, loneliness, and superfluousness of the older person as viewed by the younger person:

> Can you imagine us
> Years from today
> Sharing a park bench quietly?
> How terribly strange
> To be 70...
>
> *Old Friends*

> Long ago...it must be...
> I have a photograph.
> Preserve your memories,
> They're all that's left you.
>
> *Bookends Theme**

Television, one of this century's major mass communicators, has also played its role as an interpreter of the country's actions. In the early days of television Edward Albee wrote a brief but poignant play, *The Sandbox*. These words belong to Grandma.

...Honestly! What a way to treat an old woman! Drag her out of the house...stick her in a car...bring her in a pile of sand...and leave her here to set. I'm 86 years old! I was married when I was 30...I'm a feeble old woman...How do you expect anybody to hear me over the peep! peep!...There's no respect around here...

They took me off the farm...which was real decent of them...and they moved me into the big town house with them...fixed a nice place for me under the stove...gave me a blanket...and my own dish...my very own dish! So what have I got to complain about! Nothing, of course I'm not complaining.[5]

A society's sense of humor often reflects its attitudes towards values that it honors or devaluates. It was noted in a recent study that involved a content analysis of 2,217 cartoons from a variety of American magazines, that certain negative themes regarding the elderly recurred frequently. These included sexual dysfunction, ultra-conservative attitudes, mental incompetency, and/or physical infirmities. Even those cartoons which portrayed the elderly as competent were tinged with negative attitudes, as their main point was to depict the older adult in unusual or unexpected roles.[6]

The quality of care a society gives its needy citizens has always been a hallmark of its attitude towards human values. The scandalous conditions in some boarding and nursing homes have awakened us to the fact that we have to be rigorous in our demands for quality care in facilities that serve older adults.

Simon P, Garfunkel A: Bookends. *New York, Charing Cross Music, 1968.*

However, in recent years investigative reporting has been involved in a more sensitive and perhaps more secretive issue—that of elderly parent abuse. This condition, often referred to as the King Lear Syndrome, appears to be coming out of the closet. The abuse can range from physical violence—body burns, wounds, sexual molestation, and being tethered in cramped and dirty quarters—to verbal threatening—forcing an older person to grovel for food, or extorting a pensioner's check by threats. Some researchers feel that many adult children reach a breaking point when tending a bed-wetting, frail elderly parent. There may be guilt associated with placing a parent in an institution. For many, learning to cope with these problems is a stressful experience. There are few financial aids, day-care, or public counseling programs available to alleviate the pressures that many of these children of older adults feel. Only 11 states require professionals to report cases of elderly abuse. However, in 1978, the state of Connecticut took an even greater step by requiring anyone who deals with the elderly to report suspicious occurrences or risk a $5,000 fine.[7] There is much work that lies ahead in the area of parent neglect/abuse. As the number of older people continues to grow, this problem can only increase.

Social practices, in terms of the use of leisure time, also give testimony to the values a society holds important. We turn again to the largest mass communicator, television. Much in the way of attitudes is transmitted through this medium; not only does it reflect how others view aging, it also affects how the elderly perceive themselves. It is interesting to note that television viewing increases with age. Content analysis of television programming reveals that there is an underrepresentation of the aged—particularly older women. It has been hypothesized that isolated old people may be particularly vulnerable to television's influence in areas concerning social roles. It is especially true of this viewing group because they are less likely to test the validity of what they have seen. Besides a negative self-image, there are other repercussions. It has been positively correlated that the poor diet which stems from a heavy intake of snacks is directly related to heavy television viewing. Moreover, since television is primarily a passive experience, the older person can actually be influenced to withdraw more from the world of activity by increased television viewing. On the other hand, television can be used as a positive force. It should be noted that when certain series concerned with aging were watched on television (for example, *Getting On*), the impressions of the vitality and efficacy of older adults improved. Not only did older people feel better about their peers, but younger viewers made substantial revisions in their initial negative attitudes towards aging.[8]

Professional Attitudes

In recent years, federal funding has brought new financial support to agencies concerned with aging persons. Many professionals have begun to become actively involved in caring for older people, and professional literature concerning older adults is increasing rapidly. However, providing appropriate services, and overcoming such attitudes as older persons are uninteresting, unrewarding, or difficult to treat or care for is still a formidable task. In an interview for the *APA Monitor*, Dr. Robert Butler, the first director of the

National Institute of Aging, spoke about the concerns and needs of the elderly receiving quality health care. When asked what the role was that the mental health professions play in alleviating the mental and emotional problems that are associated with aging, Dr. Butler replied:

> Unfortunately, very little. They share society's ambivalence and negativism toward the old, but it's disguised in professional trappings. Their disinterest in the aged, [often] combined with...discrimination on the part of agencies and institutions, means that for most old people mental health services are unobtainable.

Dr. Butler continued to explain that most nursing homes rarely provide psychiatric services, even though some 50% of their patients may suffer from mental and psychological impairment. [9]

More Older Adults: New Concerns

There was a time when books and information on aging and gerontology were at a minimum. Now, we are experiencing a plethora of information about the elderly. If we note that at the turn of the nineteenth century 3.1% of the total population of the United States was over 65 and that today 10% of the total population is in that age group, we see a dramatic increase. It is estimated that more than 32 million Americans will be over 65 by the year 2000.[10] Although a new interest in aging is emerging, pervasive negative attitudes still exist.

New legislation—most notably the Older Americans Act—has been designed to increase services to the elderly. Despite the best of intentions a number of problems have emerged. Carroll Estes warns that it is the aging enterprise, and not older Americans, that has become the focus of government policy. According to Estes, this growing bureaucracy's survival depends upon continuing the dependent status of older Americans. The agencies that were created by Congress primarily to solve problems related to aging have succeeded in institutionalizing these problems. Estes argues that the needs of the agencies are replacing the needs of the aged.[11]

Once a quiet minority, older adults have become an increasing focus of attention. In the fall of 1979 *The Wall Street Journal* documented a series of articles entitled, "Aging Americans." This series was devoted to the triumphs and tribulations of the rising number of older Americans. Several issues were examined, some of which are as follows:

> 1) There will be a consistently greater life expectancy in the years ahead. The population of the very old (those 80 and above) is expected to increase dramatically. This ever increasing aging population will create greater income needs and higher pension costs. In response to the greater number of aging Americans, the federal government's health care budget will continue to rise.[12]
>
> 2) The results of retirement inflation and psychic well-being were explored. Most older persons are on a fixed income. To combat this problem some older employees are delaying retirement. Many of those who are already retired are trying to return to an already tight job market. Too often the

work they find is menial and part time.

In response to the psycho-social reaction to retirement, several studies were cited. One of these included the mortality rate of 4,000 people who retired from two tire companies. It was found that there was a sharp increase in the mortality rate three to four years after retirement. It is believed that this might be a direct result of a depression which has its roots in joblessness, boredom, a tight budget, and a sense of uselessness.

Some solutions to these problems are being sought by industry. For instance, some companies have adopted flextime. This includes alternatives in which older employees can select their own hours, permanent part time employment, sharing a full time job with another worker, and shorter workweeks. Another company has adopted a program that pays the educational costs of those older employees who are seeking a second career.[13]

3) Many families find their lives greatly changed by caring for their elderly parents. In 1900 one person in 25 was 65 years and older. Now the ratio is one in 9 and by the year 2000 it is expected to be one in 7. As a consequence, more families will find themselves caring for their elderly relatives. However, a new phenomenon has developed—increasing numbers of older adults (65 to 75) are now attending their very old (85+) parents.[14]

4) A growing number of older Americans find that they are easy victims to a variety of abuses, scandals, and fraud. These range from simple street crimes to elaborate schemes. For instance, a new report by the House Select Committee on Aging cites numerous medical insurance frauds. In one instance a 96-year-old Kansas resident had 26 insurance policies written on him within a three year time span. Another example of fraudulent practices is the Pacific Homes retirement communities scandal which involved the gross mismanagement of large amounts of the residents' funds and investments. Many residents lost their total life savings.[15]

Aging: A New Interest
in the Continuum of Life

The number of writers interested in the psychosocial development of the stages of life, with a special focus upon mid- and old-life, has increased dramatically in the past five years. Mid-life and old age are no longer thought of in terms of a plateau, but rather as definite periods of time in which specific behavioral patterns and transitions occur. This new interest in literature concerning aging, formerly the niche of behavioral scientists and psychiatrists, has produced an array of best-selling books. Perhaps this is an indication that many Americans, as they age, are beginning to become interested in the aging process itself.

Gail Sheehy's comments on old age, "...the delights of self-discovery are always available...for the mind freed of the constant strivings of earlier years, there is time in the later years to ponder the mysteries of existence without interruption..." reminds us that there exists an unusual opportunity in the winter of our lives.[16]

In *The Seasons of a Man's Life,* the authors deal with the concept that many dread old age as a time when they will become an empty, dried structure without energy, inner resources, or interests. Instead, the authors see this period as a time for a person to find a new balance between involvement with the self and society. It is a time to gather wisdom through a new understanding of the self, to reflect upon one's life work, and to come to grips with life and death.[17]

Roger Gould views adult life in terms of a struggle for adult consciousness. He holds that there are four major false assumptions that help to protect one's illusion of absolute safety, and thereby ensure the world of child consciousness. These assumptions are:

1) We will always live with our parents and be their child.

2) When we are unable to do something by ourselves, our parents will always be there to help us.

3) Our parent's simplified version of inner feelings and reality is correct. An example of this is the parent who turns on the bedroom light to prove there are no robbers, ghosts, or other mysterious beings.

4) Death and evil do not exist as realities in the world.

Although intellectually, by the time we graduate from high school we realize that these assumptions are not correct, emotionally, we do not understand this. It is the periodic shedding of these false assumptions that causes the gradual shift from the child consciousness to the adult consciousness. Finally, maturity is reached as the life of inner-directedness prevails—one owns oneself. At this stage, the world of competition and struggle for status slowly gives way to a new frame of reference—the mature inner-directed adult. Thus, this "mysterious indelible 'me' becomes our acknowledged core, around which we center the rest of our lives..."[18]

The Commercial World Takes Note

The advent of aging in America is upon us and Madison Avenue. Mid-lifers and older adults have become a lucrative market. *Prime Time* is the newest magazine created exclusively for those over 45 years of age. *Retirement Living* has changed its name and image and is now called *50 Plus.* The old theme of looking backward has been changed to looking forward. *Modern Maturity* (circulation approaching 7 million), the magazine for members of the American Association of Retired Persons, started carrying ads in early 1980. Cine-america, a new cable television network, will begin broadcasting programs designed for those over 50.[19]

Successful Aging

We have examined some of the problems of aging in America. Despite the pervasive negative attitude that runs within our culture, many older Americans have managed to continue their thoroughly successful and meaningful lives. What is successful aging?

Some of the attributes for successful aging include:

1) The older generation sharing with the younger the accumulated knowledge and experience of their lives. If encouraged, this function takes the form of counseling, guiding, and sponsoring younger adults.

2) The distinctive sense of the life cycle.

3) The definite sense of priorities set within the limits of the present—a sense of living in the moment.

4) Curiosity, creativity, and the ability to be surprised can contribute to a sense of productivity in late life.

5) The sense of fulfillment and satisfaction with one's life.[20]

Rollo May tells us that "the important issue is not whether a person is 20 or 40 or 60: it rather is whether he fulfills his own capacity of self-conscious choice at his particular level of development...The practical implication is that one's goal is to live each moment with freedom, honesty, and responsibility."[21]

Octogenarian Dr. Richard A. Kern, Emeritus Professor, believes that moderation of the following three activities is instrumental in obtaining successful old age: work, both mental and physical; rest; and diversion, including self-study and sharing activities with others.[22]

Many older people are now pursuing college study or instruction in areas that will promote second careers.[23] Attitudes towards successful aging can be reflected in these trends.

Successful old age includes the fact that the majority of older adults remain productive and maintain themselves in their communities. Less than 5% live in institutions. A full 70% live in their own homes, and nearly nine out of every ten elderly homeowners have paid off their mortgages.[24] Only 5% of older adults' income comes from public assistance programs; 45% of their income is derived from pensions that they had contributed to during their years of employment. A full 15% of their income is from their own savings.[25]

Those older adults who were creative in their youth continue to be creative in old age. Georgia O'Keefe, Imogen Cunningham, Arthur Rubenstein, Mark Chagall, and Pablo Picasso are some examples of older people who continued to predominate their respective fields while they were well past their 70s. Other older persons may initiate new careers and interests—for example, Grandma Moses—while still others experience a renaissance in their chosen profession—most noteworthy of this practice is actor George Burns. Then there are those persons who desire to spark, shape, and improve society. The founder of the Gray Panther movement, Maggie Kuhn, is an example of what an older person can accomplish in the arena of social concern.

Advocacy, Its Role and Function

All of us are in the aging game. If we live long enough, we too shall be old. A deep respect for the worth of every person at any stage in life should be an essential part of the human experience. Providers and consumers alike must stand firm in their commitment that all people, regardless of age, race, religion, ethnic, or economic background, are entitled to quality care. Each provider should therefore, assume an advocate's role for his client every time he renders that client a service.

References

1. Cousins N: Anatomy of an Illness: As Perceived by the Patient. New York, WW Norton and Co, 1979.
2. Lasch C: The Culture of Narcissism: American Life in an Age of Diminishing Expectations. New York, Warner Books, WW Norton and Co, 1979, pp 352-367.
3. Shakespeare W: As You Like It. Act 2, Scene 7, Line 139.
4. Curtin S: Nobody Ever Died of Old Age. Boston, Little Brown and Co, 1973, p 3.
5. Albee E: Three Plays. New York, Coward-McCann Inc, 1960, pp 149, 150, 152.
6. Smith MD: The portrayal of elders in magazine cartoons. Gerontologist 19:408-412, 1979.
7. Langway L, Zabarsk M, Hager M, Hick J: Unveiling a family secret. Newsweek, February 18, 1980, pp 104-105.
8. Kubey RW: Television and aging: Past, present, and future. Gerontologist 20:16-35, 1979.
9. Butler RN: An interview with Robert Butler. APA Monitor, March 1976, pp 14-15.
10. Goldfarb A, Frazier S: Aging and Organic Brain Syndrome. Ft Washington, PA, McNeil Laboratories, 1974, p 5.
11. Estes C: The Aging Enterprise. San Francisco, Jossey-Bass Pub, 1979.
12. Hyatt C: Aging Americans: As lives are extended, some people wonder if it's really a blessing. Wall Street Journal, Oct 25, 1979, pp 1, 27.
13. Stevens C: Aging Americans: Many delay retiring or resume jobs to beat inflation and the blues. Wall Street Journal, Nov 5, 1979, pp 1, 22.
14. Bennett A: Aging Americans: Caring for the elderly greatly changes lives of many US families. Wall Street Journal, Nov 16, 1979, pp 1, 4.
15. Montgomery J: Aging Americans: Preditors find elderly are often easy prey for array of rip-offs. Wall Street Journal, Nov 9, 1979, pp 1, 28.
16. Sheehy G: Passages. New York, Bantam Books, 1976, p 513.
17. Levinson DL, Darrow CN, Klein ED, Levinson MH, McKee B: The Seasons of a Man's Life. New York, Alfred A Knopf, 1978, pp 35, 36.
18. Gould RL: Transformations: Growth and Change in Adult Life. New York, Simon & Schuster, 1978, pp 39, 311.
19. A magazine for the over-45 set. Newsweek, December 31, 1979, p 50.
20. Butler RN, Lewis MI: Aging and Mental Health: Positive Psychosocial Approaches. St Louis, CV Mosby Co, 1973, pp 24-28.
21. May R: Man's Search for Himself. New York, WW Norton and Co, 1953, pp 233, 235.
22. Kern RA: Successful Aging. A One-Day Seminar on Aging. Fifth Annual Weiss-English Psychosomatic Symposium, Sponsored by the Temple University School of Medicine and the Academy of Psychosomatic Medicine, Philadelphia, November 17, 1979.
23. Hechinger FM: Education's new majority. Saturday Review, Sept 20, 1975, pp 14-19.
24. Rabushka A, Jacobs B: Are old folks really poor? Here with a look at some common views. New York Times, February 15, 1979, p A29.
25. What Do You Want to Be When You Grow Old? New York, Roering-Pfizer Pharmaceuticals, May 1976, p ii.

2
Older Adults
Speak Out

I s there a formula for vitality after age 65? How do older people spend their time? What are their interests and concerns? The value of each human being is of paramount importance. Having a forum from which the older adult can clarify these important issues and sharing that knowledge and wisdom with others is an enriching experience both for the audience and the speaker.

The older adult who is successfully living in the community has much to tell us. Studying statistics and trends are extremely helpful in determining information about any given subject. However, determining a profile of what an "average" senior citizen should be is a most difficult task. People do not seem to fit into a standard mold. Indeed, when one is speaking with an individual, it is the uniqueness of that person and his contributions to society that are of value. Each human being lives through a specific time in history and reacts to his or her experiences in a unique way. The interviews contained within this chapter reflect this uniqueness.

Each participant had to meet the following criteria:

1) Be willing to speak candidly. The person being interviewed had the choice of total anonymity or identification;

2) Be age 65 or older;

3) Be living independently in the community.

This series of interviews represents an opportunity for older people, who come from a rich variety of cultures, to share with others their thoughts and feelings concerning maintaining a meaningful life.

Interviews

Interview with: Mary Korr,* 65-year-old widow, the retired associate editor for a biological journal, currently weaving and designing latchhook rugs.

Question: Would you please highlight some of your educational and employment experiences?

Answer: *I graduated first in my class from an urban all-girl high school. I continued my studies on a scholarship at a large Ivy League university, graduating in 1935 with honors and distinction with a BA in Botany. Later I received a Master's degree in Botany.*

My first full time job, starting in 1938, was with the Department of Public Assistance, where I worked for about three years, until my daughter's birth. Three years later my son was born. Most of my time was devoted to caring for my children, but I did work for a while as a part time assistant manager of a movie house.

While my children were growing up I was very much involved in various community activities. For example, I edited the community newspaper for five years, and was a committeewoman for 16 years. I also was active in the reform movement, a successful one fortunately, in the city where I still live.

When the children were ready for college, it became desirable to have supplemental income for tuition; so I decided to go back to full time work. I applied for a job with a biological journal and was hired as an editorial assistant. Eventually I moved up to associate editor. I worked for this firm for approximately 12 years.

Question: Since your retirement, what kinds of things interest you?

Answer: *I continue to enjoy doing things with my hands. Long ago I had tried clay sculpture and ceramics, and more recently, in the 60s, I attended painting classes. After I retired in 1972, I thought I would try something different and decided on latchhook work. Once I mastered this very simple technique by using a commercial kit, I began to create my own designs for wall hangings. Since I work from a small black and white sketch, knowing the colors only in my mind, every creation in a sense becomes an adventure. I've also done some collages and a little painting. I maintain a large collection of indoor plants, and I do quite a bit of reading.*

Question: Does your arthritis get in your way as you work?

Answer: *Some achiness and stiffness develop. When that happens I simply stop for a while, then start again. If you really want to do something, you just go ahead and do it.*

Question: What makes a full and meaningful life?

Answer: *You must continue to build up your inner resources. As long as you are breathing you should be learning and growing as an individual. But you also must not forget that we all have a responsibility to the community in which*

*Used with the permission of Mrs. Mary Korr.

we live. We have to keep informed on what is going on around us, and to take positive action when necessary or desirable.

I suppose, when you get down to basics, it's our human relationships that are the most important thing in life. Other people are really our lifeline; we are all dependent on each other for emotional as well as physical sustenance. So we must remain interested in people.

Question: Could you tell me how your personal aging has affected you?

Answer: When I look in the mirror I'm constantly surprised, because inside I don't feel the age of the person whose reflection I see. I still do pretty much the kinds of things I've always been interested in, but at a slower pace, and they do seem to require greater effort. I guess when you've been used to doing things you just go right on doing them.

I think one of the bonuses growing older has brought me is greater patience with people and circumstances. The only thing that still gets me hopping mad is injustice in any form, and I hope I never lose the capacity to feel this kind of anger.

Interview with: Dr. X, 77 years old, married, retired university professor emeritus, currently involved in researching history pertaining to Chinese culture and writing Chinese poetry.

Question: Would you please highlight some of your educational and vocational experiences?

Answer: I arrived in the United States in 1923 and enrolled in a rigorous undergraduate and graduate program in mechanical engineering. Six years later, after completing my studies, I returned to China.

During that period, through a governmental position, I was involved with the educational development of Chinese children from kindergarten through the university level in both the private and public sector.

At that time, there was great flux in China. While the United States was experiencing a depression, we in China lived through a long period of war, starting around 1931. World War II brought occupation by the Japanese. Later, a revolution between Nationalist and Communist forces erupted and many were forced to flee to Taiwan.

Question: Although you are an engineer by profession, I understand you have many other interests.

Answer: Cultural development of the individual is very important to his growth and understanding of the world and himself. I have always enjoyed learning and studying a variety of subjects. Some of these have included traditional Chinese music, poetry, and art.

Question: How did you return to the United States?

Answer: In the early 50s I was invited to teach mechanical engineering at a large, private northeastern university, and I remained there until my retirement in 1972.

Question: What were your interests and duties during this period?

Answer: As a professor and teacher it is vital to be involved in learning about and understanding the latest developments. After all, one is responsible for the education of students. This means that the teacher must himself keep continuously learning. Reading current journals, papers, and books, and attending conferences are some ways in which one can continue his education. Participating in research is another. There is an obligation for one to invest his energy into contributing and adding to his special field of interest.

Question: What types of things interest you today?

Answer: *Everything is of interest—engineering, art, music, reading, talking with friends. When one gets really old, then there is time to be interested in a lot of things.*

Question: Do you have any advice you would like to share about aging?

Answer: *Yes. Retire as early as possible and live a long life! Our life today is full of stress. Knowing when to stop the stressful life is the question. Most people know when that time comes but being able to act is another question. It is a wise person who knows how and when to stop. Why press on and on? Because each person's time is an individual matter, it is very difficult to say that a specific age is the right time.*

As we go through life we experience good and hard times. No one's life is smooth because the times will not permit it. There is a saying—"If prices go up, eat less, enjoy more." We do not need anxiety. Each person should set up his own standards as he ages, and find his own baseline.

Question: You are very modest about your accomplishments and your interests. I understand that you have recently completed a book on the history of Zen and that you have also published a book of 500 of your own Chinese poems.

Answer: *I have always had a lifelong interest in these things.*

Question: What do you think about retirement communities?

Answer: *I know a number of people who enjoy this type of life. For myself, I enjoy living in the center of the city, close to cultural events. It helps to keep one independent. I can come and go as I please and take advantage of nearby museums, libraries, theaters, the cinema, lectures, and concerts. There are more options for me to choose from, and if I wish to travel to another area, I can readily take a train or a bus.*

Because of limited transportation services, suburban living would not be in my best interest. For instance, when I visit my daughter, who lives in the suburbs, I cannot even walk to get a newspaper, because nothing is convenient. For the smallest item I need the services of another person. Even if there is a transportation strike in the city, I can still walk out of my apartment and take care of my needs.

Interview with: Hermenegildo Camacho,* 65 years old, married, a retired bridge crane operator, currently involved in church and community related activities.

Question: Would you please highlight some of your previous life experiences?

Answer: *I was born in Bayamon, Puerto Rico, a suburban community near San Juan. There were ten children in our family. I have three older sisters, one*

*Used with the permission of Mr. Hermenegildo Camacho.

older brother, three younger brothers, and two younger sisters. After approximately eight years of schooling I started working in 1937 as a bridge crane operator, for a sugar refining mill in Puerto Rico, loading and unloading large bags of sugar.

In 1944 I was inducted into the United States Army and was stationed in Ponce, a city in the southern part of the island, where I was trained as an operator of land mortars. World War II ended, and I was discharged in 1945.

At that time I got work in a foundry as a bridge crane operator. I was married in December of 1948 (my wife and I have four children and one grandchild) and came to New York City in July of 1949 looking for greater economic opportunities. In my first job I worked in a spring factory. That job required tremendous physical strength, as you had to grip the wires and twist them with a pliers. My hands were always scratched and bleeding, and I often looked as though I had been in a cat fight. My wife encouraged me to seek another kind of job and suggested perhaps I should get work doing what I had some training in—bridge crane operating. So I applied for work in the Brooklyn Naval Shipyard and was able to find a job there working as a bridge crane operator.

In 1965 the Brooklyn Naval Shipyard was closed, and I was told that if I wished to stay with the government, I should apply for work in Boston or Philadelphia. The Philadelphia Naval Shipyard had the most openings, and so I came to that city with a very close friend who had worked with me in Brooklyn. I needed to find a new home for me and my family. It was very important that the house be near a church and a school. My friend and I stayed together, cooking and generally looking out for each other, until our families could be reunited with us. My wife and I and three of our children are still living in that house today.

Question: Since your retirement, what types of things do you enjoy doing?

Answer: We have always based our lives and happiness around the Church and our family. Both my wife and I belong to religious service groups within our church and parish. For instance, I serve as an usher. We enjoy participating in Mass and observing the festivals and processions.

Our family gives us great pleasure. My little grandson will be starting first grade soon, and we are very proud of him.

We enjoy our home. Just now we are putting some new cabinets in the kitchen. My brother comes over often, and we play checkers together.

I enjoy going to a baseball game or watching it on television. Sometimes there might be a good movie—a comedy or religious based film—that is of interest.

Also, I belong to the Edad de Oro—Golden Age Club—that is related to my parish. There are about 15 members. We meet in different neighborhood churches once a month. In addition we have a special monthly event. For example, recently we visited a section of the city known as Manayunk. We learned about the customs of Indians and the pioneers who had lived there, as well as the later work history, such as the mules that were used on the canal. It was very interesting. Other trips have included visits to famous shrines. The *sister involved in organizing this group also visits us individually in our homes.*

Question: What kind of advice would you give to others regarding staying active after retirement?

Answer: *It is very important to make and keep friendships. I like telling stories in Spanish that are enjoyable to others and that make people laugh. I would like everyone to get along with each other. People should see and be a part of the bright side of life. You are never alone if you are among good friends and family.*

Interview with: Abe Egnal,* 72 years old, married, retired high school teacher, currently teaching part time at a private university.

Question: Would you please highlight your educational and work experiences?

Answer: *I graduated from a large private university with a major in Business— Real Estate to be exact—and started working upon graduation in 1929, just in time for the Depression! At that time I received a position through the university's placement service, in an insurance company. Ostensibly, I was in training to be an executive. Part of the training involved insurance collection. Because of my intense dislike for this facet of the work, I quit my job and decided to go back to school to get credits that would qualify me as a teacher.*

While attending college I supported myself by obtaining part time office work. It took me about a year to qualify. In 1931 I took the teaching exams for a large city high school system. There were no regular appointments then, but I was able to secure an appointment as a full time substitute teacher at $6 a day. This meant that I went wherever I was needed. In 1933 I took as many exams as I could (federal exams, teaching, and liquor store clerk exams). At that time the Depression was full-blown, and one out of every four or five people were out of work. I was fortunate to find permanent work as a liquor store clerk.

Later, in May of 1935, I found that I had qualified for two permanent jobs— teaching high school history and social studies, and general accounting. During the summer I decided to try the accounting job in Washington, but found that I didn't like it as much as teaching, so I returned in earnest to a full time permanent teaching career.

World War II intervened, and I was drafted in 1943. My experience in the army was that of a non-commissioned officer in Information and Education. This meant that I gave lectures, showed films about the Nazis and the Japanese, and led discussions as to why we were fighting. I changed locations several times, but for the most part, my assignments were in Georgia.

In 1945 the War was over, and I returned to teaching high school until 1953. The Joe McCarthy era, a difficult and dark period, had begun. I refused to testify and be part of the hysteria of that time. Like many others who felt the same way, I was separated from the school system.

Shortly afterwards I became a detail man for a medical equipment company. In 1959 my wife and I went into the houseware business in a farmer's market.

*Used with the permission of Mr. Abe Egnal.

We only carried quality merchandise, as we had a great deal of concern that the customer should not be cheated by inferior products. Other work included my being office manager in a factory that manufactured furniture store fixtures.

Later I went back to teaching in a private school. In 1964 I became a part time and then a full time teacher in a large city community college. Then word came out that former high school teachers, who had been separated unjustly from the school system during the McCarthy period, would be reinstated with credit for their experience. Consequently, I went back to teaching high school until 1970, when I officially retired from full time work. Currently, I am teaching economics part time at a private university.

Question: Do you think it is important to develop many interests in youth that can then be used as one ages? What types of things interest you today?

Answer: *I have always been interested and active in political and social issues involving justice. This goes back to the Spanish Civil War. During that time I was incensed at Hitler and his tactics. I wanted to join with others and renounce his policy of murder and oppression. I met my wife. Leah, in 1937 at a political meeting.*

Today, I continue in my quest for a better world. I am opposed to nuclear power for the purposes of killing people. I have also been active in the Gray Panther movement.

My current involvement with the growing problems of the older adult has led me to participate in a number of official governmental agencies. I am a member of the regional council of my state's committee on aging; the advisory council of the local county area agency on aging; an official member of my county's Health Systems Agency; co-chairman of the committee of the primary care task force that is involved in planning and developing that Health Systems Agency; and a committee member of our local Meals-on-Wheels.

In terms of an individual's self-development, one must keep active both physically and mentally. I have always enjoyed playing tennis, and I continue to enjoy participating in it. Reading, listening to the news, and talking with others are ways in which one can stimulate the mind.

Man is a social animal. Our activities should be interrelated with our fellow humans. How people get along with people is the foremost problem of our times—we must keep trying to make things better and give hope to our troubled times.

Comment: In closing, I would like to share some of your written thoughts about society and aging:*

> *To justify and rationalize the exclusion of... older persons from the key roles in society, there have been accumulated characteristics that are assumed to be descriptive of older persons... It is claimed that they are not adaptive, cannot learn, are absent-minded, narrow-minded, not able to do... While some of these stereotypes may be true for some older persons they are untrue for others. Not too strangely, some of these stereotypes are applied to younger persons. The stereotypes are current and tend to mold the thinking of youngers toward the olders, and, also, of olders toward other olders. For the*

*Egnal, A: Introduction—Aging and the Aged: A Personal Perspective on Aging and Society—Intended for All People Who Are Growing Older. *Unpublished Paper, 1976, pp 16, 17.*

> *stereotypes to change to the realities it would require a change in social and economic conditions... The United States, today, is far from using its potential resources, especially its human resources. A meaningful and useful life for all, young and old, can be realized if society so wills.*

Interview with: Leah Egnal,* 70 years old, married, and a professional weaver.

Question: Would you please highlight your educational and work experiences?

Answer: *Before I was married, I worked for an exodontist, and assisted in the preparation of patients for surgery. After Abe and I married, and we started our family of two children, I became involved in the China-aide Council (1939). When the children no longer came home for lunch during school, I went back to work as a bookkeeper, but I always managed to take time in the summer to study weaving. From 1954 to 1959, Abe and I ran our own housewares business.*

I was 60 years old when I started college full time, and graduated just in time to go on social security. Initially, I was interested in the mental health field, but later became absorbed in art history and ceramics.

Weaving became a major interest, and I pursued it full time. I started by buying myself a small loom, and now I own three large floor looms. I teach both at home and at an elder crafts store—this is a store that takes in work, done by people 65+, which is judged for standard quality—and have exhibited my work in various craft shows.

Question: Would you say that continued involvement is an essential ingredient to a full and meaningful life?

Answer: *I support my husband's varied activities, and he supports my interest in weaving. For instance, he is responsible for all the carpentry work on the looms.*

I am the editor of the local, five county Weaving Guild Newsletter, and I believe in its masthead, which states, "We learn by doing and grow by sharing."

It is good to read but one shouldn't just sit in his home and read alone. We have to share with other people. It is important to be with people. One cannot stop, and must not stop growing and learning at any time.

Interview with: Mrs. L, 65 years old, married, a retired high school teacher, who currently undertakes an occasional substitute teaching assignment.

Question: Would you please highlight some of your life experiences?

Answer: *I majored in Business and minored in English, and in 1936, graduated with a BS in Education from a large private university. I was married during my junior year. My husband had graduated from veterinary school in 1933. We have been living in the same house since then.*

Our first child, a son, was born in 1940. In 1941 the Japanese attacked Pearl Harbor and we were at war. Of course, everything was interrupted. During that time, my husband was drafted and received 13 military assignments in Illinois, Kansas, Michigan, Virginia, and Massachusetts. Our second son was born when we were stationed in Westoverfield, Massachusetts.

*Used with the permission of Mrs. Leah Egnal.

18

My husband was discharged in 1946. When he returned from the service, he had to start his veterinary practice all over again. Prior to World War II he had been engaged in the artificial breeding of cattle. After the War co-ops were doing this kind of work. In essence, my husband had to find alternatives to his former practice, so he started in with small animal work. Also, he became involved in developing a small mail-order business of artificial breeding equipment and supplies. I helped out with some office work—particularly in the typing of scientific research papers. My husband was extremely interested in flea research and later was given an award for his work.

In 1961 he became quite ill and required intensive surgical treatment. Consequently, it became necessary for me to find work. I started by being a substitute teacher in a junior high school of a large city school system. I took the teaching exams, passed, and worked for 17 years teaching business—clerical practice, office practice, typing, business, English, business arithmetic—in a large city high school. Other duties included school treasurer and accounting work which involved a great deal of responsibility.

Many of my students came from disadvantaged backgrounds. I enjoyed working with young people—trying to help them. I found the school environment very stimulating. It was very demanding and challenging work. The majority of the students came to school with a lot of personal problems. Part of my responsibility was trying to find ways in which they could become successful. Hopefully, this success would continue in on-the-job situations—despite set-backs, problems, and frustrations. Obviously, this kind of work demanded a great deal of patience.

Question: What kinds of things interest you now?

Answer: *I enjoy traveling, and have been to Spain, Portugal, Morocco, England, and to many places in the U.S.A. I also enjoy visiting museums. For instance, I have made arrangements to see the opening of the Picasso exhibit, and have recently returned from visiting Hillwood, the Marjorie Post estate in the Washington DC area, that houses a fabulous art collection from the Hermitage in Russia. I play golf every day that the sun is shining! Often, my husband and I will play bridge at social gatherings.*

The financial news is of great interest to me—what to do with investments? How to fight inflation? Both the newspapers and radio talk-shows that advise one about finances are important resources. Older people are insecure because they are out of the labor market. In this time of high inflation the fixed income is a real deficit.

I enjoy watching the educational television channel—particularly historical portrayals.

Birdwatching has a special interest for me as well. I developed this interest by playing golf and seeing the birds on the field. From these observations I became interested in their social behavior. Consequently, I joined the Audubon Society, and now I frequently go on bird-watching hikes.

Question: What advice would you give to someone else regarding successful aging? How does one keep active and vital?

Answer: *I think it is easier for women because they have been raised, at least in my generation, with built-in obligations to take care of others. Their work is never done.*

Having hobbies and interests keeps people's minds and bodies alert. You need to have something to look forward to outside of the home. It is essential that one should be stimulated by the environment. For this reason, you must establish interests and hobbies before *retirement so that you can continue these interests after retirement.*

Interview with: Beatrice Elum,* 67 years old, separated, retired Practical Nurse, currently involved in the catering business.

Question: Would you please highlight some of your life experiences?

Answer: *I was born on my grandfather's 140 acre farm in the South and am the oldest of eight children. On the farm we grew cotton, corn, tobacco, and a variety of other vegetables. We used horses for plowing and prepared for planting by clearing the land with our hands. It was physically difficult work. In 1945 I came North to a large city. My work experience up to then had included farmwork, housework, and all kinds of cooking.*

In 1945 I trained for and became a Licensed Practical Nurse. My specialties were newborn and elderly care. For 15 years I practiced private duty newborn care in the home. In that time I kept records on 55 babies. My professional work also included five years in hospital nurseries.

I enjoy child care and care of the elderly best because I feel I can make them comfortable. For instance, older people need sensitive care; they like a bath and a rubdown. They like to talk, relax, and not be in a hurry. I really enjoy the contact I receive from an older person.

I have two children, a son and a daughter, and three grandchildren. I continue to live in my own home of 21 years with my daughter and granddaughter.

Being the oldest of my brothers and sisters, I still maintain responsibilities to the farm that my father left us. This means that at least annually I must go down, help to prepare the ground and see that the farmhouse, which is rented, is kept in good condition.

Most recently I have developed an interest in the catering business, and I plan to pursue this further.

Question: How would you advise another person regarding successful aging? What is your philosophy on keeping alert?

Answer: *Don't fence me in! I love to travel! Since my retirement, I have visited Mexico, California, Florida, New Mexico, Nassau, St. Thomas, Puerto Rico, and Bermuda. I love to see and learn about new things.*

Also, I am active in church work. I belong to my church's missionary club and sunshine club. It is important to be able to help other people. We provide companionship to those church members who request it. Another responsibility is to send flowers to those who are shut in at home or in the

Used with the permission of Ms. Beatrice Elum.

hospital. We also give parties to help raise money for the church.

It is important to stay informed about what is going on in the world. I enjoy following the news on television or by newspaper. Staying informed keeps one mentally alert and a part of society.

Interview with: Mrs. D, 83 years old, widow, a retired manager and co-owner of a motel, currently living independently in her own apartment.

Question: Would you please tell me something about your life experiences— where and how you grew up, and the types of jobs you have been engaged in?

Answer: *I was born in Lithuania. There were five children in my family—four boys, and I, as the only girl. Also, there were a number of children who died in infancy. There was restlessness in the land, and I personally remember pogroms. When the soldiers would come, we would run into our houses and shutter the windows to try to avoid being hurt or killed. My father was in the lumber transportation business, and he was often gone for long periods of time. In Lithuania, the early part of this century was full of turmoil—talk of revolution, and the Czar's many military engagements. My parents did not think it was a safe place to raise children—especially boys.*

America seemed to be the answer. My father left first with his younger brother to seek a new life and to find a home for the family. In the meantime, my mother was left with the responsibility of caring for the family and selling their property. As we were arranging to go, I became ill—so ill, in fact, that the doctor said that I should not be permitted to travel. By this time my parents' house had been sold, and the boat passage was already paid for. My mother had a difficult decision to make, so she went to the chief Rabbi to seek advice. He told her that she should go with the rest of the family to America, and that she should find a relative in Lithuania, who would care for me until I was strong enough to travel. He told her not to worry and that "God would provide." My mother left, and I spent two years with cousins. I was lonely and missed my family very much.

Finally, my turn came, and I too was off to America. I was about 12 years old when I stepped off the boat. We lived in a large city. I only went two years to school in the United States. Consequently, writing English has never been easy for me. My mother ran a small candy store, and later my parents had a hardware store. We all helped out. At age 14 I went to work in a shoe box factory. The work was long (6:00 am to 7:00 pm) and hard, and we received very little pay for our efforts. Later, I worked managing and selling in a small shop. The man who owned the property fell in love with me and asked me to marry him. He was upset and tried to hurt me when I told him no. I was just 16 and not interested in marriage at that time. At about age 18 I married a widower who had one child. Together, we had three children, including a still-birth.

We moved a number of times, always living near a large or small city environment. My husband and I jointly owned and managed a housewares business, a liquor store, and a motel. In between the liquor store and the motel business, my husband also was in the building business. Of all our involvements I liked the motel business, which we started in our late 50s, the best. I always enjoyed talking to people, and this gave me an opportunity to meet people in a pleasant way.

Question: At present, what kinds of things do you enjoy doing?

Answer: *I keep my own apartment, do my own cooking, and enjoy going to a number of activities at a local Golden Age Club. I recently became a great-grandmother—which was a real thrill. One of my youngest grandchildren is planning to be married in the near future. Naturally, it is very exciting. But at the same time things are harder for me to do. I get tired more easily, have difficulty seeing, have a chronic thrombotic condition and have difficulties, at times, getting oxygen to my brain. Sometimes I faint. This means I don't feel as physically confident to go out alone, and so I look for a friend to go with me when I leave for a shopping trip.*

Question: What advice would you give as to how one can age successfully?

Answer: *Always keep alert! I enjoy listening to the news on the radio or television. The newspapers are another source of current news. Stay interested in life and people. Do not isolate yourself.*

Interview with: Herman S. (Ten) Thoenebe,* 78 years old, married, retired advertising manager, and currently working part time as a columnist for five local newspapers.

Question: Would you please highlight some of your educational and employment experiences?

Answer: *I was graduated in 1924 from a large private university with a BS in Mechanical Engineering. I have taken additional course work in business management, short story writing, advertising, and management training.*

Before college I worked for a furniture factory, a laundry, a telephone company, was a YMCA switchboard operator, and an assistant to the safety engineer in lead works.

During my undergraduate days I was a staff artist for the Engineering and Architectural School's magazine as well as a member of the men's dramatics club.

Post-college employment has included engineering assistant; chief clerk of construction; advertising representative and manager; sales representative for five technical magazines; then in 1934 until my retirement in 1969, I worked for an advertising company. My work there was varied. I began working as a copy cub, then successively as copywriter, copychief, industrial director, creative director (15 years), and account executive. When I retired in 1969 I was senior vice president and director. When I started working for this company, it had 13 employees. Upon my retirement, it had 125. In the whole 35 years I was the only engineer in the company, and was in some measure responsible for the fact that half our clients were industrial.

*Used with the permission of Mr. Herman S. Thoenebe.

During my employment years I belonged to eight business associations and also was a 25-year associate member of the American Society of Mechanical Engineers.

Question: What type of community activities have you engaged in?

Answer: *In the past I have served as vestryman of my church (I am currently serving my fourth tour); consultant to my township's bicentennial commission; consultant to the committee that led in the formation of a senior citizen's center and organization; program chairman for the local PTA; creator and first editor of that school system's PTA newsletter; speaker for a number of Kiwanis club meetings and church groups; editor of my church's monthly newspaper; involved in advertising promotion of a local home and garden show; and active in promotion of the alumni club of the university from which I graduated; and am now serving as President of a local alumni chapter.*

Question: You've certainly led an active community, church, and civic life. Have you had any time for the development of hobbies?

Answer: *Yes, I have an interest in astronomy, photography, painting, woodworking, politics, reading, cooking, inventing and offering merchandising suggestions to manufacturers, playing the organ, and birdwatching with my wife.*

Question: What sort of retirement career have you participated in?

Answer: *For five years I was responsible for writing the campaigns for Operation Native Son (now Operation Native Talent). This program was conducted each year by the chamber of commerce of a large nearby city to induce graduates of local colleges to sign with local businesses. In March of last year I became a Third Degree Mason. Since 1972 I have initiated and written a column,* Gray Matter, *for five county newspapers. Occasionally, I freelance as a writer for advertising agencies.*

Question: How do you spend your day?

Answer: *I get up around 8:00 am and start working on my newspaper column, photography, or community affairs after breakfast. After lunch my wife and I take a nap from 1:00 to 3:00, and then we are ready to go again. In* Gray Matter, *I enjoy writing about thought-provoking subjects. Some of my topics have a flavor of controversy. For instance, I am not totally satisfied with our method of selecting presidents. I think it wasteful to spend all that TV advertising money—some of it with public funds—on a candidate's campaign, when the same money might be better utilized analyzing and choosing men and women who are capable of doing the best job. With all our computer technology, why not search the country for a qualified person?*

Question: I understand you are very much interested in the American Association of Retired Persons (AARP). How did you get involved in this organization?

Answer: *In September of 1970 there was an organizational meeting at a local church. They had expected 90 people and 300 came. I volunteered to write the publicity, was the first newsletter editor, and continue to be involved in this. I also am a director, chaplain, and chairman of consumer education for our local area chapter of AARP, as well as a past president. Recently, I completed two slide shows for AARP that dealt with statistics about our local membership.*

Question: What other types of things do you enjoy doing?

Answer: *A neighbor of mine once asked me, "What do you do with yourself all day long?" "At the present time," I said, "I am working on a proposal for a 25 hour day."*

I love challenge of all kinds, particularly in math. For example, after reading an article about MENSA this past year, I became interested in obtaining membership. Since in my day there were no standard tests acceptable to MENSA, becoming a member meant passing a grueling 6 hour test (it started at 8:15 am with no time out for lunch!). I am happy to say I passed all the necessary procedures.

I write literally hundreds of letters a year. If I get an idea I give it to a company for nothing. I have a number of ideas I would like to patent. For instance, I invented a machine that improves the bookbinding process. I constantly get ideas, and I don't like to throw them away.

Currently, I am writing a book about my youth. In it I relate what my neighborhood life was like between the years 1910 to 1915.

Question: Do you have any concerns that you would like to share with others?

Answer: *Yes. I enjoy living in my house. However, I am concerned about the taxes that older people have to pay. Our state real estate tax rebate system does little in the way of easing the financial burden of those on fixed incomes. We, the retired, need more consideration when it comes to taxes. For example, we pay the same school taxes as those who are currently employed. Since we moved into our home, taxes have increased 20 times! When you retire, your income is at a standstill. We juggle our investments, but we can't beat inflation. We live modestly, but we can't beat inflation. There is a lot of talk about helping the retired elderly, but there is very little real help.*

Question: In closing, what advice would you give to others concerning successful retirement?

Answer: *Keep active—there is so much to do. Pursue your interests to the fullest. Join organizations that are helpful to others and that stimulate you.*

Life doesn't necessarily begin at 40; it may begin at 60, 70¼ or 80½. I'm looking forward to 1986 and the return of Halley's comet—which thrilled me in 1910.

Interview with: Mrs. Katherine Dirks Niebuhr,* 74-year-old widow, who currently maintains her own home in a suburban community of approximately 9,000 people.

Question: Please tell me about your life, and what you are currently involved in.

Answer: *I was born on September 4, 1906 in the Ukraine in the Mennonite colony of Gnadenfeld, Molatschna. Most of the people in my village were*

*Used with the permission of Mrs. Katherine Dirks Niebuhr.

Germans who had fled religious persecution. There were ten children in my family. Three died in infancy. Four of my brothers and sisters were older than I. After the Russian Revolution, which began around 1917, we had to flee again. It was very difficult to get an American visa. My married brothers and sisters attended to their own affairs. Many of my aunts and uncles went to Canada. Luckily, my sister and I were sponsored by a Mennonite community in Pennsylvania. It was around 1922 that we came to America. In order to pay off the boat fare it was necessary for both my sister and I to work for the sponsoring community for one year. After that time we joined our parents in New York City.

There, I met my husband, Herman. When I first saw him I was immediately impressed. It was as they say in the books—love at first sight. He was a taxi driver, and we lived in New York City for 36 years. We had one child, a son. Upon my husband's retirement, we bought a bungalow and moved to a suburban community to be near our son, daughter-in-law, and two grandchildren.

Question: I notice that you speak English with only a slight trace of accent. During your years in America, did you attend any special English classes for new Americans?

Answer: No. I learned my English by listening to neighbors speak, by listening to the radio, and by reading newspapers.

Question: Would you tell me about you and your husband's retirement years and what you are doing now?

Answer: We both enjoyed gardening. Our new home gave us the opportunity to really pursue this activity seriously. Later, my husband died, and I have been a widow for quite some time now. I continue to live in the same house with my two cats and a dog. Work that requires hand skills—alterations, dressmaking, shell pictures, needlework—is especially gratifying to me. Baking is another one of my major interests—particularly around holiday time. For instance, Halloween finds me busily preparing cookies in the shapes of a pumpkin, a witch's hat, or a cat for the neighborhood children who come to call.

Question: What advice would you give to others in helping them to understand what successful aging is all about?

Answer: Keep on doing things that you enjoy doing. I would be very sad if I couldn't do things that give me pleasure. It is good to have friends and maintain strong and warm ties with both family and neighbors. Let me tell you about a very pleasant experience that I had four years ago: on my 70th birthday my son, daughter-in-law, and grandchildren threw a special party for me. Over 40 people came. It was good to know just how much everybody cared. I maintain an open-door policy—that is, my door is always open and friends know that they can drop in for tea when they pass by.

In closing, Isaac Bashevis Singer leaves us with a penetrating view regarding wisdom and aging:[1]

The novelists never told us that in love, as in other matters, the young are just beginners and that the art of loving matures with age and experience... The only hope of mankind is love in its various forms and manifestations—the source of them all being love of life, which, as we know, increases and ripens with the years.

References

1. Singer IB: Old Love. South Yarmouth, MA, John Curley & Assoc, 1979, p v, vi.

3
Theories of Growth and Aging

B efore one studies theories of growth and aging, the various aspects of the aging process should be clarified. Senescence involves the biological, psychological, and sociological changes that an individual experiences during different periods of his life. Although certain developmental characteristics occur at different times during the life cycle, each person ages at his own pace. The several components of aging include:

1) *Biological aging*—These are changes of the various biological and physiological processes that occur during the passage of time.

2) *Chronological aging*—The birth date is used to define an individual's age.

3) *Psychological aging*—These are changes in sensory functioning, perception, memory, learning, intelligence, and dynamics of personality that occur at various stages within the individual's life span.

4) *Sociological aging*—This includes the changing of roles, function, and status of the individual within the social system (ie, family, economics, government, recreation, religious affiliations, education and medicine).[1]

The theories in the remainder of this chapter represent a broad spectrum of thoughts concerning human development and aging.

The Developmental Approach

There are many theories concerning the aging process. Certainly, aging starts at the moment of conception and continues during the life span of the individual. The quality of human development as well as appropriate growth patterns are important components of developmental theory. These aspects of human growth are also important to geriatric practitioners because they help to identify the functioning level of the individual client.

The theories of Jean Piaget (cognitive development), Erik H. Erikson (psychosocial development), Lawrence Kohlberg (moral development), and Abraham H. Maslow (growth motivation) discuss developmental stages that are vital to one's maturation process.

Piaget's Theory

Jean Piaget's general theory of cognitive development is founded on two biological attributes: *organization*—the tendency for living organisms to integrate processes into cohesive systems—and *adaptation*—the instinctive tendency of an organism to interact with his environment by means of assimilation and accommodation. The schema, an action sequence composed of organized sensory-motor responses, is a basic building block of his theory. An example of an inherited schema is the sucking pattern of a baby.[2]

Piaget's earliest theories deal with speech patterns of the young child. He postulates that the communication skills of the preschooler are egocentric. The child rarely attempts to exchange thoughts with others. As the child grows older his speech becomes more socialized and he is able to consider another person's ideas.[3]

According to Piaget's theory there are five different developmental phases. Maturity encompasses the total integration of these stages. Some of the major characteristics of each phase are reviewed below.

Chronological Order	Cognitive Modality	Characteristics
Birth to 2 yrs	Sensorimotor	*The Sensorimotor Phase* During this time the infant's earliest movements are primitive reflexes. Most learning occurs through the senses and by manipulation. Behavior during this phase can be categorized as "autistic." By age two the first internalization of schemata and the use of deductive thought may be utilized to solve problems. There are a total of six separate stages within the sensorimotor phase.

2 to 4 yrs	Preoperational	*The Preconceptual Phase*

In the preconceptual phase the individual's thinking becomes more egocentric in approach. Play that emphasizes the why and how becomes the major tool for adaption. Symbolic play, simple language, and repetition are the mechanisms that are used. During this time the child is able to classify and compare items by a single attribute (for example, color or size).

4 to 7 yrs	Preoperational	*The Intuitive Phase*

In this phase the individual truly begins to use words to express his ideas. The generalization of symbols as images becomes a major portion of the cognitive process. There is a gradual awareness of the conservation of mass, weight, and volume.

7 to 11 yrs	Concrete Operations	*The Concrete Operational Phase*

This phase represents the utilization of logical thought. At this point the individual can organize objects into a series and is able to reverse operations (ie, addition and subtraction, multiplication and division). Communication and play are now used as a means of understanding the social and physical world. During this time the individual begins to gain a sense of autonomy.

11 to 14 yrs and ongoing	Formal Operations	*Formal Operations Phase*

The concept of relativity, reason by hypothesis, and the use of implication begins to emerge. The

individual is now able to understand abstract thought.[4]

Erikson's Theory

Cognitive development is but one of many aspects of human functioning.
Psychosocial development offers another area of growth. Erik H. Erikson's work
in this field details a series of eight phases, or ages, that he believes are essential
to attain human maturity.

In each of these ages, the individual struggles with two conflicting approaches
or crisis situations. Erikson uses the word *versus* to demonstrate these polar
differences. At each crisis phase the individual has options of positive or negative
behaviors. The development of the individual occurs when he is biologically,
psychologically, and socially prepared to move into the next phase. Erikson also
uses the term *basic virtue* to represent realization of those values that he
considers give meaning and spirit to human existence. Thus, each phase has its
corresponding basic virtue. In regard to the first six ages, Erikson relates his
developmental approach to Freudian psychosexual theory. The following
represents a brief explanation of these eight ages or phases.

Chronological Order	Basic Virtue	Characteristic Ages (Phases)
Infancy	Hope	*Age I: Basic Trust vs Basic Mistrust*
		It is at this time that the infant learns to acquire a sense of trust by means of feeling physically well and by experiencing a minimal amount of anxiety. Behavior during this phase is egocentric.
Early Childhood	Will Power	*Age II: Autonomy and Pride vs Shame and Doubt*
		During this time the individual begins to see boundaries between himself and his parents. Elimination and interest in the erotic areas of the body are of prime concern to the child, and he increasingly begins to assume a greater control of his body (regulation of the self vs regulation by others).

Play Age	Purpose	*Age III: Initiative vs Guilt*
		This is a period when the individual is expanding his language and mobility skills. Sexual identification also commences at this time. During this period the *id, ego,* and *superego* begin to find a mutual balance which leads to the fuller development of the personality.
School Age	Competence	*Age IV: Industry vs Inferiority*
		In this phase the individual develops the ability to win recognition by producing things. It is a time for systematic instruction. The child begins, then, to rely increasingly upon social institutions (schools, clubs, organizations).
Adolescence	Fidelity	*Age V: Identity vs Role Confusion*
		The individual physically matures into adulthood. The adolescent is constantly re-evaluating himself and his "new" body. Desire for sexual fulfillment begins to have more importance. According to Erikson, adolescence is a period of the moratorium, or delay between the child's world and the full responsibilities of the adult world.
Younger Adult	Love	*Age VI: Intimacy vs Isolation*
		The individual has the opportunity of becoming a full member of the society—enjoying both the responsibility (work world) and the liberty that is involved in adulthood. Ego-identity manifests itself during this period. This is usually the time that one acquires a mate and assumes mutual responsi-

		bilities that are involved (ie, regulate appropriate cycles of work, recreation, and procreation) with the given partner.
Adulthood	Care	*Age VII: Generativity vs Stagnation* During this phase the individual has the opportunity to guide the next generation. It is possible to achieve a sense of having contributed to mankind's future at this time.
Maturity	Wisdom	*Age VIII: Ego Integrity vs Despair* A spiritual sense pervades this final phase. It can be a time of fulfillment, acceptance, and respect for one's life style and life cycle.[5]

Kohlberg's Theory

The moral developmental theory of Lawrence Kohlberg represents another area of human functioning. According to Kohlberg there are six structured stages of development and a speculative seventh stage that reaches beyond the other stages to attain a humanistic perspective. The following are major characteristics of each stage.

Morality Level	Characteristic Stages
Preconventional	*Stage I: Punishment and Obedience* During this stage it is the physical consequence (ie, punishment, reward) that determines the value of an action. *Stage II: Instrumental Relativist* In this stage reciprocity becomes a major method of determining the value of an action (ie, "If you'll do this for me I'll do that for you").
Conventional	*Stage III: Interpersonal Concordance* Behavior is frequently judged by intent. Approved behavior (often labeled as "good or nice") is determined by one's willingness to help others. There is conformity to stereotyped images.

Stage IV: Law and Order

Approved behavior is based upon one's willingness to respond to duty and respect for authority.

Post Conventional   *Stage V: Social Contract Legalistic Approach*

Approved action is based upon individual rights, with standards agreed upon by the society. However, these are not rigid but rather can be thought of in terms of free agreement and contract (with room for amending).

Stage VI: Universal Ethical Principle

"Right" action is determined by decisions of individual conscience as related to universal ethical principles (eg, The Golden Rule).

Possible Stage VII: The Ontological-Religious Approach

This stage is still being defined by Kohlberg. It involves the contemplative experience and assumes an identification with the cosmic (infinite) perspective.[6]

Maslow's Theory

Another theoretician, Abraham H. Maslow, believed that mature human growth was dependent upon "need gratification or growth maturation."[3] His theory is built upon the assumption that human beings fulfill their needs by a positive striving to grow. Maslow suggested a hierarchy of seven needs that commence with the most basic. As each lower need fulfills itself by being appropriately and sufficiently gratified, the individual is able to move to the next need level. These hierarchical levels consist of the following needs: physiological, safety, belonging and love, esteem, the need for self-actualization, the need to know and understand, and aesthetic needs.[3]

Opposing Theories of the Aging Process

Besides a developmental point of view on aging, there also exist two theories, *disengagement* and *activity,* that are concerned with the way in which the individual and society view the aging process.

According to Cumming and Henry, it is almost inevitable that as an individual ages and his personal resources decline, his interest in the social systems that he belongs to will also decrease. This withdrawal or disengagement can be seen by a decline in the number of people that an individual interacts with, the qualitative changes in patterns of interaction, and personality changes that result in decreased involvement.[7] This disengagement process helps the individual prepare for his eventual death.

Directly opposed to the disengagement theory is the *activity* theory. The majority of geriatric practitioners and theorists are proponents of this theory. Even though an individual may recognize his increasing limitations as he ages, old age may still be regarded as a time of fulfillment and as much activity as is possible. It can be a period when the wisdom of years may be harvested and utilized by the society. Like many other fellow professionals who support the activity viewpoint, Theodore Lidz believes that those people who continue to be involved in some form of productive activity remain alert for a longer period of time than those who are less active.[8]

Havighurst, Neugarten, and Tobin's findings pose yet another approach to the theories of aging. They regard an individual's personality as the cornerstone in predicting patterns of aging. Accordingly, as an individual grows older, if his personality remains integrated, there is an increasing consistency of that personality. For example, values that an individual has always felt positively about will become more cherished as he ages.[9]

Aging Theory and the Geriatric Practitioner's Role

The practitioner's knowledge of a variety of aging theories facilitates his ability to more fully comprehend his client's behavior and capabilities. It is always important to present treatment programs that are responsive to the individual client's needs. Some examples of patient behaviors and how they relate to developmental theory follow.

The older person who is disoriented or who no longer can control his bodily functions experiences a sense of loss of self. For instance, the incontinent person must cope with the frustration of feeling like a child as he is unable to regulate himself. Consider Erikson's *Age II—Autonomy vs. Shame and Doubt* as a comparison. Although some of the client's behavior may at times be reminiscent of a child's, he should not be treated as if he were one. It should be remembered that this is a person who has experienced life, and that this chronological maturity deserves the respect of all those younger people who must deal with the older person.

In the same vein, the older individual who is assessed as cognitively functioning at a 1½-year-old level (Piaget's sensory-motor phase), should be provided with treatment that reflects these findings. A treatment program that lies beyond the client's grasp can only result in disappointment and frustration for himself as well as the practitioner.

The mentally alert older person, operating at a physically minimal level, represents yet another example of the varying complexities of human functioning. It is the practitioner's obligation to make use of all the resources of his client. The developmental theories mentioned in this chapter discuss the number of stages that are necessary to attain maturity. The older person's wisdom and life experiences are indeed great strengths and assets that the practitioner should utilize.

Another factor in resident care that has a direct bearing upon developmental theory is the relationship between the client and the institution. Institutional life may force many older people to assume behavior similar to Kohlberg's *Stage 3—Interpersonal Concordance* (good girl/boy label). For example, when the staff is preparing a special event like a trip, it is usually the quiet and cooperative patient who is permitted to participate.

In respect to Maslow's theory, the institutionalized older client's physiological and safety needs are usually met. However, higher level needs such as belonging and love, esteem, and self-actualization are usually not fulfilled. In this regard, caregivers have a very important mission, as they can provide treatment that encourages the gratification of these more mature needs.

Whether a person's life style dictates a disengagement pattern or one of activity, it is the dignity of the individual and his right to choose that should help to determine his treatment program. The practitioner can help him in his decision-making process and assist him in his efforts to accomplish specific treatment goals.

References

1. Rosen H, et al: Working with Older People: A Guide to Practice. Washington DC, Public Health Service Publications, vol 1, no 1459, glossary. 1966.
2. Guilford JP: The Nature of Human Intelligence. New York, McGraw-Hill Book Co. 1967, p 24.
3. Biehler FR: Psychology Applied to Teaching. New York, Houghton Mifflin Co, 1971, p 78, 313-322.
4. Maier HW: Three Theories of Child Development. New York, Harper & Row Pubs Inc, 1969, pp 103-150.
5. Erikson EH: Childhood and Society. New York, WW Norton & Co Inc, 1963, pp 247-273.
6. Kohlberg L: Stages and aging in moral development—some speculations. Gerontologist 1:497-502, 1973.
7. Cumming E, Henry WE: Growing Old: The Process of Disengagement. New York, Basic Books Inc, 1961, p 15.
8. Lidz T: The Person: His Development Throughout the Life Cycle. New York, Basic Books Inc, 1968, pp 438-484.
9. Neugarten B, Havighurst R, Tobin SS: Personality and patterns of aging. In Neugarten B (ed): Middle Age and Aging: A Reader in Social Psychology. Chicago, Univ Chicago Press, 1973, p 177.

4
Biological Changes
Due to Aging

A s one ages, certain biological and physical changes occur. According to
Strehler there are four characteristics that are common to senescence:

1) *Universality*—This concept asserts that specific aging characteristics
can be seen in all segments of the elderly population. For instance, if gray
hair is to be classified as a true phenomenon of aging, it must be shown that
as people grow older, all subjects will exhibit some amount of graying hair.

2) *Intrinsicality*—The varying effects of ultraviolet radiation on both the
physical and chemical properties of skin protein in young and elderly
people illustrates this characteristic. These effects depend on the changing
susceptability of the skin collagen to irradiation and are not directly
attributable to the ultraviolet light.

3) *Progressiveness*—True aging phenomena develops at a gradual pace
and is generally not reversible. The development of atheroma and the
resultant repair process which is seen by the accumulation of fibrous
plaques on the intimal surfaces of the vessels can be identified as an
example of progressiveness.

4) *Deleteriousness*—Currently, there exists much controversy regarding
this final characteristic. Accordingly, degradative and deteriorating
changes must occur when senescence begins.[1]

Basically, there are two types of aging: 1) *primary aging*—a time-related
sequence closely rooted in heredity that results in a decline of the efficiency of

various functions within the organism, and 2) *secondary aging*—a process associated with stress, trauma, and disease.

Biological Theories

Busse affirms that human beings are composed of three biological components: 1) cells capable of multiplying throughout their life span (ie, epithelial, and white blood cells), 2) cells incapable of division (ie, brain neurons), and 3) interstitial material (noncellular). He also states that the following biological theories of aging are based in part on at least one of these three components:

1) *Exhaustion theory*—This rather dated biological explanation of aging assumes that an organism contains a fixed amount of energy. When this energy storage is depleted, the individual dies.

2) *The accumulation of harmful material theory*—This theory identifies aging with the accumulation of deleterious substances. The formation of lipofuscin (brown pigment) that is found in brain neurons as well as other cells of older persons is believed to be an example of this concept.

3) *Intentional biological programming*—Senescence occurs by means of programmed changes that take place within the life cycle of an organism. A specific example would be the human erythrocyte (one of the red blood cells) which appears to be programmed to live 120 years. Most research supports the assumption that there is a definite correlation between the survival of the erythrocyte and the total life span of the human organism.

4) *Decline in the doubling capacity of human cells*—This is believed to be the causative factor responsible for senescence.

5) *Mean time failure*—Leonard Heyflick gives much credence to this theory, which states that the lifetime of an organism is directly related to the durability of its parts.

6) *Accumulation of copying errors*—Aging occurs when one's cells develop copying errors that become amplified and widespread. Death takes place when the metabolic efficiency is reduced, and ultimately, when the cells lose their capability for repair.

7) *Stochastic theories*—These theories focus upon cell loss or mutation as the main cause of aging. Laboratory studies demonstrate that the exposure of an organism to repeated small doses of ionizing radiation or to a larger sublethal dose reduces the life span of that organism.

8) *Curtis' composite theory*—Howard J. Curtis postulates that one ages because of the accumulation of defectively functioning cells in organs that are composed of nondividing cells. Further, Curtis believes that as one ages, one becomes increasingly susceptible to degenerative diseases. He asserts that an individual may develop all of the degenerative diseases at different rates before he or she dies.

9) *DNA-RNA error theory*—This theory of cellular aging assumes that as

one ages alterations occur within the structure of the deoxyribonucleic acid (DNA) molecule. These errors are then transmitted to ribonucleic acid (RNA), the messenger, and they are finally transmitted to newly synthesized enzymes. These defective enzymes could then produce substrates within the cell. The normal metabolic process might be seriously impaired. Death may result when the supply of RNA becomes too low for cell functioning.

10) *Eversion theory (cross-linkage)*—Senescence occurs when the collagen molecule (the most abundant protein in the human organism) alters its structure and changes its characteristics—especially its elasticity. This loss of elasticity accelerates the aging process.

11) *Autoimmunity*—As one ages, there is an increased incidence of autoimmune disease. This theory suggests that the gradual increase of antibodies in the plasma may be responsible for a lifelong accumulative exposure to multiple immunochemical substances.

12) *Index of cephalization*—This hypothesis proposes that the excess of brain weight in relation to its expected body weight bears a direct correlation to longevity.

13) *Genetic determinants of aging*—While there is no specific gene that can insure a long life span, there are certain genes that are responsible for defects that result in shortening one's life. It is possible to theorize that an overabundance of these genes would be responsible for an accelerated aging pace.[2]

Other theorists have proposed: 1) the *Lipid peroxidation theory* which asserts that unstable lipid portions of the lipoprotein cell membranes are continuously undergoing spontaneous peroxidation due to cosmic ray bombardment. Antioxidants such as vitamin E or alpha-tocopheral are believed to retard the peroxidation process (and presumably aging); and 2) the failure of the hypothalamus to regulate normal body functioning and rhythms.[3]

As research continues in its quest for the answer to the fundamental reasons of senescence, new theories may replace or alter the old ones. With the increasing amount of sophisticated technology that is being introduced yearly into the scientific community, one can assume that at some future date humankind will be able to understand the mystery of the aging process.

Physical and Biological Changes

The remainder of this chapter will discuss aging in terms of the physical, the biological, and the functional changes that occur within the human organism. However, there is considerable controversy as to whether these changes are due to intrinsic aging, wear and tear, or the consequences of vascular impairment and other diseases.

Throughout this section, discussion will be focused on changes in the following areas: 1) the various systems of the body, 2) the skin and subcutaneous tissues, and 3) the senses.

Systems of the Body

The Respiratory System

Three major components of the respiratory system—ventilation, diffusion, and pulmonary circulation—show loss of efficiency as one ages. Specifically, this impairment can be seen by five symptoms:

1) the decline of total lung capacity;

2) an increase in residual volume;

3) a reduction in a vital capacity. Research, conducted with 20-year-old subjects as compared to 80-year-old subjects, indicated that the breathing capacity declined from 132 liters per minute in the 20-year-old, to 50 liters per minute in the 80-year-old;

4) the decrease in the resiliency of the lungs; and

5) increased thickening of supporting membrane structures between the alveoli and the capillaries.[4]

The Skeletal System

Such skeletal changes typical of the aging process as stooped posture, stiffened joints, and porous bone structure result in a decrease of mobility, efficiency, and the capability of the human organism. These changes in appearance and function are manifested as:

1) a reduction in height;

2) poor posture. These postural alterations, particularly bent hips and knees, stooping back, and flexed neck, are primarily due to a progressive calcification and eventual ossification of the ligaments. In vertebral ligaments, this condition is often referred to as lipping vertebral. The mineralization process usually involves the elastic fibers; the erosion and ossification of cartilaginous joint surfaces as well as degenerative changes of the synovium. This process leads to an increased stiffening of the joints. The fibrocartilaginous discs undergo atrophic changes as they become thinner. These changes are particularly responsible for an increasing curvature of the spine and the atrophy of the boney structure of the vertebral and intervertebral discs and ligaments, known as kyphoscoliosis (hunched back);

3) degenerative changes in the rib cartilages and in the ligaments and joints which join the rib cage to the sternum and vertebrae. This is one of the causes of respiratory impairment;

4) changes in the temporalmandibular joints and loss of teeth, which may cause difficulty in speech and eating; and

5) porous bones. As one ages, the bones become more porous, lighter, and lose a great deal fo their elasticity. This process actually is a disease state— osteoporosis.[4]

The Nervous System

The nervous system also undergoes a great deal of change. Within the brain itself, many changes can be identified as: 1) a progressive atrophy of the gyri (convolutions) and the widening and deepening of the sulci (spaces between the convolutions); 2) a loss of the bulk of brain substances and dilution of the ventricles which contain cerebrospinal fluid; 3) the progressive loss of neurons — many of the neurons that remain acquire lipofuscin; and 4) a progressive increase of corpora amylacea (small sand-like bodies) within the brain substance.[4]

Other changes within the nervous system are reaction time increase due to the degeneration of the integrative system, an atrophy in the medullary olives, a decrease in the Purkinje cells of the cerebellum, trunk instability, and losses within the proprioceptive, kinesthetic, vestibular, and visual mechanisms. These mechanisms contribute to a characteristic gait which is considered typical of elderly people: shorter step length, higher cadence, wider walking base, and a longer time period spent in the support stage of the step rather than the swing stage. Because of the combination of the increased reaction time and postural instability, there is a greater tendency to fall as one ages.[5]

The Muscular System

The muscular system is another area that demonstrates decline during aging. Muscle atrophy, hypotonia, and muscle weakness are due to such multiple causes as the thinning of individual muscle fibers, the loss of nerve terminals, and the diminished rate of synthesis of acetylcholine. As these muscle fibers degenerate, there is an increase of fat (ie, by age 70, fat may compose one third of the total dry weight of the gastrocnemius and fibrous tissue). The muscle loses a great amount of its ability to expand and contract at will because of these changes.[5]

As a result of this muscular deterioration, other bodily functions are also affected. These consist of impairment of respiratory efficiency, impairment of efficient excretory functions, and decline in the ability to respond effectively in an emergency situation. The muscle is a major site for glycogen storage. Atrophied muscles lead to a loss of glycogen stores. This loss then results in an increased loss of reserve sugar from which is derived the energy that is required for use in an emergency.[4]

The Reproductive System

The major female reproductive change that occurs is menopause, a discontinuance of menstruation and the ability to bear children. This usually takes place at approximately 45-50 years of age. After menopause, there often is a gradual steroid insufficiency. This can cause the vaginal walls to become thinner, and many women experience an increase in vaginal itching. However, steroid replacement therapy can alleviate these menopausal symptoms. Menopause does not deny women a satisfying sex life. In fact, many women maintain pleasurable sexual activity well into their 70s and 80s.[3]

The male "change of life" is often referred to as the climacteric. Many researchers feel that much of male impotency is directly due to lack of self-confidence, and not to any physical cause. Although it may take an older man a longer time to obtain an erection, sexual capability can usually continue for as many years as the individual consistently pursues sexual activity. Men in their 60s and 70s have been known to have fathered children. Sperm has been found in men 90 years of age.[6]

Human sexuality and the sexual rights and practices of the older person are concerns to all those who are interested in the well-being of the elderly. For many years, it had been thought that the older individual was not or should not be interested in an active sex life. Traditionally, older people were supposed to lose interest in sex. If this was not the case, they were considered dirty old men/women, silly, or intruding upon the perogatives of the young.[7]

However, older adults themselves are beginning to challenge these stereotypes. There are numerous reasons why persons over 60 years of age enjoy engaging in sexual experiences. Some of these include: an opportunity to express passion; an affirmation of one's body and its functioning capacities; an affirmation of a sense of self; a means or vehicle for self-assertion; release or protection from anxiety; pleasure—the joy of being touched or caressed; a sense of romance, an affirmation of life; a defiance of the stereotypes of aging—"There may be snow on the roof but there's still fire in the furnace"; and a response to the continuous search for sexual gratification.[8]

Evidence of changing attitudes is affirmed in Celeste Loughman's recent study, which included the examination of a number of contemporary writers of fiction who challenge the myths and conventions that are usually associated with the sexual behavior of the older person. In summary, Loughman writes:

> As behavioral science confirms, the persistence of sexual impulse gives evidence that life is a continuum and that behavior tolerated in the young should not be censured in the old. Above all, the authors demonstrate that the tension between the old and society is less significant than the tensions within the themselves. More than a physical drive, the erotic impulse is an expression of functional desires for human contact, for love, for life itself.[9]

Respect of the sexual rights of residents in nursing homes and other types of institutions is a major concern for those who value the human rights of the frail older adult. Too often we find in these types of places, that the privacy of the elderly resident is ignored because he is "just another old person." However, "both men and women want their own personal sexual identity. Personal identity, at least from age two onward, has been compounded and interwoven and mixed with sexual identity. When you take someone out of the sex roles or make them so they don't function sexually to some degree, you attack not only their body but their image of themselves."[10]

The Cardiovascular System

Some of the structural changes that occur include:

1) an increase in interstitial fibrous tissue;
2) an increase of lipofuscin in the muscle cells;

3) an increase in amyloidosis (excessive deposits of starch-like material);

4) an elongation of the arteries, which become tortuous and calcify; and

5) a thickening of the supporting membranes, including capillaries.

All these structural alterations contribute to the following changes in functioning: there is a definite decline in cardiac output at rest; the heart loses some of its capacity for responding to extra work; there is a progressive increase in the peripheral resistance to blood flow; and the systolic blood pressure increases.

The Urinary Tract

In urinary tract functioning, the filtration rate in the kidney of 80-year-old persons is approximately 50% of that of individuals in their 20s. The renal blood flow is also about 50%. Polyuria (excessive urination) is common. Structural changes such as the hyalinization of the glomeruli (kidney filters) and interstitial fibrosis are believed to result in the atrophy of the collecting tubules.

The Gastrointestinal Tract

Intrinsic aging of the gastrointestinal tract produces:

1) a decline in stomach gastric mobility;

2) a reduction in gastric volume;

3) a tendency towards achlorohydria (loss of digestive acid);

4) a reduction in quantity of digestive enzymes;

5) diminished peristalsis. This may be a factor that causes constipation, a common complaint of older persons; and

6) atrophy of the mucosal lining. This is responsible for the impairment of absorption that many older persons experience.[4]

The Skin and Subcutaneous Tissues

Gray hair and wrinkles, characteristics most often associated with an elderly appearance, yield a stereotyped image of older people. These characteristics can become symbols that may alter an older person's self-perception. Some of the areas of the body that display changes in external appearance are as follows.

Skin

Wrinkles—Wrinkling is often attributed to decreased blood supply and changes in collagen and elastic fiber. This results in a loss of elasticity and resiliency of the skin. When the skin is stretched in the older person, the folds become more delineated as they return into place.

Discoloration—During the aging process, the skin undergoes atrophic processes. Consequently there are many pigmentary discolorations. Red blotches on the skin are usually caused by changes in the blood vessels beneath the skin.

Seborrheic keratoses—These are wart growths that appear to be stuck on.

Biological Changes Due to Aging

Fissures—There appears to be an increase of fissures about the mouth. This may be caused by atrophy of the epidermal layer.

Nails

Atrophy of nail tissues causes the nails to become more brittle and to grow at a slower pace.

Hair

There is a loss of hair pigmentation which results in its graying or whitening. This is believed to be due to a decrease in enzyme activity. In some cases, and especially among men, there is a loss of hair—known as balding.

Tongue and Gums

The tongue and gum areas undergo atrophic changes and become reddened. Gum shrinkage around the teeth may cause eating and maintenance problems.

Subcutaneous Tissue

This layer of tissue acts in two ways: as an insulator which helps to keep body heat constant, and as a cushion against trauma. When these tissues atrophy, it becomes difficult for an individual to regulate body temperature.

Sweat and Oil Glands

The sweat and oil glands atrophy and decrease in size and number. Because of this, older people lose their ability to sweat, and consequently, the skin becomes very dry.[6]

The Senses

The senses are the mechanisms by which the human organism gathers information about the environment. The senses help us to discern the differences between pleasant, unpleasant, and dangerous experiences. Imagine how difficult it would be to detect fire without the benefit of this type of alerting system. One would be unable to hear the crackling sound of fire, to smell the smoke, to feel the heat, or to see the flames.

Hearing

Handicapping hearing impairments increase as one ages. Within the United States, there are nearly three million people 65+ who have hearing impairments; of this number, 63,000 are classified as being totally deaf.

There are basically two different kinds of hearing loss: *conductive* and *sensorineural*. In conductive hearing loss, the sound has difficulty reaching the cochlea. This results in a loss of perceived intensity. Louder speech permits the person to hear adequately. Hearing aides are helpful for this type of disability.

Sensorineural hearing loss is characteristic of the type of degeneration that takes place during the aging process. Specifically, there is damage to some of the nerve endings in the cochlea. As a result, the ear responds to sounds in an uneven manner. There is usually a loss of one's ability to respond to high frequency sounds, such as the consonants *s, t, p, k,* and *f*. However, the low frequency sounds (usually vowels) are more readily heard. This results in the loss of the ability to discriminate words in speech. Speech is heard as the muffled droning sounds of low frequency tones. Low frequency background noises frequently mask the vowel sounds that a person can hear. Thus, if a television or an air conditioner is on during a conversation, a person with this type of hearing loss will not be able to fully comprehend what is being said. Hearing aids merely make the confused sound louder, and therefore are contraindicated.

There are other conditions that impede hearing. One of these is tinnitus, a high-pitched ringing in the ears. Another is presbycusis. This is a combination of discriminatory hearing loss and the presence of recruitment (faint or moderate sounds cannot be heard, but loud sounds can be perceived). Functionally, a characteristic of presbycusis is a gradual reduction in sensitivity to high-frequency sounds. Starting at approximately age 40, this condition increases in severity as the individual ages.[11]

Other changes in the auditory system which often result in some form of hearing loss include: a reduction in size of the opening of the ear canal (external auditory meatus) due to degenerative changes in the cartilage of the canal wall; degenerative changes in the thickness and stiffness of the tympanic membrane which in turn alters the vibratory characteristics of the eardrum; or ostosclerosis, a bony growth that forms at the point where the foot plate of the stapes fits into the oval window, may develop. This condition may cause a loss of the mechanical transmission of the vibrations. Ostosclerosis may be helped by a plantinectomy, a surgical procedure in which the foot plate of the stapes is surgically removed and replaced by a piece of vein from the back of the hand. Degeneration of the inner ear, particularly the organ of corti, can result in a loss of high sound frequencies.[12]

Vision

Visual loss can cause a decrease in mobility, frightening visual impressions, and poor orientation. By age 65, approximately 50% of the population in the United States experiences a visual acuity of 20/70 or less. At 75, three out of five persons experience some degree of visual loss.[13]

A major characteristic change due to the aging process is the loss of elasticity of the lens. This interferes with the process of accommodation—the ability of the lens to change its curvature in order to bring objects, at varying distances, into focus. In normal close vision, the ciliary muscle contracts and tension is reduced on the suspensory ligaments. The lens bulges and the individual is able to focus on near objects. In presbyopia the lens' ability to focus on near objects is reduced. It is very common for people in mid and late life to need reading glasses or bifocals to correct this condition. There are a number of other changes related to the aging process that contribute to a decrease in visual acuity: the arcus senilis (senile ring), the development of an opaque ring just inside the border between the cornea and the sclerotic coat, causes a reduction in peripheral vision. In this condition, only a diffuse light can pass through the opaque ring. As a result, an individual with this problem experiences a reduction in the visual field. There is a gradual fading of the color of the iris, due to the changing location of the pigment granules. It is possible for minute portions of these granules to be carried away by the aqueous humor fluid and to then become obstructions that could lead to glaucoma. There is a tendency for the tissue around the border of the pupil to swell, causing a decrease in the ability of the pupil to dilate. As a result, reduced amounts of light enter the eye. Reduction in visual acuity in older adults is especially prominent in dim light The tissue of the lens loses its transparency and takes on a yellow coat. Consequently, there is a filtering out of certain light wavelengths, especially short wavelengths such as blue and violet, which results in impaired color vision. Glaucoma, increased intraocular tension which can lead to the hardening of the eyeball, is a major concern of many older adults. Fortunately, glaucoma can be controlled by drugs that lower the pressure in the eyeball. The development of cataracts, or the clouding of the lens, causes increased visual impairment.[12] Formerly, cataracts were treated by removing the lens of the eye, and then prescribing corrective glasses. However, modern technology has developed the intraocular lens implant—the replacement of the eye's natural lens with a tiny piece of plastic—which is permitting many people with this problem to see clearly again without the aid of glasses.[13]

The size of the lens increases gradually so that, by age 80, it is 50% larger than at age 20. Comparably, the size of the pupil decreases and, as mentioned in the problems of the elasticity of the lens, less light is able to reach the retina. Glare and loss of the ability to adapt to sudden changes of light intensity are two major problems that older adults experience.[14]

Macular degeneration is another visual condition that is often associated with aging. The macula, a spot in the retina which contains the fovea, is responsible for distinct to fine vision. In this condition, there is a decreased blood supply to the macula. As a result the receptors are damaged and central vision is lost. Magnifiers are low vision aids that are helpful to those adults affected by macular degeneration.[12]

Gustatory and Olfactory

The taste receptors, located in the taste buds, are found on the tip, sides, and back of the tongue. Only substances that dissolve in water or saliva can truly be tasted. The purposes of taste are fourfold: 1) provides information about the environment; 2) detects harmful substances; 3) contributes to an individual's ability to choose a nutritionally-sound diet; and 4) used to motivate changes in behavior. Physiologically, taste nerve fibers have been known to project to parts of the limbic system. Classical conditioning in psychology has long been associated with food and pleasant taste as a motivating/ reward factor.

In old age, the tongue contains only about 50% of the taste receptors that were present when the individual was young. This means that most older adults' ability to discriminate and perceive the four primary taste sensations (sweet, salt, sour, and bitter) is diminished.

Since it is estimated that two-thirds of taste sensations depend upon the ability to smell, there is a strong interrelationship between these two senses. Many food substances owe a considerable portion of their characteristic flavor to the olfactory system. While there are over 20 different regions of the human brain that are attributed to receiving input from the smell receptors, the actual receptor sites are located in each side of the olfactory cleft on a piece of tissue called the olfactory epithelium. The olfactory process is initiated when airborne gaseous particles reach the olfactory epithelium by way of eddy currents. Although the olfactory receptors are sensitive, they fatigue quite rapidly.

Anosmia, or the inability to smell, renders most food bland or tasteless. This condition is usually caused by obstructions to the basal passage (eg, nasal polyps, acute sinusitis, swelling of the mucous lining of the olfactory epithelium, trauma, and tumors) and degenerative conditions of the olfactory nerves and the olfactory epithelium.[12]

Kinesthesia

The ability to perceive changes in body position and body orientation in space decreases with age. The changes are due, in part, to neurological and neuromuscular dysfunction, decline in muscular tone and strength, and dysfunction or disturbance of body mechanisms (ie, the vestibular system). Some older persons experience nystagmus, a constant, involuntary, cyclical movement of the eyeball. This causes them to perceive the ground as moving up and down. Often, the deficits that impede appropriate kinesthetic functioning compel the older person to compensate by changing his gait pattern.[14]

Tactile

Skin somesthesis includes sensations such as warmth, cold, light touch, pressure, and vibration. Pain, considered by some investigators to be a separate sense, will also be examined.

Encapsulated end organs are attributed to being responsible for temperature and touch sensitivity. Some free nerve endings are also able to signal temperature and touch sensations in addition to mediating pain.

Touch/Pressure—The Meissner and pacinian corpuscles are believed to be the receptors for light touch and pressure. The body's surface is not uniformly sensitive to touch. For instance, the lips and finger tips are extremely sensitive to touch, while the back is less so.

Vibration—The pacinian corpuscle, the encapsulated end organ in the skin, is especially identified as responding to vibration. According to Colavita, vibration is the experience of repeated rapid touch stimulations.[12]

Temperature—Temperature sensations, including hot, warm, cold, or cool, help the individual receive information about the environment. Experiments demonstrate that there are more cold spots than warm spots in the body. Cold receptors are generally located nearer to the skin surface than are warm receptors. According to some researchers, there do not seem to be separate receptors in the skin for hot sensations; the perception of hot appears to be the result of simultaneous activation of warm and cold receptor sites.

Somesthetic changes in aging—These changes include a reduction in touch and vibration sensitivity. The aged person's skin elasticity changes, and more pressure is needed to mechanically deform the tissue and stimulate the sense receptors that lie beneath the skin. This reduction in touch sensitivity may also be due to fewer encapsulated end organs and the degeneration of sensory nerves that carry somesthetic messages to the brain. An inability for older people to maintain constant body temperature is also one of the changes noticed.

Pain—Another sensory modality, pain warns the individual about things within the internal and external environments. Free nerve endings (the receptors for pain) are found mostly in the skin. They may also be found in tendons, muscles, joints, connective tissues of the visceral organs, the eardrums, and the corneas. The brain itself and some internal organs (eg, gall bladder) do not possess free nerve endings. The greatest concentration of pain occurs along the midline axis of the body and decreases toward the extremities. Thus, pain intensity varies as to body part (eg, the abdomen's pain sensitivity is approximately 20 times greater then the pain sensitivity, in the same size area, of the finger tip; the cornea of the eye's pain sensitivity is 30 times more sensitive than the abdomen's).

According to the gate-control theory of Patrick Wall and Ronald Melzack, pain is caused by the transmission of painful impulses from the site of injury in the body, through the spinal cord, and then to the brain. In this theory, there is a cluster of cells within the spinal cord, the substantia gelatinosa, that acts as a gate. When these nerve cells are activated, the pain impulses are blocked at the spinal cord level and do not reach the brain. Therefore, any procedure that increases the electrical activity in the substantia gelatinosa decreases pain by increasing the inhibitory properties of these cells. The gate control theory predicts that anything increasing the activity level in large nerve fibers should reduce pain sensations. The use of hot packs, ice packs, mustard plasters, massage, and whirlpool treatments to relieve pain substantiate the rationale of the gate-control theory.[12] Much research is still needed in this area.

Physical Conditioning: A Method for Preserving Health

We have discussed some of the changes that occur due to the aging process. However, through a regular routine of exercise, it is possible for an individual to maintain and, in some cases, improve his physical and emotional well-being.

The art of keeping physically fit has many benefits: the amount of hemoglobin to the red blood cells is increased; the skeletal tone is heightened; fat deposits are reduced; mineralization of the bones is stimulated; oxygen is used more efficiently by the muscles; the heart becomes better able to deliver a greater volume of blood per stroke, and at the same time its capacity to maintain a longer recovery period between beats is increased; nerve regulation of the heart becomes more stable; liver and kidney function is enhanced; and the individual's ability to relax, control emotions, and tolerate fatigue are improved.[15] If a new drug were developed that could achieve all these things, local pharmacies would be depleted of their stocks in a very short time. It is no wonder that the lethargic, television-viewing American of all ages is currently enjoying a physical fitness renaissance.

According to a recent NIH publication, the regular and intelligent use of exercise is considered to be a tool in preventive and curative medicine.[16] Any exercise program should be properly prescribed and adequately supervised. Individuals participating in physical fitness conditioning activities should be cautioned not to over-exercise. It is important for everyone to be aware of the Safe Exercising Pulse Test. An individual should know his *resting pulse* (the average heart beat, taken three days in a row and evaluated upon awakening, but before getting out of bed), and his *maximum pulse,* the fastest rate his heart can safely beat (this should be determined by a physician). The safe exercising pulse is established by subtracting the resting pulse rate from the maximum pulse rate. To insure that there is no overexertion, one should keep the heart rate within ten to 13 beats of the safe exercising pulse. As a point of interest, Dr. F. Kosch found the maximum heart rate of 17 men between the ages of 70 and 79 to be from 155 to 161.[15]

A recent study concerning Master Athlete Paul E. Spangler, a retired 77-year-old physician from California, demonstrates that an individual can consistently achieve well-being in late life. Dr. Spangler, a 1975 National AAU Master's class IV-b Champion (competition for athletes 40 years and older) in 400, 800; 1,500, 5,000, and 15,000 meter races, underwent intensive physiological testing. Dr. Spangler's physical functioning exceeded those people of comparable age who were more sedentary; his physical condition was similar to other Master Athletes, and his functioning approached standards that are often achieved by much younger runners. Observable age-related decrements were noted in measures of maximal pulmonary ventilation, maximal oxygen consumption, and maximal heart rate.[17] This remarkable person demonstrates that while one can never be 20 at 77, an individual is capable of maintaining excellent health standards throughout his life.

Dr. Raymond Harris suggests that exercise programs should include four basic elements: 1) relaxation; 2) exercise designed to enhance endurance and to condition the heart, the lungs, and the circulatory system; 3) stretching exercises designed to improve joint mobility; and 4) muscle strengthening exercises.[18]

When initiating an exercise program, the geriatric practitioner should always receive clearance from the client's physician. The scope of the program and its plan should be discussed thoroughly and approved by a competent medical authority. As the program progresses, the participant's physical condition should be monitored by qualified health personnel. Some therapeutic goals that a generalized group exercise program can achieve are listed below.

Psychological/Social Functioning

1) Improve one's ability to engage in the appropriate release of tension.

2) Improve one's ability to engage in the appropriate release of emotions such as anger, hostility, anxiety, fear, frustration, and aggression.

3) Improve social interaction skills.

4) Develop and improve awareness of physical appearance.

Cognitive Functioning

1) Improve attention span.

2) Increase awareness of body parts.

3) Improve the ability to follow directions and visual cues.

Physical Functioning

1) Increase range of motion and mobility.

2) Improve muscle tone and muscle strength.

3) Improve flexibility, coordination, and balance.

4) Improve gross motor and fine motor functioning.

5) Improve functioning of the cardiovascular and respiratory systems.

6) Increase kinesthetic awareness.

7) Improve endurance.

There are many factors to be taken into consideration concerning exercise programs. One should not confuse exercise and overexertion. Exercise programs should begin gradually and never reach a frenetic pace; to get the most benefit from each exercise, the participant should strive to achieve full range of motion and generally not exercise beyond the point of pain. There is a need for a consistent routine of time (many elderly people prefer midmorning), place, duration of each session (30 to 40 minutes), and number of sessions per week. While it is recommended that exercise be carried out daily, it has been noted that group exercising two or three times weekly and individualized exercising on the other days usually provides a reasonable compromise. There should also be a routine order of exercise. Start with loosening up postures—walking briskly, breathing deeply—and then include a variety of body parts such as scalp, face and eyes, neck, shoulders, elbows, wrists, hands, fingers, abdomen and hips, upper back and chest, lower back, knees, ankles, feet, and toes. This will insure the most efficient and beneficial management of the program.[19] Specific progress can be shown by measuring joint range of motion, grasp, weight loss, and balance tolerance at the beginning and at the conclusion of each session. A graph charting this progress is also helpful.

It is vital that the program include exercise that utilizes all the joints of the body as well as the major and minor muscle groups. Persons using wheelchairs should not be excluded as many exercises can be done from a seated position.

To insure effective communication it is essential that the trainer speak clearly, give visual cues and/or demonstrations when necessary, and explain the purpose of each exercise prior to the activity.

While equipment is not necessary, male participants in particular respond well to a gym-like atmosphere (eg, basketball equipment, punching bags, exercise bicycles). However, it should be noted that isometrics or weightlifting (physical activity that develops the voluntary muscle groups by means of short, rapid, forceful movement) do little to enhance total body conditioning. In fact, there is evidence that this kind of stress on the muscle bundles during contraction has a tendency to impede circulation.[20]

Can a generalized exercise program be effective? Frekany and Leslie evaluated the flexibility of the ankle, hamstrings, and lower back of 15 female subjects— residents of nursing homes and participants of a Golden Agers Club whose ages ranged from 71 to 90—after a seven month involvement in a weekly generalized program (TOES, The Oaknoll Exercise Society). The results demonstrated a statistically significant (p. < .05 level) improvement.[21] The findings of another study, Stamford, Hambacker, and Fallica, indicated that significant cardiovascular and psychosocial improvement were noted in institutionalized geriatric patients who participated in an exercise program.[22]

The Senior Actualization and Growth Explorations (SAGE), an innovative experimental health program for elderly people in preventive mental health groups and in nursing and convalescent homes, utilizes a variety of exercises and training techniques such as Hatha Yoga, meditation, Tai Chi Chuan, relaxation, group breathing, foot massage, visualization discussions, guided imagery, gestalt dream interpretation, Feldenkrais exercises, biofeedback, and autogenic training. This program has been especially effective with depressed older people. Its stated aim is to restore vitality to the older adult.[23]

Exercises and related techniques that can be utilized by older adults are described and clarified in the following materials:

1) Administration on Aging. The Fitness Challenge in the Later Years: An Exercise Program for Older Americans. Washington DC, US Government Printing Office.

2) Cantu RC: Toward Fitness: A Guided Exercise for Those with Health Problems. New York, Human Science Press, 1980.

3) Delza S: Body, Mind in Harmony: Tai Chi Chuan (Wu Style): Ancient Chinese Way of Exercise. New York, Cornerstone Library Publications, 1972.

4) Devi I: Yoga for Americans. New York, The New American Library, 1968.

5) Frankel LJ, Richard BB: Be Alive as Long as You Live. Charleston, WV, Preventi-care Publications, 1977.

6) Hornbaker A: Preventive Care: Easy Exercise Against Aging. New York, Drake Pub Inc, 1974.

7) Kalish A: SAGE (three videotapes). Clarmont Office Park, 41 Tunnel Road, Berkeley, CA, 94705.

8) Leslie K, McLure JW: Exercise for the elderly. Des Moines, IA, Univ Iowa, 1975.

9) Geriatric Exercise Manual. Norristown State Hospital Occupational Therapy Department, Norristown, PA 19401.

10) Royal Canadian Air Force Exercise Plans for Physical Fitness. Ottowa, Canada, 1962.

Physical conditioning may also be accomplished by participation in sports such as swimming, ice skating, boating, tennis, golf, ping-pong, social events such as square, folk, and ballroom dancing, and special organizations such as bicycle clubs, and nature hiking groups.

The Service Provider's Function

Much of this chapter has dealt with the physical, biological, and functional decline of the older person. Whatever the situation, it is the treatment of the whole person—not just an isolated body part—that should reign supreme.

Because so many areas of decline and dysfunction overlap, human care personnel should be well acquainted with the complete spectrum of the aging process. For instance, if one is treating a confused, depressed older person, it is important to be aware that this person may also be experiencing a kinesthetic loss. If this is true, then appropriate self-help aids (ie, grab rails in the hall) and proprioceptive input should be considered as much a part of treatment as reality orientation and life review.

It is essential that the service provider be aware of the consequences of decline that are associated with intrinsic aging. The caregiver who comes armed with as much information as he can acquire is able to deal more competently in initiating and maintaining effective treatment programs than one who has kept his scope of knowledge in narrow confines.

References

1. Hall DA: The Aging of Connective Tissue. New York, Academic Press Inc, 1976, pp 3-4.
2. Busse EW: Theories of Aging. In Busse EW, Pfeiffer E (eds): Behavior and Adaptation in Late Life. Boston, Little Brown and Co, 1969, pp 12-25.
3. Butler RN, Lewis MI: Aging and Mental Health: Positive Psychosocial Approaches. Saint Louis, CV Mosby Co, 1973, pp 102, 272-273.
4. Rosen H: Working with Older People: A Guide to Practice. Washington, DC, Public Health Service Publication, 1966, Vol 1, No 1459, p 13-17.
5. Hasselkus BR: Aging and the human nervous system. Am J Occup Ther 28:17-18, 1974.
6. Liang DS: Facts About Aging. Springfield, IL, Charles C. Thomas Pub, 1973, pp 8-11, 35, 36, 43.
7. Johnson WR: Sex Education and Counseling Special Groups: The Mentally and Physically Handicapped, Ill and Elderly. Springfield, IL, Charles C. Thomas, 1975, p 33.
8. Butler RN and Lewis MI: Sex After Sixty: A Guide for Men and Women in Later Years. New York, Harper and Row, 1976, p 136.
9. Loughman C: Eros and the elderly: A literary view. The Gerontologist 20:182-186, April 1980.
10. Boderick C: Sexuality and aging: An overview. In Solnick R (ed): Los Angeles, University of California Press, 1978, p 6.
11. Battle D: A speech therapist considers speech and learning problems for the elderly. In Deichman ES, O'Kane CP (eds): Working with the Elderly: A Training Manual. Buffalo, New York, DOK Pub Inc, 1975, pp 51-53.
12. Colavita FB: Sensory Changes in the Elderly. Springfield, IL, Charles C. Thomas, 1978, pp 35-39.
13. Altman LK: Cataract surgery advances with lens implants. The New York Times—Science Times, Tuesday May 6, 1980, p C 1.
14. Shore H: Designing a training program for understanding sensory losses in aging. Gerontologist 16:157-165, 1976.
15. Stonecypher DD Jr: Getting Older and Staying Young. New York. WW Norton Inc, 1974, pp 207-209, 211.
16. Special Report on Aging: 1979. U.S. Report of HEW-NIA. (NIH Pub No 80-1907) February 1980, p. 24.
17. Webb LJ, Urner S, McDaniels J: Physiological characteristics of a champion runner. J Gerontol 33:286-290, 1977.

18. Harris R: Leisure time and exercise activities for the elderly. In Craig T (ed): The Humanistic and Mental Health Aspects of Sports, Exercise, and Recreation. Chicago, American Medical Association, 1975, p 100.
19. Leslie DK, McLure JW: Exercises for the Elderly. Des Moines, IA, Univ Iowa, 1973, pp 7-10.
20. Exercises and your heart. Consumer Reports, May 1977, p 25.
21. Frekany GA, Leslie DK: Effects of an exercise program on selected flexibility measurements of senior citizens. Gerontologist 15:182-183, 1975.
22. Stamford BA, Fallica A, Hambacker W: Effects of daily physical exercise on the psychotic state of institutionalized geriatric mental patients. Res Q Am Assoc Health Phys Ed 45:34-41, 1974.
23. Fields S: Sage can be a spice in life. Innovations 4:11-18, 1977.

Bibliography

Jennekins FGI, Tomlinson BE, Walton JN: Histochemical aspects of five limb muscles in old age. J Neural Sci 14:259-276, 1971.
Serratrice G, Roux H, Aquaron R: Proximal muscle weakness in elderly subjects. J Neural Sci 7:275-299, 1968.
Strehler BL: Time, Cells and Aging. New York, Academic Press Inc, 1962.

5
Primary Diseases
of the Elderly

S tatistics indicate that 86% of older persons have some form of chronic
health problem.[1] It is not unusual for the elderly to experience two, three,
or four diseases or areas of dysfunction simultaneously. Many of these chronic
physical problems are accompanied by varying degrees of pain.

Mental Dysfunction

During late life one is most likely to develop some form of mental illness,
specifically a functional or organic brain disorder.[2] These two types of mental
illness have very different origins. Functional disorders which include such
affective disorders as depression paranoia, schizophrenia, neurosis, personality
disorder, alcoholism, and drug dependence, appear to be emotionally based,
while organic disorders are firmly rooted in a physical foundation.[1]

Functional Disorders

Depression

Depressive illness tends to increase with advancing age. In fact, suicides
account for 27.9 deaths per 100,000 population of people in the 75-85 age
bracket.[3]

Depression can manifest itself in many ways—self-reproaches, negative self-
concepts; a specifically altered mood which shows itself in terms of apathy,
loneliness, or sadness, a retarded activity level, a definite loss of libido (expressed

by insomnia and increased anorexia), and regressive and self-punitive wishes (such as desires to escape, hide, or die).[4]

With an older person, depression is complicated by several external factors. First is the repeated experience of *loss*—a spouse or friend, a talent, a body part or function. A second factor is the relentless *attack* of nature, either physically or psychologically, on an aging body, causing discomfort, injury, and pain. Third is the frustrating *restraint* imposed on older life by various disorders. Examples are the bed rest required by certain diseases, the restricted activity prescribed for heart patients, even the economic limitations imposed by a fixed income. The combined and repeated experience of these factors results in a constant state of *threat*, evoked at the smallest sign of an impending loss, attack, or restraint.[5]

It is often difficult to distinguish between depressive and organic states. However, the major types of depression which most affect older adults include mood disorders (both involutional melancholia and manic-depressive psychoses), psychotic depressive reactions, and depressive neuroses.

Involutional melancholia (or involutional psychotic reaction) was originally associated with menopause, but is now associated with aging in general. Onset of the disorder occurs during the ages of 40 to 50 in females and 50 to 65 in males. The depression characteristic of this disease can be manifested in guilt feelings, reduced self-regard, anxiety, insomnia, somatic preoccupation, agitation, and delusions. It is not linked to a previous history of manic-depressive illness.

Manic-depressive psychoses are marked by periods of severe mood swings which may occur as cyclic episodes of one mood alone or of both extremes. Psychopharmacology has made remarkable strides in helping clients who suffer from manic-depression. Specifically, lithium therapy has proved 70% effective. Alternate drugs, such as carbamazepine, are being developed to help the remaining 30%.[6]

Psychotic depressive reactions are severe symptoms of depression that can be attributed to a definable life experience (such as a serious loss or disappointment). In such a state, a person has only a tenuous grip on reality, and his ability to function may be greatly impaired.

Depressive neuroses—also termed depressive reactions or reactive depressions—are the most common neuroses of older persons, often initiated by loss of a loved one, disappointment, criticism, or a threat (both imagined and real).[1]

Current research on depression is focusing more and more on the biochemical factors involved. Many typical depressive behaviors can be related to such specific biochemical changes as higher salt retention within the cells, production of larger amounts of cortisol, a hormone that comes into play during periods of body stress, heightened heart and respiration rate, clenched body musculature, and apparent disorganized hyperactivity of the central nervous system, causing nervous circuits to operate inefficiently.

Perhaps the most important recent findings concern the biogenic amines, substances that are released by the brain's nerve cells, and appear to affect and alter moods. Some scientists now believe that a balance of norepinephrine (a biogenic amine credited with being a primary factor of arousal and alertness), serotonin (another amine believed to be associated with drowsiness), and perhaps other lesser known biogenic amines is essential for maintaining normal moods. Other scientists believe that the enkephalins and endorphins (pain killers which occur naturally in the brain) may be more important than the biogenic amines in affecting mood.

In 1972, the MHPG (3-Methoxy-4-Hydroxyphenylglycol) compound, which derives from norepinephrine, was discovered in the urine and in the cerebrospinal fluid of human and animal subjects. Dr. Schildkraut, a professor of psychiatry at Harvard, believes that MHPG will prove clinically helpful both in determining the different types of depression, and in predicting how well a patient will respond to different types of antidepressants.*

Nondepressive Functional Disorders

Besides the depressive disorders, there are a number of psychiatric illnesses which affect older adults: schizophrenia, paranoia, several types of neuroses and personality disorders, and psychophysiological disorders.

Schizophrenia, a disease marked by disturbances of thought, mood, and behavior, is characterized by hallucinations, poor contact with reality, delusions, diminished control of impulses, and inappropriate behavior and attitudes. "...The schizophrenic finds it difficult to organize thoughts and direct them toward a goal. It appears as if associations lose their logical continuity. Thus, thinking becomes confused, abrupt, and bizarre."[1] Many people experience thought-blocking, a poverty of ideas, with the common result that the same theme may be repeated many times with little variation. Hallucinations (sensory experiences in the absense of appropriate stimuli) and delusions (misunderstanding the meaning of real stimuli) may cause a schizophrenic to become hostile, suspicious, and withdrawn. Specifically, a person suffering from schizophrenia may believe that a song on the radio is especially meant for him, and that there is a definite and special purpose or meaning for it to be played. Thus, fantasy and reality become hopelessly intertwined.[7] The disease as it affects the elderly, falls into two major types: *chronic* and *senile*. Chronic schizophrenia refers to a disease whose symptoms originated in adolescence. Persons with this type of schizophrenia have carried their behaviors and mental disturbances from adolescence into late life. Senile schizophrenia refers to the disease which develops only in late life; it is a rare disorder.[1]

Perhaps the biggest breakthrough in the treatment of schizophrenia has been the advent of the anti-psychotic drugs, introduced in the United States in the mid-1950s. It is believed that when the neurotransmitter, dopamine (dopamine receptors are situated in the areas of the brain where feelings and thoughts are processed), is blocked, many schizophrenic symptoms are diminished. These drugs (eg, *phenothiazines* such as Thorazine, Mellaril, and Stelazine; *thioxanthenes* such as Taractan and Navane; and *butyrophenones* such as Haldol) are helpful in decreasing agitation and combativeness, and in reducing delusions and disordered thinking. While none of these drugs cures schizophrenia, they are aids in improving a person's ability to function.

*Scarf M: From joy to depression: New insights into the chemistry of moods. The New York Times, April 24, 1977, pp 31-37.

However, in long term treatment, continued use of these types of drugs may lead to the development of tardive dyskinesia, a neurologic disorder with symptoms that include twitching of the legs and arms, and grotesque, involuntary movements of the facial muscles.[8]

These powerful drugs, also known as neuroleptics, have been increasingly used in geriatric care facilities where they may be prescribed to control disruptive behavior. A growing number of psychiatrists have objected to the use of these drugs as a "replacement for talking to people—making them feel cared about and cared for."[9]

Paranoid states are psychotic disorders manifested by a delusion, usually of a grandiose or persecutory nature. The delusion may cause disturbances in mood, behavior, and thinking, although it does not impair intellectual functioning. Paranoia tends to occur when a person suffers from an adverse condition such as blindness, deafness, isolation, or infection. It is believed that the isolation from human contact which occurs with hearing loss or blindness results in the misinterpretation of incoming stimuli.

Neuroses, while they may impair thinking and judgment, do not manifest as gross a distortion of reality or as profound a disorganization of personality as do schizophrenia and paranoia. According to psychiatric theory, neuroses are the result of attempts to resolve unconscious emotional conflicts. Characterized by anxiety, neurotic conditions are very common in late life.

The neuroses that appear most frequently in old age include depressive, hysterical (both dissociative and conversion types), obsessive-compulsive, phobic, and hypochondriacal neuroses. With dissociative hysterical neurosis, the older person becomes extremely anxious—to the point of personality disorganization. This state often results in amnesia, confusion, fatigue, and stupor. With conversion hysterical neurosis, a person manifests emotional conflict through physical symptoms; his autonomic nervous system is not involved. A person suffering obsessive-compulsive neurosis repeats thoughts or actions, unable to discontinue the pattern. Someone in a phobic state repeatedly exhibits an intense fear of something; this fear displaces some real feared object or event.

With hypochondriacal neurosis, a person is overconcerned with his own well-being. He may complain of various bodily ailments for which there is no actual physiological basis. These ailments serve his needs in a variety of ways: punishment for guilt, a method of controlling others, a symbol of his deterioration and age, a displacement of anxiety, a method of inhibiting undesired behavior, a means of reducing interpersonal contact, and a method by which he can identify with a deceased loved one who may have experienced similar symptoms. There is a great deal of overlap between hypochondria and depression.

Personality disorders cover a whole group of old age disorders which are the result of personality defects developed over a lifetime. The following are examples of deeply ingrained maladaptive patterns of behavior often observed in older adults: schizoid, paranoid, inadequate obsessive-compulsive, cyclothymic, hysterical, explosive, asthenic-antisocial, and passive-aggressive.

In psychophysiological or psychosomatic disorders the physical symptoms are caused by emotional factors. However, there are definite differences between this disease state and conversion reactions or hypochondria. Psychophysiological disorders involve the autonomic nervous system; they do not help to reduce anxiety. The symptoms are physiological rather than symbolic. Since actual structural change occurs, these disorders pose a definite somatic threat. The most common psychosomatic reactions of older people are pruritus (of the ani and vulvae), psychogenic rheumatism, irritable colon, nocturia (frequent urination at night), cardiac neuroses, preoccupation with bowel habits, and hyperventilation syndromes.[1]

Organic Disorders

Fifteen percent of people in the 65 to 75 year age bracket and 25% of people 75 years and older have been diagnosed as "senile." Currently, most professionals refer to this mental state as "organic brain syndrome."*

Organic brain syndromes are psychiatric disorders that reflect brain cell loss, or impairment of brain tissue function. They fall into two basic types: *acute* (reversible) and *chronic* (irreversible).

There are five traditional signs which indicate organic brain dysfunction: impairment and disturbance of memory, impairment of intellectual functioning, orientation, judgment, and labile or shallow affect.[1] However, psychiatric, neurotic, and behavioral disorders may complicate the clinical picture of any organic brain dysfunction.

Acute brain syndrome may result from:

1) cerebral hypoxia, decreased oxygenation of the blood caused by anemia, pulmonary disease, and similar factors;

2) increased cerebral oxygen requirements such as those found in thyrotoxicosis and febrile states;

3) insufficient supply of a necessary metabolic substance such as nicotinic acid and thiamine;

4) a disruption of cerebral metabolic processes, manifested in endocrine disorders, head trauma, toxic states, or fluid and electrolyte imbalance; and

5) impaired cerebral blood supply, which is seen in cardiac disease, hypertensive encephalopathy, and decreased blood volume.

One consistent characteristic of acute brain syndrome is that the pathology is reversible. Other symptoms of the disorder include a fluctuating level of awareness, hallucinations (particularly visual), disorientation, aggressiveness, delusions of persecution, anxiety, and lack of cooperation.[1]

Chronic brain syndrome, diffuse brain damage with massive loss of cortical and limbic neurons, can be caused by a number of circumstances, including:

1) episodic and recurrent blood loss, caused by infections with high fever,

*Altman LK: Medicine—Senility is not always what it seems to be. The New York Times, May 8, 1977, p E9.

cardiac arrhythmia, anemic states, myocardial infarction, and blood pressure drops;

2) erosion of vulnerable areas of the brain which are poorly supplied by collateral blood vessels, leading to erosion of the total mass of brain tissue;

3) occlusion of the arterioles due to thromboses or emboli, which results in a critical loss of cerebral tissue; and

4) cerebral degeneration of unknown origin, such as that manifested by presenile sclerosis, which can occur at any age.

The emotionally laden term *senility* refers specifically to chronic brain syndrome. The primary characteristic of this syndrome is its irreversibility. Dr. R. N. Butler considers organic brain syndrome to be divided into two categories: *senile psychosis,* senile dementia and senile brain disease, and *psychosis,* which is associated with cerebral arteriosclerosis.[1] On the other hand, Dr. A. I. Goldfarb believes that organic brain syndrome should be classified as *uncomplicated* (irreversible cognitive impairment without any appreciable degree of thought, behavioral, or mood disorder) and *complicated* (irreversible cognitive impairment that is accompanied by disturbances of thought, content, behavior, or mood).[10]

Senile Psychosis

In senile psychosis there is a progressive decline in mental functioning associated with structural changes within the brain caused by atrophy and degeneration. Early features of senile psychosis include errors in judgment, decline in self-care habits, loosening of inhibitions, impairment of abstract thought, restlessness, depression, and anxiety. These symptoms are precursors of greater impairments.

Arteriosclerotic Psychosis

While senile psychosis shows a steady mental decline, arteriosclerotic psychosis is characterized by an uneven downward progression. This disorder is associated with' the arteriosclerotic impairment of the cerebral blood vessels. Early symptoms include dizziness, headaches, and a decrease in vigor. Another important characteristic is erratic impairment of memory.

Presenile Dementia

Presenile dementia refers to a group of cortical brain diseases—Alzheimer's disease and Pick's disease being the most common—which clinically resemble the senile dementias seen in older persons. Presenile dementias, however, usually occur in adults 40 to 50 years old, although, like senile dementias, they can occur in persons over 65. These diseases are characterized primarily by personality disintegration and intellectual deterioration. Both Pick's disease and Alzheimer's disease are clinically similar except that the former is characterized by lack of initiative, the latter by aggression. Both diseases are invariably fatal.[1]

Alzheimer's Disease

While many specialists once believed that Alzheimer's disease occurred most frequently in people under 65 years of age, it is becoming increasingly clear that this disorder is the most common cause of severe intellectual dysfunctioning in older adults. It is now estimated that one half of the elderly with severe intellectual impairments suffer from Alzheimer's disease. Approximately one fourth of this group are victims of vascular disorders, brain tumors, abnormal thyroid function, infections, pernicious anemia, adverse drug reactions, and hydrocephalus.

Neurofibrillary tangles, an accumulation of abnormal fibers in the cerebral cortex, were first described in 1906 by Alois Alzheimer. In recent years highly sophisticated instruments such as the electron microscope have revealed a number of other changes in the brain that are characteristic of this disease. Throughout the cortex are scattered groups of nerve endings that degenerate and disrupt the passage of electrochemical signals between the cells. These areas of degeneration are known as plaques. Disturbance of intellectual function increases as the number of plaques and tangles increases. As a consequence, the individual becomes forgetful about recent events, and as the disease progresses, confusion, irritability, restlessness, and agitation increase.

Although the exact cause for Alzheimer's disease is unknown, scientists have identified a 90% reduction in cholineacetyltransferase (a brain enzyme that is involved in the passage of nerve signals) in persons suffering from this condition.[11] NIA research grantees at the University of Toronto have shown that the brains of people dying of Alzheimer's disease contain large quantities of aluminum. Further study indicates that aluminum forms crosslinks between DNA strands and could therefore be responsible for the lesions that are characteristic of this disease.[12]

Treatment usually includes the judicious use of tranquilizers to lessen agitation and anxiety. Appropriate nourishment and exercise are indicated, and activities of daily living should be maintained as close to a normal level as is possible. Memory aids such as calendars, written reminders about routine safety measures, lists of daily tasks, and directions on items that are most frequently used are helpful.[11]

The importance of being aware of the clinical differences between dementia (true senility, eg, Alzheimer's disease) and pseudodementia is a prime concern for service providers. In both illnesses the client presents as being in a confused state.

In dementia: the onset is insidious with a slow progression; except in the early stages, the patient is not upset over his deficits and there is a tendency for him to evade or deny the problem; there is no history of loss or significant life event that triggered the problem; the patient will try to maintain social acceptance and the ability to experience some pleasures; the affect is generally bland and may be shallow and labile; confabulation is a common occurrence; there is an increase of agitation at night (true in both dementia and pseudodementia); mental status examinations are usually consistent with remote memory being more intact—daily mental status examinations remain unchanged; deficits have no dynamic significance for the client; and families tend to recognize the problems late.

In pseudodementia the onset is subacute with a relatively rapid progression; one can usually elicit a history of loss or stressfully significant life event; the patient will often emphasize his disability and highlight his failures; there is general evidence of social withdrawal; the patient tends to be anhedonic; affective change is prominent as the client usually becomes angry and irritable; confabulation is rare; the client's mental status examinations are internally inconsistent and both recent and remote memory are severely impaired on an equal basis—daily mental status examinations fluctuate; and families tend to recognize the illness early (usually because the client is difficult to handle).

In pseudodementia the confused state can often be alleviated with treatment that is appropriate for depression.[13]

New Hope for the Intellectually Impaired

Through biochemical research, it is hoped that some of the problems of memory impairment in old age can be solved. NIA grantees have discovered, in studies comparing aged and young animals, that both groups are able to compensate for brain nerve cell loss. Each nerve cell in the brain both sends and receives input from thousands of other nerve cells. In some instances, when nerve cells are destroyed, the remaining cells are able to form new connections, compensating for those that were lost. This is known as reactive synaptogenesis. Researchers have demonstrated that aged rats (equivalent to 80 human years) exhibit this ability to regrow new brain circuits. However, regrowth in the older animals is much weaker, and it often reforms improper connections to existing brain cells. Certainly, further studies as to why improper connections are made need to be conducted. If ways could be found to enhance the proper type of regrowth, the damage caused by organic brain syndrome and other degenerative changes in the brain could be reduced.[12]

The peptide, MSH/ACTH 4-10, is a brain protein that is a derivative of two pituitary hormones. According to researchers Allen E. Willner and Charles J. Rabiner of Long Island Jewish-Hillside Medical Center, MSH/ACTH 4-10 has been found to improve visual retention, reduce anxiety and help concentration in healthy subjects, to improve task comprehension and workshop performance in the mentally retarded, to improve visual memory in elderly senile patients, and to improve mild memory problems in older persons.[14]

Diagnostic Methods

The arrival of the CAT (computerized axial tomography), a revolutionary new X-ray technique, has made possible a more definitive neurological diagnosis of organic brain syndrome. Quick and painless, the CAT X-ray can actually show a shrunken brain. Scientific technology is moving at such a rapid rate that even this new method may soon become outdated. An experimental tool, called the Dynamic Spatial Reconstructor (DSR) is being developed at the Mayo Clinic in

Rochester, Minnesota. This new device dissects the living body without harming it. The chief difference between the CAT scanner and the DSR is that the CAT scanner constructs images "resembling two-dimensional salami-like slices, while the DSR dices the body. Then, electronically, the DSR reassembles the cubes to form a moving, three-dimensional life-size X-ray image of the body." Since it stores data, the system can then be asked to reconstruct parts of the scanned region at any desired angle or location. The impact of this new tool, when fully developed, will most certainly be enormous. It will be a way of getting direct confirmation as to what is actually happening in all parts of the body without performing any type of vivisection.[15]

The PET (positron emission tomography) is yet another revolutionary scanning process. It examines the brain's activities by way of a glucose-like substance which is tagged with a radioactive marker.[16]

Previous clinical diagnostic measures such as the EEG, the static and dynamic brain scans, and ultra-sound were time consuming, sometimes painful, and not very accurate.

Other diagnostic evaluations and assessments, however, are helpful in determining the severity of the condition. They include the Mental Status Evaluation (Perlen S, Butler RN), the Mental Status Questionnaire (Kahn RL, Goldfarb AI, Pollack M, Peck A), the Short Portable Mental Status Questionnaire (Pfeiffer E), and the Double Simultaneous Stimulations of the Hand and Face (Goldfarb).

Physical Dysfunction

Parkinson's Disease

Parkinson's disease, a degenerative disorder of the central nervous system, is the third most common chronic disease of late life. Parkinsonism may be classified in two ways: *symptomatic*—a result of cerebral arteriosclerosis, encephalitis, toxicity, or high dosages of phenothiazines—and *idiopathic*.

Parkinson's disease is characterized by several physiological changes in the brain. Researchers believe that Parkinsonism may be caused by the failure of the degenerating neurons in the substancia nigra to transmit dopamine (the precursor of norepinephrine) to the striatum.[17]

Changes within the extrapyramidal tract are responsible for such characteristic Parkinson symptoms as rigidity, loss of balance, and tremor. Loss of dopamine transmission permits the cholinergic pathways to predominate. The following are specific characteristics commonly associated with Parkinsonism:

1) *Involuntary motion*—Parkinsonism tremor, initially involving the flexion and extension of the thumb and index finger, results in what is commonly referred to as "pillrolling". This type of tremor may also be found in the other fingers, wrists, forearms, and ankles. It is most pronounced when the client is at rest, and increases with emotional stress or fatigue. It is absent during sleep and supressed during activity.

2) *Rigidity*—This phenomenon, affecting both flexor and extensor muscles, takes two forms: *leadpipe* and *cogwheel*. Leadpipe rigidity refers to increased resistance throughout the entire range of motion when the upper and lower extremities are passively moved. Cogwheel rigidity occurs in a jerky intermittent manner; there is impairment of fine motor movements of the upper extremities. The typical Parkinsonism posture is displayed in flexion of the head, shoulders, hips, and knees, with the client forward of the normal center of gravity.

3) *Impaired motor function*—As the client becomes less mobile, he moves in a more deliberate manner, often referred to as "freezing." In the early stages of the disease, his gait is slow and there is reciprocal loss of arm movements. In the more advanced stage, his gait is shuffled and his steps smaller. Eventually his fine motor control is severely impaired.

4) *Dysfunction of the cranial nerves*—The ocular, facial, and oropharyngeal nerves cease to function appropriately. The malfunctions may take several forms: difficulty in swallowing, chewing, and facial movements; disturbances of eye function such as convergence and oculogyric crises (ocular fixation in one position for a prolonged period); and dysfunctions of speech, including decreased volume, monotonous tone, and poor enunciation.

5) *Impairment of equilibrium*—The client loses his righting or protective reactions and is unable to maintain a standing balance.

6) *Disorder of the autonomic nervous system*—These include increased salivation, perspiration, bladder malfunction, greasy skin, intolerance to heat, and diminished peristalsis.

Medical treatment for Parkinson's disease involves a variety of drug therapies such as anticholinergics, antihistamines, Levodopa, and Sinemet (this combination of Carbodopa and Levodopa does not manifest the unpleasant side effects of Levadopa alone).[18]

Joint Disease and Osteo-Disorders

Arthritis (from the Greek roots *arthron,* meaning joint, and *itis,* meaning inflammation) is one of the most common and oldest of chronic diseases. Although there are many kinds of arthritis, this discussion will focus on the types which most often involve the elderly—osteoarthritis, rheumatoid arthritis, and gout.

Osteoarthritis

A noninflammatory degenerative joint disease, osteoarthritis is extremely common among elderly people. It is a progressive disorder of the movable weight-bearing joints. During the course of this disease, there is a pathological deterioration of the articular cartilage and formation of new bone at the margins of the joint and in the subchondral areas.[19] This degenerative process can be traced to such reasons as impaired blood supply, heredity, the wear and tear of daily living, a single severe injury, continued minor trauma, and excessive strain and wear on specific joint areas (eg, desk workers may develop this disease in the neck and spine, while obese people may develop osteoarthritis in the knees).[20]

Specific changes in cell cartilage, including the loss of density which is exhibited by the presence of fibrillations, and increased erosion, usually cause the body to produce extra calcium in the form of osteophytes, or bony spurs. This combination of osteophyte formation and cartilage degeneration often produces stiff and immobile joints. A specific example is Herbeden's nodes, which are enlargements of the distal interphalangeal joints found in many women with osteoarthritis.

People with degenerative joint disease often complain that they experience stiffness and pain upon rising in the morning, during damp weather, after prolonged static positioning, and during periods of fatigue.

Medical treatment of this disease includes chemotherapy (aspirin is the drug of choice); local support in the form of splints, crutches or a cane when necessary; heat; specific exercises designed to correct muscle atrophy; and surgical procedures such as debridement, arthrodesis (joint fusion), arthroplasty (new prosthetic articulating surface), osteotomy (a new section of a bone is used to alter the weight-bearing surface), and total joint replacement.[19]

Rheumatoid Arthritis

Rheumatoid arthritis, a disease process that can occur at any age, usually begins within the joints as an inflammation of the synovial area. It is characterized by edema, vascular congestion, cellular infiltrate, and fibrin exudate of the synovium. Usually the synovial fluid decreases in viscosity and becomes turbid. During the course of this disease there is a distinctive tendency towards spontaneous exacerbation and remission.

Although there is no specifically-known cause for rheumatoid arthritis, many theories exist. Some scientists believe it to be caused by such infectious agents as mycoplasma or viruses; others think that such immune mechanisms as antigen antibody complexes (the interaction of IgG and rheumatoid factors) cause the disease; while others feel it is caused by Lysosonial enzymes.[19]

At onset, the symptoms of rheumatoid arthritis are insidious (aching and stiffness are usually poorly localized to the joints). As the disease progresses, many patients complain of stiff joints upon awakening. Joints of the extremities are frequently involved. Tenosynovitis is extremely common, with the extensor and flexor tendon sheaths about the wrist being most often affected. Carpal tunnel syndrome may also be manifested. Joint involvement in rheumatoid arthritis tends to be bilaterally symmetrical.

The disease often results in serious deformities. Fixed deformities are caused by the inflammation and subsequent fibrosis in ligaments, capsule, and musculotendinous apparatus. Subluxation (slipping of one articular surface past another) is usually caused by erosion of bone and cartilage as well as the destruction of supporting soft tissues such as ligaments and joint capsules. Characteristic hand deformities include ulnar drift, subluxation of the metacarpophalangeal joints, enlargement of the proximal interphalangeal joints, boutonniere deformity (the flexed proximal interphalangeal joint is forced through the extensor hood), and swan neck deformity (contraction of the intrinsic hand muscles, producing hyperextension at the proximal interphalangeal joint and flexion at the distal interphalangeal joint).[19]

Medical treatment of rheumatoid arthritis includes chemotherapy (aspirin being the most effective drug) and a variety of orthopedic and surgical procedures including splinting, insertion of a metal cup in the hip joint, complete replacement of joints by artificial devices, tendon repair, and synonectomy.

Gout

With gout, blood deposits of uric acid crystals form in the kidney, various joints, and certain cartilages. These chalky deposits, called tophi, are directly caused by an increase of uric acid in the blood. The disease is characterized by recurring attacks of acute painful swelling in a variety of joints, most commonly the big toe (50% of all cases) and the elbow. Eighty-five percent of the cases are men, and the usual period of onset is after the age of 40.

The factors believed to be instrumental in precipitating gout attacks are injury to the joint, eating food that contains excessive amounts of purine (such as duck, goose, or sweetbreads), excessive alcohol, and physical and mental stress.

Treatment involves the control and prevention of future attacks as well as the long-term reduction of hyperuricema. Both can be accomplished through chemotherapy using uricosuric agent drugs such as colchicine, phenylbutazone, and oxyphenbutazone. These drugs aid in the elimination of excessive uric acid. Appropriate diet—foods with little purine or alcoholic content—is also recommended.[20]

Osteoporosis

A common problem among elderly persons, osteoporosis is not actually related to the arthritic complaints. It is characterized by the thickening of the bone cortex, a compensatory reaction that occurs on the periosteum. These new bone deposits are responsible for changing the actual shape of the bone. Because of these structural changes, the older person becomes less able to withstand trauma, and is therefore predisposed to an increasing amount of bone fracture.[21]

In terms of treatment, NIA investigators have discovered that when individuals experience a vitamin K deficiency, there is a resultant decrease in the protein osteo-calcin which in turn causes bone calcium loss. Vitamin K is now believed to be vital to calcium bone turnover. By selecting foods that are easily digested the elderly often exclude green vegetables, cauliflower, potatoes, and liver—all rich in vitamin K. If research continues to demonstrate a strong relationship between vitamin K, calcium metabolism, and osteoporosis, then a vitamin K-rich diet could very well serve as a method of treatment.[12]

Heart Disease

The number one cause of death in the United States, heart disease, actually covers a heterogeneous group of diseases which affect the heart. It can be broken down into three categories: cerebrovascular disease, diseases of the circulatory system, and cardiovascular-renal diseases.

1) *Cerebrovascular disease*—attributed to vascular lesions that affect the central nervous system. These lesions are generated by ischemia (infarction of the brain that may be caused by atherosclerosis, thrombosis, or cerebral embolism) and cerebral hemorrhage.

2) *Diseases of the circulatory system*—these include the following disorders: rheumatic fever, chorea, rheumatic valvular disease, rheumatic endocarditis, myocarditis, arteriosclerotic and degenerative disease, acute and subacute endocarditis, acute myocarditis, acute pericarditis, functional diseases of the heart, hypertensive heart disease and hypertension, arteriosclerosis (atherosclerosis of the coronary arteries which can manifest itself as myocardiac infarction, angina pectoris, coronary insufficiency, sudden death, congestive heart failure, and cardiac arrhythmias), aneurysms, peripheral vascular diseases, arteriol embolism and thrombosis, and diseases of the veins.

One of these diseases, arteriosclerosis, is a primary disorder that affects many older people. Arteriosclerosis is a generic term that refers to a number of different conditions which cause hardening of the arteries. Atherosclerosis is just one of these conditions. In this illness the center of a fibrous plaque is filled with a greasy, porridge-like material. This chronic disease begins in childhood and progresses with age. Myocardial and cerebral infarctions, presently the most common immediate causes of adult death in the United States, are complications.

3) *Cardiovascular-renal diseases*—these involve a combination of heart disorders (ie, hypertensive heart disease) with other diseases such as chronic nephritis and renal sclerosis.

The exact cause of heart disease has not yet been determined, but the following items are considered risk factors: genetics, gross obesity, social and psychological stress, high serum cholesterol levels, elevated arterial blood pressure levels, smoking, and such disorders as diabetes mellitus, hypothyroidism, myxedema, and rheumatic fever.

Medical treatment of heart disease varies with the specific problem. Chemotherapy in the form of anticoagulant drugs can be effectively used to help prevent complications of acute heart attacks (thrombosis and embolism). Numerous drugs are also available to help lower blood pressure levels. Surgical treatment includes replacing damaged arteries with artificial ones, bypassing damaged segments, and in rare cases, transplanting the heart itself. Mechanical devices such as alternating- and direct-current cardiac defibrillators, cardioverters, and cardiac pacemakers are used to restore the heart rate to a more normal beat.[22]

Cerebral Vascular Accident (Stroke)

At least two million people now alive in the United States, have suffered a stroke. Approximately 80% of all stroke victims survive the initial episode.

Often they are left with some form of residual disability. The female-male ratio is about 2:1.[23]

Stroke can result from any of three major factors:

1) Occlusion caused by thrombosis—clotting of the cerebral vessel;

2) Rupture of a cerebral vessel caused by high blood pressure or a flaw in the vessel wall which results in an aneurysm; or

3) Occlusion caused by an embolism—a fragment of a clot that becomes dislodged from the heart or blood vessels and plugs the cerebral vessel.

All these factors result in an inadequate supply of oxygenated blood to parts of the brain, which demands more than one fifth of all blood pumped from the heart. The CAT and PET scans are helpful in determining specific areas of brain dysfunction. Warning episodes of stroke include brief attacks of speech loss, weakness of the limbs, and loss of consciousness.

Medical treatment of the stroke patient involves the use of high oxygen pressure chambers, blood vessel surgery, and chemotherapy to improve blood circulation, control fat metabolism, and hypertension.[22]

The rehabilitation process of the stroke patient more often takes place in a specialized facility. Principles of restorative care rests on four basic tenets:

1) Definitive diagnosis—determining the basic reason for a symptom's existence.

2) Prevention of secondary disabilities—recognizing the problem early, preparing a preliminary treatment plan, utilizing corrective measures to alleviate the handicap as early as possible, and continuing corrective treatment measures throughout the duration of the handicap.

3) Developing functional abilities and using existing ones to ensure maximum utilization of compensatory mechanisms.

4) Preservation of the client's dignity.

Issacs believes that a comprehensive examination that assesses motor function, communication, cognition, sensation (eg, light touch, deep pressure, pin-prick), proprioceptive difficulties, somatoception (sensation that one's arm/leg does not belong to him), visual impairments, and automatic function/dysfunction (bowel and bladder) is essential.[24]

Wolcott states that there are four basic recovery stages and that the rate of progress during the initial days or weeks depends upon the client's general exercise tolerance, functional return in the extremities, and motivation. In each of the stages of recovery (acute, post acute, convalescent, and follow-up) the rehabilitation team members, usually consisting of physicians, therapists, nurses, counselors and a social worker, are responsible for utilizing their skills and knowledge to improve the patient's functioning level.[23]

The most common impairments of surviving stroke patients are:

1) *Hemiplegia*—paralysis of one side of the body.

2) *Aphasia*—a condition that results in a decrease of language ability,

affecting understanding, reading, writing, speaking, calculation, and gesturing. A more comprehensive description of aphasia follows this section.

3) *Dysarthria*—oral production of speech is impaired, and is usually the result of a central or peripheral nervous system lesion that causes weakness, uncoordination, or paralysis of the speech musculaculture. One, more, or all of the following motor aspects of speech may be affected: phonation, resonance, articulation, respiration, volume, rate of intonation, voice quality, and rhythm.

4) *Apraxia*—inability to plan voluntary motor movements.

5) *Paraphasia*—verbal output impairment which is usually due to a posterior lesion in the brain. It is characterized by inconsistent sound substitutions and additions (phonetic paraphasia—splork for fork) or associated words (verbal paraphasia—knife for fork). (Shultz AR, Unpublished research.)

6) *Bilateral problems*—a left cerebral lesion can cause a deficit in right/left discrimination, and an inability to understand and use the concepts of right and left. Those persons with bilateral dysfunction tend to have problems in motor planning and verbal communication.[25]

7) *Unilateral visual/perceptual neglect*—the individual tends to neglect visual stimuli on the impaired body side. This type of neglect occurs in any activity that requires a symmetrical visual exploration of the environment. It is characterized by the individual bumping into objects, dressing only one side of the body, ignoring food on one side of the plate, or reading only one half of a page.

8) *Homonymous hemianopsia*—a visual field defect. Often patients with this condition are able to compensate well for their hemianopsia and demonstrate little or no visual neglect.[26]

Aphasia

Aphasia, a symptom-complex condition, is now believed to be the direct result of a lesion to the left side of the cerebral hemisphere. This usually results in decreased language competency. Aphasia can be classified as *receptive* and *expressive*.

The receptive aphasic has difficulty comprehending spoken (auditory aphasia) or written (alexic aphasia) symbols. Specifically, he confuses words that sound alike when spoken, such as *moat* and *boat;* he indiscriminately mixes words that are associated in experience and meaning, such as *sky* and *blue;* he suffers a reduced naming and reading vocabulary (his reading is further hampered by associated errors and perceptual confusions); and he has difficulty understanding abstract words such as *peace* or *hope,* as well as difficulty comprehending words which indicate relationships, such as *if* and *but.*[27]

In expressive aphasia the individual is not able to adequately express his ideas in writing or speech. His written and spoken vocabularies, especially nouns, are impoverished. When writing, he may reverse letters, confuse similar letters, and exhibit phonetic spelling. His speech often consists of telegraphic utterances, such as, "Eat apple," or "Drink tea." Since he has difficulty utilizing words that express conditions, relationships, and qualities, his sentences are often ungrammatical. He may also exhibit a specific impairment in his speech delivery—hesitancies, slowed or quickened speech rate, faulty word pronunciation, reversal, omitting, and incorrect usage of sounds or syllables.[28]

Pure receptive and expressive aphasia rarely exist. Instead, aphasic disability is associated with multiple dysfunction of language modalities such as comprehension of spoken language, reading, writing, and speech. Specific perceptual-motor or sensory-motor deficits may be superimposed upon this condition.[27]

Cancer

"...Cancer is a term applied to a group of diseases having in common the transformation of normal body cells into abnormally growing parasitic cells."[22] The basis of the illness is the cancer cell. While there are numerous known agents that can transform healthy cells into cancer cells, there is as yet no known single cause for the transformation. Scientific studies show that cancer cell nuclei differ from normal ones in several respects: they are larger, vary in shape, do not adhere to each other as much as normal cells, and they show deviations in the number and appearance of chromosomes.

Diseases of the cancer family have certain common characteristics: invasiveness into surrounding tissues, metastasis (transfer of a part of a cancer to another body part), hemorrhaging in tumor areas, a wasting away of the host, deviations in structure and function from the normal, and occurrences of superimposed infections.

The most common sites for cancer in males are the skin, lung, prostate, large intestine, stomach, rectum, and bladder. Common female sites are the breast, cervix, uterus, large intestine, corpus uteri, ovary, stomach, and rectum.

Many factors can precipitate the disease: unnecessary exposure to ionizing and ultraviolet radiation, non-hygienic measures in occupations which involve exposure to cancer-producing dust and chemicals, excessive exposure to tobacco, and heredity.

Medical treatment of this condition involves the surgical removal of the cancerous areas, radiation therapy, and chemotherapy.[22]

Emphysema

Emphysema is derived from the Greek word "emphystma" which means body inflation. With this disease the passages leading to the lung alveoli, the smaller bronchioles, and the blood vessels become constricted. Little oxygen can reach the alveoli. Consequently, carbon dioxide accumulates in the air sacs. There is a constant decrease in arterial saturation of oxygen. As the disease progresses, the alveoli become enlarged and their elastic tissue is lost. There is a definite decrease in vital capacity and maximum breathing capacity. In the most severe cases there may be brain damage and an enlarged, weakened heart.

Many physicians believe that emphysema originates with a bronchial infection.[29]

Diabetes Mellitus

This disease can be defined as the body's inability to metabolize carbohydrates normally. These carbohydrates, in the form of glucose, accumulate and result in an increase of blood sugar. Eventually, this leads to sugar in the urine.

The exact cause of diabetes is unknown. Originally, it was believed that diabetes was the direct result of deficient insulin action. However, recent research indicates that diabetes may be a multihormonal disturbance.[30] Researchers in San Francisco have been able to produce human insulin by means of genetically engineered bacteria, recombinant DNA technology. Large scale production is expected shortly.[31] Though its cause is unknown, the disease can be closely related to four factors: obesity, heredity, stress and urbanization, and arteriosclerosis—which is responsible for 60% of all diabetic deaths.

Some symptoms of diabetes include repeated infections, gangrene, early cataracts, pruritus (especially in the genital areas), undue exhaustion, impotence, extensive pyorrhea, and sudden refractory changes in the eyes.[32]

At present, treatment includes insulin therapy, cleanliness, and a measured balanced diet which is low in calories and high in nutrients. Although there has been much interest in the use of oral hypoglycemic agents such as Orinace, insulin remains the most effective form of chemotherapy.[30] To avoid insulin shock, the diabetic must account for an increase in exercise or routine by a corresponding increase in his between meal intake.[33]

If this disease is not treated, diabetic coma will result. This usually develops slowly over a period of hours. The symptoms, in their progressive order, include increased urination and thirst; drowsy restlessness, loss of appetite; nausea, vomiting, and pain; an increase in temperature; Kussmaul respiration (hyperventilation with deep, regular sighing); dry skin; beet-red tongue; acetone on the breath; rapid heart beat; and finally, unconsciousness. Bed rest, forced fluids, insulin, and cleansing of the bowels are the primary forms of treatment.[32]

Accidental Hypothermia

Hypothermia is an abnormally low body temperature of 95°F (35°C) and under. The exact cause is unknown. In Britain 10% of a random population of people 65 and over were classified as potential hypothermia victims. The actual number of elderly deaths in the United States attributed to this condition is not known. Based upon the British studies and statistics, at least 2.3 million elderly in the United States could be vulnerable.

Risk factors include those who live alone and therefore cannot get help if they have an accident, those whose body heat regulatory systems are not working properly, those who take drugs that hamper the body's ability to regulate temperature (eg, phenothiazines that are commonly used to treat depression or nausea), and those who live in substandard housing—an estimated 30% of the older American population.

Symptoms of hypothermia include: bloated face; skin color which may be pale and waxy, or oddly pink; trembling on one side of the body or in one leg or arm, but no shivering; irregular and slowed heart beat, slurred speech, very slow, shallow breathing, low blood pressure; and drowsiness.

Hypothermia must be treated by a physician. Rewarming must be done slowly—no more than one degree per hour—and the blood pressure must be held steady. A body temperature under 90°F (32.2°C) must be treated as a medical emergency, including hospitalization.

There are a number of protective measures that the older person should observe: rooms should be kept at 70°F (21°C); prolonged exposure to the cold should be avoided; adequate warm clothing should be worn; the bed should have several blankets; and if possible, susceptible people should try not to be alone for long periods of time.[34]

Hyperthermia

The three basic types of hyperthermia are heatstroke, Neuroleptic Malignant Syndrome and catatonia. Older people are particularly susceptible to hyperthermia.

Heatstroke—This condition may be caused by overactivity, heat or high humidity, overheating of the home or care center, and possibly certain drugs. The onset is sudden; the person may collapse in just hours. The mouth often becomes dry and the skin may be either dry or sweating. The core temperature range is usually between 105-108°F. Treatment precautions include maintaining an appropriate environmental temperature; minimizing antipsychotic medication; and avoiding drugs with anticholinergic affects. During hot weather the older person should drink fluids, avoid exercise, prevent agitation and overactivity, wear loose-fitting clothing, avoid seclusion, and stay away from alcoholic beverages. Specific treatment calls for the immediate transfer to a hospital. The cooling process should then be administered by qualified professionals. These procedures include removing the client from the heat source, removing the client's clothing, applying cool water to the body, face and limbs, maintaining the airway, and massaging the limbs so that vasoconstriction can be reduced.

Neuroleptic Malignant Syndrome—The cause for this problem is often related to antipsychotic drugs. The client may experience sweating skin, excessive salivation; leadpipe rigidity (akinesia) and a temperature of 103-106°F. There is a gradual onset. It is best treated by stopping the intake of antipsychotic drugs.

Catatonia—The cause for this condition is generally not known, but it often occurs in hot weather. The onset is gradual and may take days or weeks. The client experiences sweating skin, a possible dry mouth and waxy flexibility. The temperature generally ranges from 100-110°F. Sedation is recommended in treating this condition.[35]

To prevent dehabilitating conditions in the elderly, these suggested precautions should be followed:

Immobilization—Prolonged immobilization, unless contraindicated, may create the following problems: pressure sores; bowel and bladder dysfunction that can lead to infection and renal stones; and increase in the risk of heart disease (eg, thrombophlebitis, pulmonary emboli); a negative balance of nitrogen, potassium, and sodium; muscular weakness; weight loss; a negative calcium and phosphorus balance; psychological demoralization; and cardio-vascular and respiratory deconditioning.

Gradual, physical exercise under medical supervision, and appropriate treatment of the psychiatric condition are recommended to combat this problem.

Transfer Trauma—When an elderly client is being transferred from one area to another, the older person may experience a loss of support, and a definite loss of familiar surroundings. This often leads to feelings of low self-esteem, poor physical health and poor interpersonal relationships.

Most importantly, the older adult may experience immense challenges to his body. This is known as the Selye General Adaptation Syndrome. It is composed of three stages: 1) an alarm reaction is sounded; 2) an increase of steroids occurs; and 3) a period of exhaustion, in which the older person can no longer produce an adequate steroid supply. This may result in some form of failure of the various systems of the body.

In order to combat these problems, appropriate preparatory counseling, before, during and after relocation is recommended. This includes allowing the client to make, to some degree, his own decisions. There should be a minimal amount of environmental change, and the highest priority should be given to providing supportive human contact.[35]

Other Medical Conditions That Frequently Affect the Elderly

Cystocele, rectocele, prolapsed uterus. A herniation into the anterior (cysto-cele), or posterior (rectocele) vaginal walls is a frequent disorder in older women. Symptoms include a feeling of heaviness in the pelvic area which is accompanied by difficulty in urinating or defecating. A prolapsed uterus is the downward displacement of the uterus. In all three instances, surgery is the treatment of choice.

Decubitus ulcers. Decubiti or bedsores are most often the result of skin break-down caused by prolonged pressure on boney areas of the body. In severe cases, extended care and treatment are necessary. The client should be turned at regular intervals to prevent continued pressure on any given area.

Gallbladder disease. Gallstones, usually formed around insoluble substances in the bile, block the duct or move around in the duct, cause extreme pain, nausea, and an inability to digest fatty foods. Surgical and nonsurgical methods may be employed to alleviate the situation.

Hiatus hernia. This condition is most often associated with obese elderly women. In this condition, a small section of the stomach slides up through the opening where the esophagus passes through the diaphram. The symptoms that are most prevalent include heartburn, regurgitation, difficulty in swallowing, belching, chest pain, and indigestion. Unless this condition becomes severe, it is usually treated nonsurgically.

Prostate enlargement. Although the cause of this condition is not definitely known, it is common among aging males. If the prostate, which surrounds the urethra at the neck of the bladder, becomes enlarged, urine flow may be painful, reduced, or obstructed. Partial obstruction over a period of time may lead to incomplete bladder emptying, pressure on the kidneys, and infection. Surgery is the usual method of treatment.

Cystitis. This is a bacterial inflammation of the bladder that is often found in older women. The symptoms include frequency and urgency of urination, burning or pain on urinating, and at times, blood in the urine.

Pyelonephritis. This bacterial infection may cause structural damage to the kidneys, uremia, and progressive renal failure. The symptoms most often associated with this condition are fever, chills, fatigue, weight loss, pain in the region of the kidneys, and gastrointestinal disturbances.

Uremia. Chronic renal failure is due to the retention of urea in the blood which the kidneys fail to excrete. Uremia may result from decreased blood flow to the kidneys, obstruction of urinary output, and kidney disease. Adequate fluid intake is extremely important as it helps to prevent dehydration.[36]

Providers, the Elderly and Disease

Since most older people experience at least two chronic diseases simultaneously, it is essential that service providers, specializing in geriatrics, acquire a firm knowledge base of the diseases most prevalent among them. Understanding the progressive characteristics of these diseases is paramount in implementing and enforcing appropriate, substantive programs.

Multidisorders also require that providers be aware of the precautionary measures associated with the involved diseases. For example, a depressed retired carpenter suffering from emphysema comes to a senior center looking for membership in one of the many clubs. Because of his former skills, a woodworking club would seem an appropriate choice to alleviate his depression. However, the accumulation of dust particles associated with woodworking projects would severely aggravate his emphysema. Instead, the aware service worker talks with him about his former and present hobbies and interests. It is learned from his conversation that the client had enjoyed playing cards, and it is suggested that he might like to attend this group.

Competent and efficient geriatric specialists are needed to administer appropriate programs that encompass an understanding of the total individual. Continued study of disease and its corresponding treatment methods and modalities is necessary if this holistic approach is to become a reality.

References

1. Butler RN, Lewis M: Aging and Mental Health: Positive Psychological Approaches. St Louis, CV Mosby Co, 1973, pp 34, 50-60, 69, 74-80.
2. Butler RN: The life review: An interpretation of reminiscence in the aged. In Kastenbaum R (ed): New Thoughts on Old Age. New York, Springer Pub Co Inc, 1964, p 274.
3. Kastenbaum R, Aisenberg R: The Psychology of Death. New York, Springer Pub Co Inc, 1972, p 252.
4. Beck AT: The Diagnosis and Management of Depression. Philadelphia, Univ Penn Press, 1973, pp 4-7.

5. Levin S: Depression in the aged: The importance of external factors. In Kastenbaum R (ed): New Thoughts on Old Age. New York, Springer Pub Co Inc, 1964, pp 179-188.
6. Trotter RJ: Psychiatry for the 80s. Science News 119:349, 1981.
7. Bernhein KF, Lewine RR: Schizophrenia: Symptoms, Causes, Treatments. New York, WW Norton & Co, 1979, p 25.
8. Clark M, et al: Drugs and psychiatry: A new era. Newsweek, Nov 12, 1979, pp 98-104.
9. Sobel D: Psychiatric drugs widely misused, critics charge. New York Times, Science Times, June 3, 1980, pp C1, C2.
10. Goldfarb AI, Frazier S: Aging and Organic Brain Syndrome. Ft Washington, PA, McNeil Laboratories Inc, 1974, pp 6-7.
11. Alzheimer's Disease: Quand A. Washington DC, US DHEW, NIH Pub 79-1646, September, 1979, pp 1-13.
12. Special Report on Aging: 1979. Washington DC, US DHEW, NIH Pub 80-1907, February, 1980, p 18.
13. Ravetz RS: Depression and Pseudodementia. Geriatric Psychiatry Lecture Series, Norristown State Hospital, September, 1981.
14. Trotter J (ed): Brain peptide packs a wallop. Science News 117:56, January, 1980.
15. Raloff J: Noninvasive Vivisection. Science News 118:284-285, November, 1980.
16. Kiplinger AH (ed): Seeing Mental Illness. Changing Times 12, May, 1981.
17. Bardeu A: Long term assessment of levodopa therapy in Parkinson's disease. Can Med Assoc J 112:1379-1380, 1975.
18. Davis JC: Team Management of Parkinson's disease. J Am Occup Ther 31:300-303, 1977.
19. Rodman GP, McEwen CG, Wallace SL: Primer on Rheumatic Diseases. New York, Arthritis Foundation, 1973, pp 25-31, 78, 80-82.
20. Crain DC: The Arthritis Handbook: A Patient's Manual on Arthritis, Rheumatism, and Gout. New York, Exposition Press, 1972, pp 15-27, 31, 80, 109-121.
21. Rosen H, et al: Working with Older People: A Guide to Practice. Washington DC, Pub No 1459, Vol 1, August, 1966, p 14.
22. DeBakey ME, et al: The President's Commission on Heart Disease, Cancer, and Stroke: Report to the President. Washington DC, US Government Printing Office, Vol 12. February, 1965, pp 1, 14-162, 459.
23. Wolcott LE: Rehabilitation and the Aged. In Reichel E (ed): Clinical Aspects of Aging. Baltimore, Williams and Wilkins Co, 1979, pp 155, 160-164.
24. Issacs B: Stroke. In Brocklehurst JC (ed): Textbook of Geriatric Medicine and Gerontology. New York, Churchill Livingstone, 1978, p 208.
25. Siev E, Freishat B: Perceptual Dysfunction in the Adult Stroke Patient. Thorofare, NJ, Charles B Slack Inc, 1976, pp 29, 32.
26. Bouska MJ, Biddle EM: The Influence of Unilateral Visual Neglect in Diagnostic Testing. Atlanta, presented at the Annual Convention of American Speech and Hearing Association, November, 1979.
27. Schnell HM, Jenkins JJ: Reduction of vocabulary in aphasia. In Sarno MT (ed): Aphasia: Selected Readings. Englewood Cliffs, NJ, Prentice-Hall Inc, 1972, pp 5, 17.
28. Battle D: A speech therapist considers speech and hearing problems for the elderly. In Deichman ES, O'Kane CP: Working with the Elderly: A Training Manual. Buffalo, 1975, pp 57-58.
29. Dubos R, Maya P: Health and Disease. New York, Time-Life Inc, 1965, p 96.
30. Laufer IJ, Kadison H: Diabetes Explained: A Layman's Guide. New York, Saturday Review Press, 1976, pp 35, 72, 97.
31. Trotter RJ (ed): Human insulin: Seizing the golden plasmid. Science News 114:195-196, September, 1978.
32. Beardwood JT, Kelly H: Simplified Diabetic Management. Philadelphia, JB Lippincott Co, 1954, pp 4, 109-110, 113.
33. Danowski TS: Diabetes Is a Way of Life. New York, Coward-McCann, Inc, 1964, p 77.
34. A Winter Hazard for the Old: Accidental Hypothermia. Washington DC, DHEW, Pub 78-1464, 1978.

35. Craig TJ: Mortality among elderly psychiatric patients: Clinical implications. Geriatric Psychiatry Lecture Series. Norristown State Hospital. September, 1981.
36. Saxon SV, Etten MJ: Physical Change and Aging: A Guide for the Helping Professions. New York, Tiresias Press, 1978, p 183.

Bibliography

Critchley M: The Parietal Lobes. New York, Hafner Pub Co Inc, 1966.

Falconer MW, Altamura MV, Behnke HD: Aging Patients: A Guide for Their Care. New York, Springer Pub Co Inc, 1976.

Friedland RP, Weinstein EA (eds): Hemi-Inattention Syndromes. New York, Raven Press, 1977.

Heilman D, Musella L, Watson R: The EEG in neglect, abstracted. Neurology 23:437, 1973.

Heilman KM, Valenstein E (eds): Clinical Neuropsychology. New York, Oxford Univ Press, 1979.

Lesonoff-Caravaglia G (ed): Health Care of the Elderly: Strategies for Preservation and Intervention, Vol 1. New York, Human Science Press, 1979.

6
Coping with Death and Dying

B irth and death are two aspects of mortal existence that touch all humanity—old, young, rich, and poor. It was written long ago, "What man shall live and not see death?" (Psalms 89:48).

Life and Death—
A Comparative View

Modern western society tends to dichotomize death and life. Death is regarded as the cessation of biological and physiological functioning or, within a religious context, as the end of worldly affairs and the beginning of a new spiritual existence. Whatever the focus, the western world views the transition from life to death as abrupt, irreversible, and final.

In ancient times there was a limited life expectancy. Only a few people survived beyond the years of early maturity. The sight, sound, and smell of death were not kept away from communal life. There was no sense of possessing any control over the forces of nature. The extended family provided all the necessary strength and continuity. Individualism, as we know it, was not yet developed. The well-being of any one person was seen in relationship to that individual's performance and obligation to the group.

The modern conception of death is a world apart from ancient beliefs. Transposition, insulation, technology, and decontextualization are primarily responsible for these new attitudes toward death. Today, our life expectancy is almost twice that of our ancestors. Because of this factor, our society tends to transpose death from an immediate and perpetual menace to one of remote possibility. Our way of life keeps us well insulated from the perceptions of death. Instead of the tribe or clan, we have developed a technical team of death specialists, consisting of medical personnel, the clergy, death or grief counselors, and those trained for mortuary work. Technological growth and scientific discovery have increased our power for reshaping and modifying our planet. Science is seen as the master and man the controller. No longer do we participate in a society built upon accepted dogma, lineage, or tradition. In previous times the individual relied upon deeply entrenched communal attitudes in his throughts and practices about life and death. Today an individual is held responsible for his own ideas and actions.[1]

The American view of death and life, based upon a Judeo-Christian foundation, is different from that of other societies. The early Greeks believed that the living could visit the land of the dead. The Buddhists conceptualize life as continuous; death is seen as a time when the soul migrates from one form to another. In the Shinto religion, death is thought of as joining one's ancestors, who continue to consult with the living.[2]

Societal Attitudes

Death in our culture is distant, depersonalized, and camouflaged (eg, a cemetary is often referred to as a "memorial garden," and a person does not die, but "passes away"). In the last 60 years Hollywood has produced numerous cowboy shoot-outs, war scenes, mystery thrillers, gangster films, and adventure stories. In almost all these movies, death occurs during a dramatic moment. On the other hand, there have been few movies of the slow death of a terminal patient, or the disintegration of the personality during senility. Apparently, there are few people who would be willing to watch. Our society prefers to remain removed from the more normal occurrences of death, protected from any direct association with one of humanity's most common experiences.[2]

However, a recent survey conducted by the National Opinion Research Center at the University of Chicago revealed that education (socioeconomic status is included within this context) and age, not sex or race, were the primary factors that affect a person's perceptions and attitudes towards death. For example, there was a definite positive correlation between acquired formal education and planning for death with wills, life insurance, or cemetary lots.[3]

Although men and women may make certain preparations for their eventual demise, there still exists a definite feeling of hostility toward death. As far as can be discerned, the human being is the only animal who consciously knows that one day he will die. Some social scientists believe that the fear of death is universal, and that no one is ever really free of it.

Perhaps death's certainty has caused Americans to cope by using mechanisms such as avoidance, denial, and repudiation.[4]

Factors Affecting Coping Techniques

Jeffers and Verwoerdt affirm that seven factors are critical in determining the type of coping techniques that an individual can use when facing death:

1) chronological age and distance from death;
2) physical and mental health;
3) various frames of reference such as religious orientation, socioeconomic, and occupational status;
4) community attitudes;
5) family and personal experiences relating to death;
6) attitudes of people within the immediate environment;
7) the individual's psychological maturity and integrity.[5]

The Dying Process

Many books and articles have been written about the various stages that are associated with dying. Kubler-Ross believes that denial, anger, bargaining, the organizing and completing of unfinished business, depression (reduction of interests, mourning past losses, silently passing through preparatory grief), and acceptance (if the person has been permitted to grieve), are necessary stages of death and dying.[6]

Weisman postulates that death from terminal old age consists of the following phases: 1) repudiation of getting older; 2) denial of the extensions of aging; 3) denial of irreversible decline; 4) impaired autonomy; 5) a yielding of control and counter control; and 6) cessation of life.[7]

Attitudes of Professionals and Institutions Towards Death

Because most people feel that terminal old age is only a pause before life's cessation, the death of an old person in a hospital can be regarded in an almost casual way. Many confused elderly people are placed in an institution where they cope by renunciation, capitulation, nullification, and/or resolution. A strategic equilibrium is achieved between control and counter control. Although choice and control may be relinquished, there is an attempt on the part of the patient to preserve his social worth.[7]

Kubler-Ross states that our retirement and nursing homes are a sad reflection on our lack of appreciation for elders. Despite the fact that some retirement centers may have swimming pools and card rooms, she feels that we deprive our elderly of a chance to serve—an opportunity to offer the wisdom, experience, and skills they have acquired over a lifetime. She also believes that if this right to serve others is denied, most older people may wish to die simply because life is not worth living. Kubler-Ross suggests that nursing homes and retirement centers should integrate their activities with children's programs, such as in day-care centers, where the elderly can be given an opportunity to help.[6]

In the review of a case history of a terminally ill patient, a team of professionals consisting of a physician, a psychiatrist, a minister, and a social psychologist agreed that in the area of death and dying most health care professionals impose emotional isolation upon the dying person, treat him in a routine manner, and as if he were an irresponsible child who cannot cope with his situation on an adult level; in other words, most helping professionals are unable to communicate to the client and respond to his immediate needs and interests in an appropriate and adequate manner.[1] It is tragic that with so little time left, the dying client is often robbed of the very meaning of life— consciousness, self-control, and decision-making.[8]

Social Death: A Consequence of Institutional Attitudes

The concept of social death begins when the institution, accepting the impending death of the client, loses its concern for the dying individual as a person and starts to treat him as if he were already dead. David Sudnow tells of two incidents that demonstrate this attitude. While at a 140-bed acute care hospital, he observed a nurse who spent several minutes trying to close the eyes of a dying woman. When asked why she did this, the nurse replied that the lids were more difficult to close after death, as the muscles and skin became stiff, and that this made for greater efficiency for ward personnel to prepare the body.

In another incident Sudnow observed that newly admitted patients who were near death (low blood pressure, erratic heartbeats, nonpalpable pulse) were frequently left on the litter on which they had arrived and wheeled to a supply room or laboratory. Staff explained that this was necessary as it meant that a clean bed did not have to be used.

This investigator also noticed that as death approached, the attention shifted from a concern about life, and possible comforts, and the administration of medically prescribed treatment, to activities that involved the timing of events of biological death (ie, vital signs). Most patients in this particular hospital died unattended in a coma. Patients in this condition were considered to be unconscious. Thus, personnel talked freely in the patient's presence as if he were not there.[9]

Where People Die

Until the 20th century, most families cared for the sick and dying at home. With the advent of greater scientific and technical knowledge there has been a definite shift away from the home towards institutional care. In 1949, 49.5% of the population of this country died in institutions such as convalescent and nursing homes, hospitals, and other types of domiciliary institutions. By 1958, 60.9% of all death occurred in institutions. The number of people who have died in institutional settings rose on an average of better than 1% annually during that time period.

A number of other nations have outdistanced us in the average person's life expectancy; in this country it now appears to have reached a plateau at just above 70 years. However, in Australia, Denmark, the Netherlands, New Zealand,

Norway, and Sweden, life expectancy may be as much as two or three years higher than comparable figures for the United States.* These statistics indicate that our total health care delivery system and life style could be improved.[10]

In our society, the loss of the extended family has also contributed to an increase of mortalities within the hospital or nursing home. Deaths now occur in settings that are removed from children and young adults. Instead of the warmth and support that is needed at this crucial time, most dying patients experience isolation, rejection, and loneliness.

New Programs on Death and Dying

Health care institutions, local Ys, adult centers, high schools, and colleges are offering many sensitivity courses on death and dying. Television specials that deal with the subject have contributed to an increasing awareness that death is a part of the life cycle.

The hospice concept, patterned on programs in Great Britain, is emerging in several areas of America. One of these, in New Haven, Connecticut, is now providing care for the terminally ill patient of any age who wants to remain at home as long as possible. The service, free to clients through funding by the National Cancer Institute, offers professionals and trained volunteers to provide care in the home. Emphasis is placed on pain control and helping the family deal with their feelings, as well as with the client's. Hospice workers also offer support to grieving families after the client has died.[11]

As of January 1, 1980, 880 clients and families have been served by the New Haven Hospice since its inception in 1974. The Hospice inaugurated inpatient services at Bradford, CT, in July of 1980. This facility, the first of its kind in the United States, offers a backup and a resource for home care. The Hospice also offers courses through its Institute for education, training and research.[12]

The NIA has become concerned about the quality of the last days of a person's life. In the *Special Report on Aging: 1979*, the hospice movement is cited for having a humanistic approach in the care of the terminally ill. According to this report, four major elements are crucial to sound and meaningful hospice care:

1) The education and training of medical, nursing, and allied health personnel to be sensitive to and aware of the rights, problems, and needs of the dying person;
2) The discovery of new therapies for managing pain and other discomforts of those in the last days of life;
3) The provision of home care, so that people can remain at home for as long as possible; and
4) Attention to both the immediate and long-term needs of grieving survivors.

Training programs that offer orientation programs, carefully designed to properly sensitize volunteers to the nature of hospice work, are also an important aspect of any hospice program.

*United Nations Demographic Year Book, pp 562-583.

The NIA has recently commissioned a paper on bereavement as a mortality risk factor. Bereavement requires a variety of adjustments (eg, changing relationships with children, realignments with the family, and the development of new intimacies). However, few social supports have been developed to help people at this critical time. The Institute is now supporting additional studies involving the nature of bereavement so that we can better understand the impact of it, and through this understanding develop meaningful programs to deal with these problems.[13]

It should be noted that not every terminal patient is a hospice candidate. Usually the criteria for hospice includes the following:

1) the patient has a progressive terminal disease, usually with an estimated prognosis of six months or less;

2) the patient and usually the family have agreed to admission;

3) pain or other symptoms are out of control and require hospice expertise;

4) the referring physician has determined that curative/life-extending treatment is not appropriate;

5) the referring physician agrees to continued cooperative care while the patient is being treated by the hospice team;

6) the patient is not comatose with a prognosis of less than 48 hours to live, unless the primary reason for admission is to meet the needs of the family; and

7) the hospice team is available to serve the needs of the patient, family, and significant others.

When the resources are limited, priority should be given to those patients whose need is greatest and who are least able to manage.

In recent years hospice care has become more prevalent. All hospice care, regardless of the setting in which it is given, emphasizes the coordinated team approach. There are at least five settings in which this service can be administered: *Free Standing Hospice*—a physical structure distinct and autonomous from any other institution; *Institution Based Hospice*—a program which exists within an institution, such as a nursing home or hospital; *Home Based Hospice*—care is centered in the home, usually through a home care agency that specializes in such a program; and a *Consortium*—a service which involves a central hospice organization that provides intake, assessment, and some direct care. Often the central organization contracts with home health agencies and inpatient units to provide hospice care to clients as needed.[14]

Service Providers
and the Dying Patient

Kubler-Ross contends that a person can communicate with the senile terminal patient through touch, love, and excellent nursing care.[6] Providing care to enhance the quality of the last days includes a deep understanding of the worth and value of each individual. Recognition of their needs and desires is paramount. Listening and supporting the patient at this critical time is essential.

By dealing with death and dying, the geriatric specialist has an insight and understanding into his own life and death. No professional should ever feel that it is worthless to stroke the brow or wipe the sweat off the face of a dying elderly patient. The mature care giver realizes that life is as important at its end as it is in its beginning. The continuum of life is an experience that each one of us shares.

References

1. Kastenbaum R, Aisenberg R: The Psychology of Death. New York, Springer Pub Co Inc, 1972, pp 191-193, 206-208, 218.
2. Knutson AL: Cultural beliefs on life and death. In Brim OG, et al: The Dying Patient. New York, The Russell Sage Foundation, 1970, pp 41, 43, 48.
3. Riley JW Jr: What people think about death. In Brim OG, et al: The Dying Patient. New York, The Russell Sage Foundation, 1970, pp 35-40.
4. Feifel H: Attitudes toward death in some normal and mentally ill populations. In Feifel H: The Meaning of Death. New York, McGraw-Hill Book Co, 1959, p 114.
5. Jeffers FC, Verwoerdt A: How the old face death. In Busse EW, Pfeiffer E: Behavior and Adaption in Late Life. Boston, Little Brown & Co, 1969, p 171.
6. Kubler-Ross E: Questions and Answers on Death and Dying. New York, Macmillan Pub Co Inc, pp 1, 142-148.
7. Weisman AD: On Dying and Denying: A Psychiatric Study of Terminality. New York, Behavioral Pub Inc, 1972, pp 137, 145-150.
8. Levine S, Scotch NA: Dying: an emerging social problem. In Brim OG, et al: The Dying Patient. New York, The Russell Sage Foundation, 1970, p 218.
9. Sudnow D: Dying in a public hospital. In Brim OG, et al: The Dying Patient. New York, The Russell Sage Foundation, 1970, pp 192-195.
10. Lerner M: When, why and where people die. In Brim OG, et al: The Dying Patient. New York, The Russell Sage Foundation, 1970, pp 9, 21-22.
11. Frazer V, Thornton SM: The New Elders: Innovative Programs By, For and About the Elderly. Denver, Obenchain Printing Co, 1977, p 20.
12. The Connecticut Hospice. In Serving Connecticut and the Nation. New Haven, CT, Vol 5, Spring 1980, pp 1-4.
13. Special Report on Aging: 1979. Washington,DC, US DHEW, NIH Pub 80-1907, February, 1980, pp 305.
14. AIP Update—hospice care. Health Systems Agency of Southwestern Pennsylvania Bulletin, 5, No 2, February, 1981.

Bibliography

Breindel CL: Should hospice be encouraged? American Health Care Association Journal 5(September):40-44, 1979.
Cohen KP: Hospice: Prescription for Terminal Care. Gaithersburg, MD, Aspen Systems Corp, 1979.
Dubois PM: The Hospice Way of Death. New York, Human Science Press, 1979.
Kubler-Ross E: On Death and Dying. New York, Macmillan Pub Co Inc, 1971.
Wass H (ed): Dying: Facing the Facts. Washington DC, Hemisphere Pub Co, 1979.

7
Society and the
Older Adult

S ince the advent of social security, initiated under Franklin D. Roosevelt, age 65 (and under recent legislation, age 70) has become the established cutoff point between the working world and the world of retirement. After retiring, the adult becomes more isolated as most of the familiar social supports (ie, the family, job status, income) begin to diminish. It takes enormous personal strength on the part of the older person to face the many losses that are a part of this life period.

Anthropologists Look at
American Retirement

Clark and Anderson documented the results of a number of studies concerning changes in role, status, and morale. Their comment: "... Old age, for most of our subjects, is a time of dramatic change in one's social (and of course personal) significance," aptly describes the difficulties that many American elderly experience.[1]

These investigators have developed an index that contains eight social statuses. They attribute their definition of *status*—a position occupied by designated individuals in a social system—and *role*—a behavior resulting from patterned expectations attributed to that position—to the work of Linton.[2] Roles are learned on the basis of one's statuses. These are subdivided into two groups as follows:

—Kinship (ascribed status) = spouse, parent, grandparent, sibling
—Nonkin (achieved status) = friend, employee, organization member, religious person

In their studies, Clark and Anderson discovered that people under 70 occupy more statuses than do people 70 and over, and that occupancy of a relatively large number of social statuses was characteristic of the wealthier subjects. However, they noted that, "If an aged individual is bereft of social alliances, neither an adequate standard of living nor good physical health diminishes his risk of mental breakdown in later life."[1]

Other studies revealed that there were a number of traits that most mentally healthy elderly felt were essential characteristics for promoting successful retirement. These were:

1) *Independence*—Sufficient autonomy to permit continued self-integrity.

2) *Social acceptability*—Congenial relationships with others.

3) *Adequate personal resources*—Reasonable amount of comfort in mind, body, and physical environment.

4) *Ability to deal with external threats and losses*—Possession of resiliency, stamina, and endurance, as well as the ability to take appropriate action when necessary.

5) *Ability to cope with changes in the self*—Substitution of skills when necessary; emphasis on continuity of personal growth and development.

6) *Having significant personal goals*—Some degree of a passionate involvement with life and its meaning.[1]

Adjusting to the Permanent Loss of a Job

According to the theories of Friedman and Havighurst, work assumes the following five universal functions:

1) *Provides income*—Income is the substance from which the physical necessities and luxuries of life are obtained.

2) *Regulates life activity*—Work usually determines the hour that one rises, the time that one eats, the length of vacations and holidays, the types of clothing one wears for at least five days out of seven, and one's residential area, including rural, urban, or suburban life style associations.

3) *Offers identification and status*—When a person is introduced to another the question, "What do you do?" is invariably asked. One is identified with the occupation pursued.

4) *Provides opportunities to associate with others*—During the work period one usually comes into contact with other individuals. Coffee breaks and lunch hours are often shared with co-workers.

5) *Makes available opportunities for a meaningful life experience*—This is especially true if one enjoys and takes pride in work.[3]

If these are the attributes that work provides, the adjustment to these losses will present paramount changes in the individual's life patterns. New activities should offer similar satisfactions to those a worker experienced during the years of employment.

Retirement often means facing society on a fixed and lower income than one was accustomed to prior to separation from the work world. Savings of a lifetime may be spent quickly by prolonged illness. In the past 30 years we have been experiencing periods of great inflation. This too, unfortunately, aids in impoverishing many older citizens. Thus, the very needs and staples of life can become luxuries.

Retirement and Leisure Time

A growing number of investigators believe that despite legislative action raising the mandatory retirement age, workers who are financially able to retire will continue to do so. Changes in the mandatory retirement age will have great impact upon employers—namely, higher costs and greater diversity in retirement age patterns. Management consultants predict that employers will respond to these changes by implementing pre-retirement counseling programs that are targeted at making retirement as attractive as possible. However, such programs will most likely only be successful to the extent that they are purposeful, timely, realistic, and relevant to the needs of the individual worker.[4] Successful retirement requires that the retiree develop new interests, or continue to expand interests that had been acquired prior to retirement. Purposeful activity is essential to the well-being of a healthy individual.

Havighurst believes that leisure activity performs three major functions: gives pure enjoyment; prepares one for the future; and extends the limits of one's behavior. However, it should be noted that the variety of leisure possibilities is limited by such practical concerns as transportation, money, and physical health.

According to documentation of current trends, there appears to be definite patterns of free time activity that are established upon retirement. These activities can be organized into the following categories:

1) *New and challenging activities*—Individuals interested in these activities enjoy becoming involved in new pursuits (eg, writing books, painting).

2) *Service pursuits*—People interested in these types of experiences give a large portion of their free time and energy to performing useful activities for their community, family, special interest group, or religious organization.

3) *Expressive pleasure experiences*—Individuals engaged in this category commit their free time to activities that involve sheer pleasure, not as a means for improving society.

4) *Mildly active pursuits*—Adults within this pattern involve themselves in routine leisure activities that may take two or three hours a day (eg, regularly planned visits to a tavern or park to play cards or checkers and talk with friends).

5) *Ordinary routines*—Individuals associated with this pattern spend their day involved in ordinary habits (eg, shopping, cleaning, preparing and eating meals), exercising little initiative for other activities.

6) *Apathetic utilization of time*—People within this category have few, if any, interests. They do not anticipate involving themselves in any major undertakings. They usually spend their time sitting in a chair or sleeping.

7) *No or little free time*—This category is the least common pattern. These individuals participate in so many role activities that they literally have no energy left for non-contained free time experiences.[5]

In any discussion concerning the use of leisure time, there needs to be a recognition of the importance of the role that personality and background play in direct relationship to the degree of activities involvement that an individual is willing to commit himself to. In this regard, meaning and relevance are two key concepts. "...Activities have been considered to have meaning to an individual if they are familiar to the individual, arouse positive associations, and tend to elicit approval from others who are respected and admired."[6] The meaning that specific activities have for an individual can usually be determined from information concerning that person's history, age, socioeconomic status, family history, work history, hobbies, and interests. The relevance and value of any activity depends upon the sociocultural background of the individual.

Coping with Changing Roles

Old age is a time in which the American society does not readily assign clearly defined roles. In fact, it is a time for permanent disengagement from two firmly entrenched social structures—the nuclear family and the occupational system.[7] The older person actually loses a sense of who he is when terminated from the work force. No longer a teacher, chemist, or active parent, his identity suddenly vanishes. He, therefore, becomes a person without a place.

In other parts of the world where respect and honor are accorded the elderly, it has been found that these older people rarely retire from the work world of their community. For instance, centurians from the South Altay and Caucasus areas chair many community functions. They are considered to be wise and to have a special place in their society. It is not uncommon for people from these regions to live well beyond 100 years.[8]

Coping with Physical Loss

In an earlier chapter, the physical changes that occur with aging were discussed. Not only is there physical decline, but often disease accompanies these physical conditions. The older person must then learn to cope with and adjust to these changes. More energy is needed and spent in the care and maintenance of the body. Because of these types of concerns, whole new patterns of life need to be initiated. Examples of this can be seen in the older person who can no longer dine out because of gastrointestinal problems, or the person who can no longer drive a car because his visual acuity has declined.[9] A great deal of independence must be relinquished as a person becomes increasingly dependent upon others to perform services that that person previously had been able to do. As the social world begins to diminish, separation from the community and loneliness often become an established consequence.

Coping with the Loss of Life Partners, Family, and Friends

The elderly spend tremendous amounts of emotional and physical energy directed toward grieving and the resolving of grief. It is a time when the deaths of a spouse, brother, sister, or close family friend may be steps apart. For many it is the beginning of a solitary life and great change. The family residence may become unmanageable or unwanted by the remaining partner. Funeral arrangements, burial preparations, and the disposition of the spouse's personal effects are some of the emotional yet practical aspects that accompany the mourning process. For most women, who outnumber men by three to one, it is unlikely that they will be able to find another partner.[10]

Dealing with New Housing Needs

The repair, cleaning, and maintenance of a house that one has lived in for 25 years or more may become increasingly too burdensome. Moving away from lifetime memories and the decline of complete independence is another in a long series of losses that many older people experience. Some housing alternatives may be foster homes, retirement centers, smaller apartments, boarding homes, moving in with children, cooperative housing, or for the more physically impaired, a nursing home. Often certain adaptive devices (ie, raised toilet seats, grab rails) need to be employed to encourage as much independence as possible.

Unfortunately, many residential halls and nursing homes still retain the custodial climate of their predecessors—the almshouse or the poorhouse. Most older people believe that these places are degrading. Some of their complaints of the traditional institutional model are that the institutions are custodial in nature; the residents are expected to play a passive role rather than one that reflects physical and mental activity; the individuality of the client is compromised for group conformity; the staff is impersonal and over-professional; and many of these institutions expand in size beyond the optimum level so that the per capita cost can be reduced.[3]

The elderly who live in the community face a number of disadvantages when seeking appropriate places to live. For instance, the older adult is often less able to effectively search for improved or appropriate housing for himself; most present housing stock is in unsatisfactory locations, such as in deteriorated neighborhoods or in areas with poor access to shopping and needed medical or social services; the proposed effectiveness of housing allowances may be offset by compensatory rental raises; and housing allowance programs are often unable to foster an age-dense environment, and cannot provide access to the everyday needs of the older person.[11]

Some of the housing options that are available to older adults who live in the community were briefly touched upon earlier. Specifically, these can be organized into the following categories:

Government assisted housing programs. This group includes programs such as: direct grants for construction of public housing authorized for the elderly, and accounts for approximately 25,000 operating units; direct-loan interest subsidy programs; rental programs; purchase programs; rehabilitation of existing housing stock programs; and relocation payments programs.

Non-federally aided retirement communities. This category consists of the following types of housing arrangements: commercial retirement villages such as the Leisure Worlds of California, Maryland, and New Jersey, and Sun City, Arizona; life-care retirement centers, usually sponsored by churches and other non-profit corporations. They offer full services, usually including a medical facility on the grounds.

Social programs. These may be federally, state, or church assisted, such as foster homes, adopt-a-grandparent programs, or sheltered housing.

Private housing. One quarter of all elderly live alone in retirement hotels, boarding homes, their own home, or in an apartment.

Family arrangements. A full two-thirds of all elderly individuals live in family settings.[11] However, the most recent statistics indicate that greater numbers of Older Americans are not living with their children.[12]

Intermediate housing programs. In this type of arrangement homes are remodeled into apartments that are clustered in an area conveniently located near an institution for the elderly, thereby creating availability of the institution's social and medical services. Otherwise, independent living continues.

Halfway house programs. These provide a more protective and structured orientation than a boarding home.[11]

Lawton aptly sums up a number of social deprivations that affect the wellbeing of the elderly—low income; inadequate housing; crime-ridden neighborhoods (more than 60% of all older adults live in metropolitan areas); lack of safe public transportation; lack of centralization of medical and social facilities; growth of the nuclear family.

It is suggested that planners, designing living arrangements exclusively for the older adult, should provide the elderly with the widest range of environmental options, including a recognition of life-enriching and life-sustaining opportunities. In this respect the older person may need a number of security devices such as controlled temperature in the tub/shower to prevent accidental scalding, shower seats, nonskid tub/shower surfaces, flush door jambs, grab bars, safety shut-off for gas burners, stove burner controls in front of the stove (to prevent burns from reaching over a hot stove), nonskid backing on rugs, refrigerators that do not utilize low drawers, wall light fixtures (to prevent the older person from being tempted to stand on a chair while changing light bulbs), slow-closing elevator doors with a sensitive reopening mechanism, and doors that do not swing shut with force. Other security devices of an electronic nature could be used to prevent personal attack, robbery, or to prevent accidents (eg, emergency electronic devices or telephones in bedroom, bathroom, or kitchen areas).

In designing appropriate living areas for the older adult, there are a number of other considerations that should be included: convenient clothes and small article storage; mirrors at eye level; and adequate illumination. Each room should have at least one wall switch-controlled light. There should be more than the usual number of built-in lights, and night lights should be placed at corners leading to the bathroom, and inside the bathroom. Long hallways should be avoided because of their dehumanizing nature (eg, lack of outside light, bare walls, and the glare that is often created from regularly spaced ceiling lights on glossy floors).[11]

The following are also suggestions which are helpful in securing a safe environment for the older person: Surfaces should be painted or carpeted with contrasting colors so that there is a distinct boundary between stair steps, thresholds, etc. Fasten all carpet firmly. Eliminate or mark all uneven floor surfaces, and do not cover them. Chairs should offer firm support and have strong arms that can be utilized as one arises. All other furniture should have four sturdy legs, or else be securely anchored.[13]

We have discussed specific types of living arrangements that affect the independence of the older adult. The living environment can also be effectively used to increase the social awareness of the older person. L.H. Snyder describes a number of modalities, devices, and living arrangements that are critical to enhancing socialization and safety among the elderly. For instance, she suggests a number of ways to improve illumination:

Glare reduction. Glare can be minimized through the use of horizontally louvered widow shades that can be lowered to allow natural light in while at the same time blocking out the sun; shielded artificial light sources; cone lighting (source recessed); valence lighting; tablecloths and placemats put on shiny formica tabletops and work surfaces; and non-reflective floor tiles.

Creating adequate lighting arrangements. These illuminating techniques can be concentrated in areas such as doorways, work areas, and floors so as to provide the minimum level of lighting that is essential to the social and physical well-being of the older person.[14]

Upon examining the mobility needs of the elderly, it becomes apparent that there are a number of transportation barriers that they must confront daily. Some of these are excessive steps at subway and train stops, lack of shelters to protect them from the elements, and a paucity of vehicles that can serve the handicapped.

The Elderly Look For New Solutions

Although this is a period of multiple losses for most older individuals, many elderly people are becoming more vocal in making society aware of their needs. The National Caucus for the Black Aged, the Gray Panthers, the Senior Action Alliance Centers, the American Association of Retired Persons, the National Council of Senior Citizens, and the Gray Bears are some examples of action groups which assume an advocate role for older people.

Magazines such as *Modern Maturity* and *Retirement Living* that focus on the needs of the older consumer are becoming more popular.

In recent years, the federal government has also been taking an increasingly active role in providing funds for services and programming for older persons. The most significant legal action has been the passage of The Older Americans Act.

Legislation

The Older Americans Act

This act was first established on July 14, 1965 (PL 89-73) and was amended by PL 90-42 (July 1, 1967), PL 91-69 (September 17, 1969), and PL 93-29 (May 3, 1973). The purpose of the latest amendments, known as *The Older Americans Comprehensive Service Amendments of 1973,* was to strengthen and improve the original Older Americans Act of 1965. There are now a total of ten titles:

Title I: Declaration of Objectives

The purpose of this title is to make available comprehensive social service programs to older Americans and to provide the opportunity for them to participate in the development of these programs.

Title II: Establishment of the Administration on Aging

The Administration on Aging, headed by the commissioner on aging, is placed within the Office of the Secretary of Health and Human Services. It provides for the creation of a National Information and Resource Clearing House for the Aging. In addition, this title establishes a Federal Council on Aging.

Title III: Grants for State and Community Programs on Aging

The Administration on Aging is committed to work with state agencies on aging (sometimes referred to as the Area Agency on Aging) in developing statewide plans for the delivery of social services to older citizens. Special grants may be given to projects involving housing needs, transportation needs, continuing education, pre-retirement information, services to the handicapped, and for demonstrations which are available to public and private nonprofit agencies.

Title IV: Training and Research

Direct grants and contracts may be awarded to research and development projects in the field of aging. Funds are also available for the specialized training of employed persons or those persons preparing for employment in programs devoted to aging. There are also provisions for establishing and supporting multidisciplinary centers of gerontology.

Title V: Multipurpose Senior Centers

This section provides for the construction, acquisition, alteration, and renovation of multipurpose senior citizen centers. Included also are funds for mortgage insurance and grants for staffing these centers.

Title VI: National Older Americans Volunteer Program

Authorization was granted to establish the Foster Grandparents Program and other Older Americans Community Service Programs (transferred to the Action Agency in 1971). These are designed to involve older Americans in programs that benefit persons of all ages. Some examples include:

RSVP (Retired Senior Volunteer Program)—These are service volunteer programs in public and nonprofit institutions.

SCORE (Service Corps of Retired Executives)—Under this program retired businessmen advise novices in the field of business management.

VISTA (Volunteers in Service to America)—This program, designed for persons of all ages, provides community service projects for at least one or two years duration.

PEACE CORPS—Volunteers of all ages are involved in community programs in foreign countries for usually a two-year tour of duty.

Title VII: Nutrition Programs

The purpose of this title is to promote greater coordination between nutrition programs and the social service programs that were provided in Title III (ie, Meals-on-Wheels, congregate meals served in senior centers, synagogues, and churches).

Title VIII: Amendments to Other Acts

This section provides opportunities for older Americans to participate in programs of continuing education that are expanded by amending the following acts: Library Services and Construction Act, National Commission on Libraries and Information Service Act, the Higher Education Act, and the Adult Education Act (ie, book mobiles, library services offered to bed-bound patrons).

Title IX: Community Service Employment for Older Americans

Community service jobs are provided for low-income Americans 55 years of age and older in the following fields: education, recreational services, social services, conservation, economic development, and environmental restoration. Most of the programs utilize the experiences of demonstration projects that are conducted by the Department of Labor under its Operation Mainstream Program. Some of these programs are Operation Green Thumb for men (conservation and landscape), and Operation Green Light for women (community service programs). Both of these programs are sponsored by the National Farmers Union. Other community service programs are the Senior Aides, sponsored by the National Council on the Aging, and the Senior Community Service Aides, sponsored by the National Retired Teachers Association.

Title X: Middle-Aged and Older Workers Training Act

The main objective of this title is to provide manpower training programs and other services to improve and increase job opportunities for the middle-aged and older citizen.

Other Federal Regulations,
Acts, Laws, and Programs
Affecting Older People

The mission of the law PL 93-296 is the creation of the National Institute on Aging (NIA). Its purpose is to conduct and support social, biomedical, and behavioral aspects of training and research as related to the aging process, the diseases of the elderly, and other special problems of older Americans. There are two types of research programs. Intramural research is conducted in Baltimore at the NIA, which was formerly known as the Gerontology Research Center. Extramural research is administered by the Adult Development and Aging branch. Included in this program is the development of many multidisciplinary centers for aging research.

Some of the areas of research interest that the NIA has been concerned with are: treatable brain disease; the quality of the last days of life; the nutritional needs of the aging; older women; geriatric medicine; longevous populations; cellular and animal resources; geriatric dentistry; osteoporosis and Vitamin K; calorie counting and fat cells; developments in cell biology; compensation in old animals for nerve cell loss; the changes of taste and smell with age; new methods to measure and study permeability of the blood-brain barrier; cardiovascular disease and intellectual decline with aging; Alzheimer's disease and its relationship to aluminum; the results of the Baltimore Longitudinal Study; the use of psychological tests in predicting death within five years of testing—this may prove useful as part of a routine health assessment for elderly patients, and may also serve to alert physicians of impending problems; antecedents of health in middle-age; and institutional adaptation of the aged.[15]

The National Institute of Mental Health Grant Programs for Staff Development in Hospitals, a federally-funded staff development program, is designed to improve the development of patient treatment within public mental health hospitals, including those within state hospital systems. The program includes inservice training for nonprofessionals and professionals. The content may include orientations, continuing educational courses, refresher programs, and special courses for teachers who conduct the training. Because of the large numbers of older patients within the state hospitals, this type of grant program can have a positive effect on the type of care that these elderly citizens receive.

Programs Supported by the
Social Security Administration—
Hospital/Medical Coverage

In the Hospital Insurance Program (included in Title XVIII: Medicare), hospital insurance services are offered to any person 65 or older and to those entitled to social security or railroad retirement benefits. A dependent spouse 65 or older is also eligible for this coverage. In each benefit period covered protection includes hospital inpatient care, posthospital extended care, and home health visits by nurses and other allied health workers from a participating home health agency. Physician's fees are not covered. These benefits, financed under social security, are based upon contributions from workers, their employers, and self-employed people made during their working years. This portion of the contribution is held in a special Hospital Insurance Trust Fund.

The Supplementary Medical Insurance (included within Title XVIII: Medicare) is part of the social security program which helps to pay for physician's bills, outpatient hospital services, and rehabilitative outpatient health care services. This program, financed by voluntary supplemental extensions of Medicare's hospital insurance program, is not financed by payroll deductions.

Under the Medical Assistance Program (under Title XIX: Medicaid), grants are provided for individual states to administer programs that assist certain people:

1) public assistance recipients who are aged, blind, disabled, or dependent children.

2) those who are medically needy but are not public assistance recipients and who represent the same group as mentioned above. These citizens may have sufficient income for daily needs but not enough finances to cover medical expenses.

3) any child below the age of 21 whose parents cannot afford medical care.

Possible Funding Sources for Geriatric Day-Care Programs, PL 92-603 (under Title XVIII Part B, and Title XIX of the Social Security Act), provides for the opportunity to implement geriatric day-care programs.

Model Cities Funding: The National Council on the Aging (through Title IV, Part A of the Social Security Act of 1971 and Titles I and XVI of the 1972 Social Security Act) is responsible for funding special services in model cities.

New Federal Directions

During the summer of 1981, Congress overwhelmingly endorsed the basics of President Reagan's initial three-part plan for transferring major areas of responsibility from the federal government to the states (Fiscal Year—"FY"—1982). The Omnibus Budget Reconciliation Act of 1981 is proposed to actually cut more than $35 billion from projected 1982 federal spending. Most of these budget cuts are from social programs, many of which directly affect the elderly.

At the same time, Congress also consolidated scores of categorical human services grant programs (these are specifically targeted to fulfill particular purposes) into a handful of umbrella block grants. Thus, the federal government is now seen as turning in a new direction. Previously, Congress had tended to strengthen the enforcement of federal standards. The categorical grant programs were administered under close federal supervision, which included following strict guidelines on putting the money where it was most needed and on citizen participation. Under the block grants financial support is provided for general areas of need while allowing the states much more discretion in utilizing the dollars as they see fit. President Reagan favored the block grants as a way of giving state and local officials the flexibility from paperwork in administering federal programs. However, critics believe that 50 separate sets of bureaucracies will be needed to handle the new block grants, thus, possibly increasing redtape.[16]

Through the years, high inflation, deficit spending, increased taxation, and the wasting of resources have brought increased concern to many Americans. Even the ability of the federal government to fund its social security program has come into question. There is now a new mood in Washington in dealing with these problems.

Resources

Amendments and alterations to existing laws are constantly taking place. Information regarding current public health care programs and regulations may be obtained by writing to the *Federal Register,* the National Archives of the United States, Washington, DC. Another source that includes information regarding federal benefits and programs is the Printing Office of the Department of Health and Human Services, Social Security Administration, Washington, DC.

The federal government is not the only source of third party payments to medical services. Supplemental health insurance policies for older Americans are provided by Blue Cross/Blue Shield; National Council of Senior Citizens, American Association of Retired Persons; and many other commercial carriers.

White House Conferences on Aging

There have been two White House Conferences on Aging: 1961—called by President Eisenhower, and 1971—called by President Nixon. A third was scheduled for 1981. Previously, President Truman had called a National Conference on Aging in 1950.

The 1971 White House Conference on Aging was attended by more than 3,000 people. Some of the many issues discussed were: improving the transportation needs of the elderly, providing better housing for older adults, improving the medical delivery system, increasing nutrition programs, and improving the financial status of older people. One significant aspect of the 1971 Conference was that the elderly themselves were encouraged to testify and to participate in the development of future programming.[17]

Looking Towards the Future

Within the past 25 years, older Americans have become increasingly conscious about the quality of their lives and how to better them. Legislation, conferences, and a variety of services from both the public and private sectors have been established to combat and improve the multiple problems that older citizens face.

As the population of the United States grows older, new life patterns may begin to emerge. Some thoughts to consider might be extending the retirement age to a later date, partial retirement, or a shorter work week. One can feel certain that as our population's needs shift, so too will the attitude within our society.

The Service Provider's Role

The dynamics of aging should be well understood by care givers before they become practitioners. These dynamics not only reflect how the elderly feel about themselves, but also what society expects of them.

Although most elders are experiencing physical decline, a lower standard of living, and emotional losses, the life experience and maturity of the older person should definitely be a contributing factor in determining methods of dealing with their problems. An understanding of these varying components should be the foundation for developing appropriate treatment plans.

Geriatric specialists should also be knowledgeable about the latest legislative programs that are offered to older persons. This will enable providers to inform their clients of the services that are available and to have a more thorough understanding of current funding sources. With this information, geriatric practitioners can then become involved in initiating creative and meaningful treatment opportunities for their clients.

References

1. Clark MA, Anderson BG: Culture and Aging: An Anthropological Study of the Older American. Springfield, IL, Charles C Thomas, 1967, p 135, 142, 177-232.
2. Linton R: The Cultural Background of Personality. New York, Appleton-Century-Crofts, Inc, 1945.
3. Barron ML: The Aging American: An Introduction to Social Gerontology and Geriatrics. New York, Thomas Y Crowell Co, 1961, pp 78, 89.
4. Edmunds EP, Elias JW: Middle-Aged Workers' Retirement Expectations: Implications for Retirement Planning. Paper presented at Annual Meeting of Gerontological Society, Washington, DC, November 28, 1979.
5. Havinghurst RJ: After work: then what? In Kalish RA (ed): The Later Years: Social Applications of Gerontology. Monterey, CA, Brooks/Cole Pub Co, 1977, pp 152-153.
6. Cynkin S: Occupational Therapy: Towards Health Through Activities. Boston, Little, Brown and Co, 1979, pp 38-39.
7. Blau ZS: Old Age in a Changing Society. New York, Franklin Watts Inc, 1973, pp 12, 138.
8. Medvedev ZA: Caucasus and Altay Longevity: A biological or social problem? Gerontologist 14:381-387, 1974.
9. Ingraham MH, Mulanaphy JM: My Purpose Holds: Reactions and Experiences in Retirement of TIAA—CREF Annuitants. New York, Teachers Insurance and Annuity Association, 1974, p 59.
10. Butler RN, Lewis MI: Aging and Mental Health: Positive Psychosocial Approaches. St Louis, CV Mosby Co, 1973, pp 29-30.
11. Lawton MP: Planning and Managing Housing for the Elderly. New York, John Wiley and Son, pp 29, 31-51, 122-148, 211-217, 1975.
12. Lawton MP: Growing Old: It's social meaning. Geriatric Psychiatric Series, Norristown State Hospital, September, 1981.
13. Saxon SV, Etten MJ: Physical Change and Aging: A Guide for the Helping Professions. New York, Tiresias Press, 1978, p 183.
14. Snyder LH: Environmental changes for socialization. J Nurs Admin 1:44-48, 1978.
15. Special Report on Aging: 1979. Washington, DC, US DHEW, NIA-NIH Pub no 80-1907, February 1980, p 23.
16. Meeting Human Needs: The new block grants. Nat Voter Vol 31, 3:23-25, 1981.
17. Smith BK: Aging in America. Boston, Beacon Press Inc, 1973, pp 199-217.

Bibliography

Butler RN: Why Survive? Being Old in America. New York, Harper & Row Pub Inc, 1975.

Friedman EA, Havighurst RJ: The Meaning of Work and Retirement. Chicago, Univ Chicago Press, 1954.

Harris L: The Myth and Reality of Aging in America. Washington DC, National Council on the Aging, Inc, 1975.

Toward a national policy on aging. White House Conference on Aging. Vols 1, 2, Washington, DC, DHEW, 1971.

8
Communicating
with Elders

N o matter what gerontologically related career one has chosen, the ability to communicate with older people—in terms of their needs, feelings, and understanding—is an essential aspect of any type of relationship. For an in-depth focus on: an understanding of what is meant by communication; the role that culture plays in relationship to communication; the fundamentals of communication; how to communicate; and a variety of communication techniques that can be utilized by older adults, please see Appendix A, pp 159-165.

Promoting opportunities for communication is a major concern for both elderly clients and for those who work with them. Social interaction programs should be constructed around the needs, interests, capacities, skills, and functioning levels of the people involved. The following programs can be used to ease communication difficulties with older adults, especially those with mental or physical dysfunction. The programs are ranked in order, with the least complex first.

Sensory Training

Leona Richman developed a program designed to help clients who manifest severe psychomotor retardation and deficits in discriminating between and responding appropriately to environmental stimuli. These persons suffer from sensory deprivation that is based upon disuse, malfunction, and psychological retreat from the environment. They usually assume the role of the nonparticipant.

Richman holds that sensory discrimination can be trained and greatly developed by practice. The goal of sensory training is to increase tactile discrimination and sensitivity of feelings through stimulation of all sense receptors, thereby increasing the regressed geriatric patient's ability to interact with the environment. The receptors are stimulated in isolation and then simultaneously in a multi-sensory approach. The following modalities are emphasized:

1) *Tactile*—discrimination of textures and body contact;

2) *Kinesthetic and proprioceptive*—awareness of one's movements in relation to joints and body parts;

3) *Olfactory*—discrimination and identification of odors;

4) *Vision*—controlled eye movements and development of the ability to look;

5) *Audition*—attention to sounds and vibrations; and

6) *Cognitive and social stimulation*—promotion of social interaction, stimulation, and awareness of verbal responses.

The program is initiated with the group seated in a circle. Participants are seen in the group setting, but each member is given individual attention. The trainer introduces each member by name. Much tactile contact—hand touching, holding, shaking—between members is encouraged. Each sense is stimulated separately. For example, in the kinesthetic and proprioceptive portion of the program, each participant is asked to identify and move various parts of the body.

Discrimination between objects makes a person feel the environment is more real and manageable. Specifically, objects of varied textures are presented (eg, a piece of wood, a sponge, a ball) to each group member to feel and describe to the group. Similar procedures are followed to exercise the olfactory, visual and auditory senses.

Self and body awareness is promoted through the use of mirror identification or by blowing soap bubbles, which makes a person more aware of his bodily processes. Breathing, then, takes on a more concrete form.[1]

Sensory training may be divided into two groups: primary, which contains the most regressed patients, and requires concrete and structured activities, and secondary, where tasks are more challenging. For instance, at this more advanced level the patient may be asked to compare two sensory stimuli.[2]

Once a client has successfully completed both levels of the sensory stimulation program, he should be encouraged to participate in other types of awareness and social interaction programs.

Reality Orientation

Many elderly clients in long-term care institutions experience a multitude of cognitive, emotional, and physical impairments. The symptoms most often associated with these conditions include confusion, anxiety, depression, social withdrawal, disorientation, emotional liability, impaired judgment, impaired recent memory, lack of self-confidence, and lethargy.

In 1958, Dr. James Folsom initiated the reality orientation technique at the Winter Veteran's Administration Hospital in Topeka, Kansas. It was later refined at the Veteran's Administration Hospital in Tuscaloosa, Alabama, in 1965.

Reality orientation is based on the assumption that repeated basic information (eg, the client's name, the place, time of day, day of week, date, name of the next meal, and special events) can reinforce learning and ameliorate disorientation and confusion.

This type of program can be initiated by any staff member, family member, or volunteer who comes into frequent contact with the client. Formal reality orientation classes usually consist of four or five class members and an instructor. The classes should meet the same time every day at least five times per week. During this time, basic information can be reinforced by the following aids: reality boards made of wood with movable slots so that appropriate information may be displayed, blackboards, slates, bulletin boards, felt boards, mock-up clocks, name tags, calendars, and large colorful pictures of food or other familiar objects.[3]

Classroom procedure includes the reinforcing of appropriate social skills as well as cognitive awareness. For example, the use of appropriate salutations should be enforced—"Hello, I am Mr. ——. What is your name?" saying good-bye at the end of the session, and thanking each participant for attending. Initially, activities should be of a simple nature, such as identifying familiar objects, photographs, writing one's name on the blackboard; they should gradually increase in complexity as the class members become less confused.

Within the classroom the following methods and procedures can be utilized:

1) A calm and friendly atmosphere is essential;

2) When addressing a class member, the instructor should always look directly at him and speak in a slow, clear voice;

3) It is important that each member be given adequate time and opportunity to respond;

4) If a class member does not know the answer to a question, the instructor should always tell it and then ask him to repeat it.

5) Immediate recognition and reinforcement of correct responses are important ingredients of this program.

After the client has completed the basic reality orientation course, an advanced course consisting of spelling, reading, math, writing, and discussion of current topics, may be initiated. Upon completion of the formal reality orientation program, graduation exercises are held. At this time a diploma inscribed with the client's name and graduation date, and stating that the client completed the prescribed reality orientation course is presented to him at a graduation ceremony. The staff as well as friends and relatives, should be invited to attend.

Twenty-four hour informal reality orientation should take place at the same time the formal program occurs. This consists of improving the client's awareness of person, time, and place at any time staff, a family member, or a volunteer has contact with him.[4] The following is an example of informal reality orientation:

> An aide finds Mr. Jones walking in the corridor at 1:00 am. The staff member states, "Mr. Jones, it is one o'clock in the morning. Is it difficult for you to sleep? Here is your room and your bed. Your name is on your bed." The aide points to the name card, reads it, and says, "It is time to rest now."

Recently, classroom reality orientation has come under criticism by some investigators for its inability to increase autonomy or happiness among the elderly. Schwenk suggests that more research is needed before a sound determination can be made.[5] Despite this recent criticism many nursing homes, residential care centers, and state and federal facilities that serve the elderly continue to use both forms of reality orientation with success.

Attitude Therapy

Attitude therapy, a consistent rehabilitative team approach, is helpful in reinforcing desirable behavior and in eliminating undesirable behavior. This approach is often used in conjunction with reality orientation programs. It involves five major attitudes that are used with five types of behavior patterns. The professional team decides what attitude would be most effective with each client. Everyone coming into contact with this client would then utilize the designated attitude. The therapeutic attitudes include the following:

> 1) *Active friendliness*—this attitude is most frequently prescribed for clients undergoing reality orientation. It is most successful with older adults who are withdrawn and apathetic. Active friendliness is a supportive, ego-building attitude that provides feelings of self-worth and accomplishment. The staff should seek the client out on a one-to-one basis and sincerely praise him for his accomplishments.

> 2) *Kind firmness*—depressed elderly adults usually respond to this approach. The staff should help the client focus on something else besides his own unhappiness. When using kind firmness, it is important that the client know exactly what is to be done and that the staff member expects his requests to be completed.

> 3) *Passive friendliness*—this approach is useful for older persons who are suspicious and frightened by active friendliness. Staff should wait for the client to make the first move and then respond by showing interest and concern.

> 4) *No demand*—older people who are distrustful, fearful, and who experience global anger respond best to this type of approach. Although activities and friendship are offered to these individuals, the client should be made aware that the only thing that is expected of him is not to hurt himself or others.

> 5) *Matter-of-fact*—this attitude is prescribed for residents who demonstrate

character disorders, anxiety reaction, psychosomatic manifestations, seductive, and manipulative behavior. The staff should respond to the client's pleas, complaints, and maneuvers in a reality-based, calm, consistent, and casual manner.[3]

Remotivation

This technique is usually begun following the successful completion of a reality orientation program. Its purpose is to encourage moderately confused older individuals to become more interested in their surroundings by focusing on simple, objective topics that are not related to the person's emotional problems. Another goal is to strengthen the client's ability to communicate and socialize with others. A remotivation series generally continues for 12 weeks, with one session per week, each session from 30 to 60 minutes long. The group size consists of five to twelve clients. Each session makes use of a five point outline.

1) *Climate of acceptance*—the remotivator greets each member by name and thanks him for attending. Pleasant remarks relating to the well-groomed appearance of some members (ie, "Mrs. Green, that is a very cheerful dress you are wearing."), and comments about the weather or news generate an atmosphere of warmth and acceptance (five minutes).

2) *Bridge to reality*—a topic concerning the "real world" helps the participants to focus their interests outside of their own concerns. Three techniques may be utilized to introduce the topic: poetry, quotations, or newspaper articles; bounce questions; and visual aids. The remotivator should encourage the group members to participate in the discussion o read portions of a poem or article (15 minutes).

3) *Sharing the world*—the remotivator stimulates discussion in a specific direction by utilizing a list of 10 or 12 questions that have been prepared in advance. The therapist should be knowledgeable about the discussion topic and be able to answer any questions that may arise (15 minutes).

4) *Work of the world*—the objective of this part is to encourage the residents to think about work in relation to themselves. Discussion concerning the clients' past tasks as well as current activities in which they might be involved are helpful (15 minutes).

5) *Climate of acceptance*—the final section includes a time for the remotivator to review the high points of the discussion, announce the time and date of the next meeting, and express his appreciation to the group members for attending (five minutes).[3]

Structured Learning Therapy (SLT)

Structured Learning Therapy is a psychoeducational skill training program composed of modeling, role playing, performance feedback, and transfer training. The procedure consists of training small groups of participants who are deficient in a particular skill to improve their deficiences. The steps are:

1) The trainee observes a modeling display of the trainer expertly performing the skill behaviors being taught.

2) The trainee is given the opportunity and encouragement to rehearse or practice the behaviors that had been previously modeled.

3) Each trainee is given approval or praise as their role playing behavior becomes more and more like the behavior of the model.

4) Each trainee will be exposed to these processes in such a way that there is a strong likelihood that the skills acquired during the training setting will not only be maintained but will also generalize to other real life situations.

Specifically, in the area of social interaction and communication the concrete training of the four skills necessary for holding a conversation with others could be utilized—beginning a conversation, carrying on a conversation, listening, and ending a conversation. In each area of conversation, these skills are broken down into simple steps. For instance, in beginning a conversation there are four major skill components to be learned: 1) greeting the person; 2) making small talk; 3) deciding if the person wants to talk back; and 4) beginning the topic.[6,7]

A recent study, one of the first to examine the effects of interpersonal skill training with the elderly, indicated that all elderly inpatients involved in the project were able to acquire the target skill of starting a conversation and that there was evidence of transfer of skill training.[8]

Opportunities for Increased Learning

For those older persons who display a minimal amount of confusion, there are other types of group interaction programs that can be utilized to stimulate greater cognitive and social awareness. News, fashion, sports, literary reviews, travel, interest, and history clubs are topical groups that can foster discussions and social involvement. An eclectic group that discusses a variety of subjects is another approach.

An atmosphere where learning is expected generates a conducive climate for positive reflection and the development of the self. During the discussion period certain attitudes and skills are essential if communication is to take place:

1) The ability to assess what is being said and to discriminate and analyze the important issues from the nonimportant issues.

2) The ability to understand and respect another person's viewpoint.

3) The ability to express one's own point of view so that others can comprehend the speaker's intent.

At the beginning of each meeting, as in any normal social situation, the participants introduce themselves. A light refreshment may be served to provide a relaxed, pleasant atmosphere. Experience has shown that the optimum sized group appears to be from five to 12 members. Specific goals that can be achieved are:

1) the development of concepts in communication;

2) the development of friendships;

3) to provide a forum to stimulate thinking;

4) to emphasize constructive thinking by means of a classroom model.

Important to the older person's sense of self is the supposition that elderly people can be considered capable of learning and achieving in the present, with expectation of future achievement. The following list of books and magazines can be useful with these groups.

Books

Carson R: The Sense of Wonder. New York, Harper & Row Pubs Inc, 1965.
Cooke A: America. New York, Alfred A Knopf Inc, 1974.
Cowley M: The View from 80. New York, Viking Press, 1980.
Maclay E: Green Winter: Celebrations of Old Age. New York, Reader's Digest Press, 1977.
Merle S (ed): Vacation Land USA. Washington DC, The National Geographic Society, 1970.
Sherman D (ed): The Best of Life. New York, Time-Life Books, 1973.
Steichen E: The Family of Man. New York, The Museum of Modern Art, 1955.

Magazines

Donovan H (ed): Sports Illustrated. Chicago, Time-Life, Inc.
Grosvenor M (ed): National Geographic. Washington DC, The National Geographic Society.
Thompson E (ed): Smithsonian. Washington DC, Smithsonian Associates.

Programs that provide opportunities for increased learning act as agents that positively affect the emotional and cognitive well-being of elders. Geriatric care givers should help the elderly learn to be an essential and normal part of the life process. When given the opportunity to participate in meaningful group settings, elderly people can achieve a more intense awareness of themselves and their environment.[9]

Senior Center Humanities Program

The National Council on the Aging and the National Endowment of the Humanities are sponsoring an exciting project—the Senior Center Humanities Program. The stated aim of extending the humanities outside academic institutions is the foundation upon which specific goals were drawn. These objectives include:

1) Enriching and stimulating the lives of older Americans through involvement in the humanities;

2) Diversifying senior center programming to include intellectually meaningful educational courses; and

3) Expanding the number of senior center participants by attracting

people who might not normally be interested in current programs.

A number of units, under the current series entitled, "Self-Discovery Through the Humanities," have been implemented. These are:

1) Exploring Local History
2) Images of Aging in Literature: A Family Album
3) The American Family in Literature and History
4) Americans and the Land
5) The Remembered Past: 1914—1945
6) Work Life
7) In Search of Meaning
8) In the Old Way

The program includes tape recordings of the readings, large print books with photographs and questions concerning the topics at the end of each section, and certificates of participation. Recipient leaders are requested to fill out a questionnaire at the end of each unit.

Any number of sites have been utilized. Some of these include college senior centers, nursing homes, hospitals, retirement homes, libraries, day-care centers, and church/religious affiliated organizations.[10] The program may be obtained by writing:

National Council on the Aging
600 Maryland Ave SW
West Wing 100
Washington, DC 20024

The Life Review

The life review, a natural and normal process, is utilized by many older persons as they become more aware of their approaching death. Health personnel can enhance this process by incorporating specific techniques and methods, applicable towards self-reflection, into the client's treatment program. In order to do this, one must first understand the meaning of the process.

> The life review is conceived of as a naturally-occurring universal mental process characterized by the progressive return to consciousness of past experiences, and particularly, the resurgence of unresolved conflicts; simultaneously and normally, these revived experiences and conflicts are surveyed and reintegrated. It is assumed that this process is prompted by the realization of approaching dissolution and death....[11]

The characteristics of this process include a progressive, often spontaneous, and unselected return to past experiences. If there is no opportunity to resolve these conflicts, an individual may become depressed, filled with guilt and anxiety, and panic-stricken. On the other hand, successful reintegration of former conflicts can lead to the righting of old wrongs, a feeling of accomplishment and pride, a sense of serenity, and an acceptance of mortal life.

In older people the life review occurs in a number of ways, such as a tendency to reminisce, tell stories, and participate in mild nostalgia. Many elderly people will tell their life story to anyone who is willing to listen. Others will conduct a monologue without an audience. Whatever the case, it is extremely important that this process take place.

Health personnel should be encouraged to listen with care and concern to the reminiscences of the elderly. The review of past experiences is not a preoccupation with the self, nor should it be thought of as boring, time-consuming, and meaningless. Instead, the life review represents a necessary and natural healing process, and those interested in helping the older adult should do everything possible to encourage its usage.

Helping an elderly individual to participate in his life review can take many avenues. One specific example is that of an elderly female patient of more than 80 who was given the opportunity to see her life's art work (representing some 50 years of painting) in a specially arranged art show. During the show she mused, "You know it's not bad, not bad at all. In fact it's quite good." Later she related that the show had given her inner peace and that she was "now ready to meet her maker."

Compiling family albums and scrapbooks as well as studying one's genealogy are examples of methods which help to enhance the life review process.[12] Too often, health care personnel tend to discount the listening aspects of therapy as actually being helpful. Instead, their focus is often upon medication, management, or activities. It is paramount in this process that there be an interested and caring listener.

Spectrum of Social Options

Besides various communication and socialization programs, older adults also need unstructured and quiet times. Snyder suggests that a spectrum of social options be available to the older person. This should include opportunities to participate in the following social patterns: solitary, dyads (two people); family-sized groups (three to six people): neighborhood groups (seven to 20 people); community groups (21 to 40 people); and full assemblage (over 40 people). Accordingly, the task becomes one of providing each older individual with opportunities for experience along this spectrum. Too often we do not recognize the need of the older adult to spend time alone, or in unstructured groups, or observing activities from the sidelines; nor do we earnestly try to persuade the older adult to exercise their freedom of choice with regard to these options.[13]

Communication Techniques with the Handicapped Elderly

Hearing Loss

It is normal practice to have an annual sight test, but uncommon for a person to have an auditory examination on a regular basis, unless there is pronounced hearing loss. Auditory decline can lead to suspicious and paranoid behavior, depression, and social isolation.[14]

The following list contains suggestions for communicating with hearing impaired older adults.

1) Speak clearly and with moderate speed;
2) Do not shout;
3) The speaker's face should be clearly visible;
4) The speaker should have the client's attention before initiating any attempts at communication. The speaker should position himself so that he is directly facing the client;
5) Stand still while speaking;
6) Use visual stimuli whenever possible (ie, gestures, written messages, pictures);
7) Rephrase sentences if the hearing impaired person does not appear to understand the original statement. Some words seem alike when spoken, such as *up* and *cup*;
8) Minimize loud background noises such as papers shuffling, chairs scraping, excessive radio or television volume;
9) If the client wears a hearing aid, make certain it is working effectively.[15]

If the client is an appropriate candidate, he can be instructed in the use of sign language.

There are a number of commercial mechanical aids that are available to people with hearing impairment. Some of these are:

Hearing aids. The use of a hearing aid should be indicated only after a qualified professional has determined if the person in question is in need of such a device. All hearing aids contain a microphone, used for collecting sound waves and converting them into electrical impulses, and a receiver, used for converting amplified electrical impulses into vibrating energy. There are two types of receivers: an *air conductor,* a custom-made device that requires a tight fit, as it is inserted into the ear canal and stimulates the auditory system by delivering vibrations to the eardrum; and a *bone conductor,* a post articular device that is worn behind the ear and delivers vibrations to the temporal bone. In the elderly, these devices should be designed to amplify high frequency sounds more than low, since most older adults develop conditions which affect the loss of the higher sounds. If the degree of sound amplification is different in each ear, a binaural system is suggested. For those individuals with unilateral hearing loss, the Contralateral Routing Signal (CRS) system is suggested. This device consists of a microphone and amplifier that is designed to only pick up sounds on the impaired side.[16]

Electrical devices. The Bell System offers specialized communications equipment that can be utilized by people with impaired hearing: a bone conduction receiver; a code-com set; and numerous types of amplification mechanisms. The code-com set converts sound into sight signals by means of a flashing light, and into sound by means of vibrations on a disc the size of a half dollar. Thus, people who are only deaf, or deaf and blind can use this device.*

Telephones and door bells that flash, and emit a low frequency ring are now available for the hearing impaired. Also, earphones that plug into television sets are helpful aids that allow many hearing impaired to enjoy television without disturbing others.[16]

The Aphasic

With aphasia, a multimodality language disorder, the client may experience difficulty in comprehending or expressing spoken or written symbols. This language disturbance may be accompanied by distress, inappropriate affect (eg, fear, anger, crying, euphoria) frustration, and perseveration (ie, inappropriate repetition of an activity or word after the original stimulus has gone). Appropriate language patterns in the aphasic can be enforced by using the following suggestions:[9]

1) When a client, whose reception is better than his ability to express, is attempting to tell you something but cannot complete his thought, utilize one or all of the following: ask the client yes or no questions; ask him to point to or show the object of his conversation; attempt to give the client a starter phrase, such as, "You would like your ——;" ask if he is able to write the one word he is unable to say; and, attempt to stimulate as much spontaneous speech as is possible by having a one-way conversation with the client.

2) When a client exhibits reduced comprehension, inability to understand questions, or follow directions, the following suggestions are recommended: reduce the length and complexity of your sentences; use more visual input; attempt to give your input before the client tries to speak; attempt to glean meaning from the client's verbalizations; and then ask to show him what you think he is saying.

3) General suggestions include: do not speak louder, but attempt to talk naturally and at a slightly slower pace; even if the client has severe comprehension problems, he may still be able to understand meaning and intent through your facial expressions, physical closeness, and inflection patterns; even if you think the client will not understand you, attempt to explain what you are doing and why; set a specific day-to-day routine; give the client time to process your input and time to try to communicate something to you; attempt to verbalize for the client what you think he might be feeling but is not able to communicate; and stay alert to all non-verbal messages, eg, body posture, facial expression, gesturing (Schultz AR, unpublished outline).

Visual Impairment

In trying to communicate with a blind, or a near-blind person, or an older adult with visual problems, one should sit or stand near that individual, well within an appropriate hearing distance, and speak in a clear, moderately-paced voice.

*Services for Special Needs. Bell Telephone, PE-161, July, 1975, pp 4-7.

Touching and utilization of the tactile senses can also be helpful.

For those who experience visual problems and who are in need of devices to help them negotiate their environment more effectively, there are a number of materials that are available: optiscope enlargers (usually magnifies four times its size), plastic script guides, hand magnifiers, elastic line writing guides, large print telephone dials, movable illuminated magnifier lamps, bath security rails, soap-on-a-rope, and adapted adult games, such as dominoes with raised dots, checkers with round and square pieces that fit into sunken holes, and large print or braille playing cards. Most of these items can be purchased from the following sources:

American Foundation for the Blind
Aids and Appliances Catalogue
15 West 16th Street
New York, NY 10011

Be OK Self Help Aids
Fred Sammons, Inc.
P.O. Box 32
Brookfield, IL 60513

Hammocker-Schlemmer
147 East 57th Street
New York, NY 10022

Oscar B. Stiskin
Dealer for Ulverscraft Large Print Books
P.O. Box 3055
Stamford, CT 06905

Recent technology has also contributed greatly in enhancing the lives of older adults with visual handicaps. Some of these include the laser cane—it is used to detect street curbs, stair treads, moving objects, and overhanging objects at head height. Another is a battery operated, hand-held calculator. Known as *Speech Plus,®* it identifies, in a clear voice, each key as it is pressed down. Pocket-sized scanning instruments identify and announce the denomination of paper money. *The Optican®* permits a blind person to read conventionally printed matter such as books, newspapers, and personal letters by converting the printing into tactile sensations which can be detected with the index finger.[16]

In helping the visually impaired older adult, it is important for health personnel and the family to be aware of a variety of ways they can assist the older person to interact with the environment as independently as possible. Some of these include environmental changes which can be utilized in institutions to assist older people who experience varying degrees of visual loss. Color coding of door jams at entrances to specific areas, or the entire area itself painted in one color, deliberate use of visual boundaries, and large print calendars on walls, all help to orient older individuals to their environment.[14]

In the home, color coding, redundant cueing, and deliberate use of visual boundaries can also be used, as well as large print labeling of frequently used items, such as spices or medicines. Whenever possible, the elder should be instructed in organizing techniques for the performance of activities of daily living. This might include an analysis of kitchen or cooking patterns that could result in a more efficient arrangement of cooking and dining equipment.

Leisure materials such as large print or talking books, newspapers, and magazines may be borrowed from the public library. The Division for the Blind and Handicapped at the Library of Congress, Washington DC, maintains a free national library service for the use of the blind, partially sighted, and physically handicapped. Through its local regional libraries, such items as braille and large print books, magazines, record players, headphones, pillow phones for listening in bed, braille music scores, music instruction on cassettes and records, and large print musical scores can be obtained.

In the United States, there are 70 Radio Information Centers that are available to handicapped individuals. A special receiver enables the listener to hear a wide variety of programming that may include newscasts, reading of local and national newspapers, shoppers' guides, recipes, nonfiction and fiction stories, magazines (including *Time, People, Fortune, Family Health,* and *Sports Illustrated*), armchair travel, variety hour, science programs, and health programs.

The following is a list of periodicals that are available in large print:

Dialogue
Dialogue Publications, Inc.
3100 South Park Avenue
Berwyn, IL 60402
    Quarterly
    A variety of articles, poems, and stories

Guideposts
Guideposts Associates, Inc.
Carmel, NY 10512
    Monthly
    Interfaith subject matter

Musical Mainstream
National Library Service for the Blind
  and Physically Handicapped
(Music Section)
Library of Congress
Washington, DC 20542
    Bimonthly
    Contains original and reprinted articles plus additions to the National Library Service Collection

New York Times/Large Type Weekly
New York Times Company
Large Print Edition
P.O. Box 2570
Boulder, CO 80302
    Weekly
    Current events, news

Reader's Digest
Louise Todd
Reader's Digest Large Type Edition
P.O. Box 241
Mt Morris, IL 61054
　Monthly
　Contains a variety of short articles

Sunshine Magazine
Sunshine Magazine/Large Print Edition
P.O. Box 40
Litchfield, IL 62056
　Monthly
　Articles for the family

World Traveler
Alexander Graham Bell Associates
4317 Volta Place NW
Washington, DC 20007
　Monthly
　Social studies and science topics

Besides this list of periodicals, the National Library Service also maintains a reference circular for the blind and physically handicapped, entitled *Reading Materials in Large Type.*

Treatment Programs and the Consumer

A number of programs have been discussed that can be utilized to improve the older adult's socialization and communication skills. Perhaps the most important aspect to remember about treatment is that the older adult should be involved with his treatment program as much as possible. In this way, the client's motivation, an essential part of any treatment program, can be kept at a maximum. In treatment, health personnel have several roles:

1) to interest the consumer to help plan and participate in his treatment program;
2) to provide appropriate and meaningful treatment that has achievable goals; and
3) to alter treatment as necessary to meet the client's needs.[9]

Resources

Caregivers of geriatric services need to be aware of available resources such as geriatric evaluations, addresses of associations and organizations involved with the concerns of the older adult, and pamphlets and books that are of interest to the geriatric consumer.

Assessment and evaluation of client progress is an on-going, essential aspect of documentation. Initial assessments are particularly important, as they provide a baseline from which the effectiveness of treatment can be determined or measured. Periodic assessments are also important, as they provide the health professional with continuous knowledge of the client's problem areas and development. When treatment is terminated, the caregiver should administer a final assessment of the client's performance, using the same evaluation instruments throughout the entire treatment process.

Evaluation and assessments are problem solving tools for defining current needs or conditions, determining outcome, planning, and research. Evaluation is specifically necessary where there is a choice among alternatives in professional caregiving.

Tests used to evaluate client performance vary considerably, although they can be grouped into five general areas:

1) *General purpose*—classify, describe, select, and/or predict.

2) *Degree of standardization*—norms are standardized distributions of scores by specified subjects that are based on extensive research with large representative samples of such subjects. When an assessment instrument is administered to a large and representative sample of the population as part of the standardization process, the evaluation tool becomes more useful, as it can then be used to compare the scores of persons who have been evaluated. Thus, the score made by an individual can be properly interpreted; it can be seen to be high, low, or average.

3) *Comprehensiveness of measurements*—measures extreme performances, such as the best or least effective level of functioning, or typical performance.

4) *Administration methods*—group or individual, time, ease, and specified skills spent in giving and scoring of the test(s).

5) *Degree of established validity and reliability*—test validity involves three components—content, criterion-relatedness, and construct. Specifically, *content validity* is the systematic examination of the items contained within a test that are used to determine the effectiveness of the representative sample of behavior that is being measured. *Criterion-relatedness* involves predictable and concurrent measures. These are employed in diagnosing the existing status of the patient. *Construct validity* is the extent to which a test measures a theoretical trait. This type of validity may involve internal consistency or correlation with other tests (ie, a positive correlation with variables that are theoretically related) and the degree of obtrusiveness or non-obtrusiveness of a test.[17]

The objectivity of a test is important. An assessment instrument should lend itself to administration and scoring without the results being affected by the personal judgment of the assessor. If the data source is viewed as a continuum, then one end consists of the client's own responses as the source of information, or *client data*. This is obtained from situations in which the client is his own scribe. At the opposite end of the continuum are the observer's responses, or *observer data*. This includes the observer's interpretation and judgments that are often based upon constructed group norms against which an individual client's responses are compared.

The obtrusiveness of the data collection procedure is another important factor. *Instrument data compilation* involves collecting information by means of a questionnaire form, various mechanical tests and devices, and simulated or artificial environments that act as an impetus for collecting information about the client. On the other hand, *non-reactive data collection* utilizes traces of client behavior that were not initially performed for purposes of measurement.[17]

The following list, representing a variety of geriatric evaluations, cites where each assessment can be found:

Double Simultaneous Tactile Stimulation (Face-Hand) Test
Found in: Bender MD, Fink M, Green M: Patterns in perception in simultaneous tests of the face and hand. Archives of Neurology and Psychiatry 66:355-362, 1951.

Instrumental Self-Maintenance/Instrumental Activities of Daily Living Scale
Found in: Lawton MP: Assessing the competence of older people. In Kent DP, Kastenbaum R, Sherwood S (eds): Research Planning and Action for the Elderly. New York, Behavioral Pub Inc, 1972, p 134, and,
Found in: Brody EM: Long-Term Care of Older People: A Practical Guide. New York, Human Science Press, 1977, p 347.

General Awareness Assessment, Liddle J
Geriatric Assessment, Murphy E
Geriatric Sensory Evaluation, Stravinskas L, Lewis S
Found in: Lewis S: The Mature Years: A Geriatric Occupational Therapy Text. Thorofare, NJ, Charles B Slack, Inc, 1979, pp 142-152.

Geriatric Interpersonal Evaluation Scale (GEIS)
Found in: Plutchik R, Conte H, Lieverman M: The development of a scale (GEIS) for the assessment of cognitive and perceptual functioning in geriatric patients. J Am Geriatrics Soc 9:614-623, July, 1971.

Geriatric Rating Scale (040 PLUT)
Found in: Plutchik R, et al: Reliability and validity of a scale for the assessing of functioning of geriatric patients. J Am Geriatric Soc 18:1-500, June, 1970.

Nurses Observation Scale for Inpatient Evaluation (NOSIE 30)
Available from: Central NP Research Laboratory (ISIE)
Veterans Administration Hospital
Perry Point, MD 21902

Measurement of Life Satisfaction
Found in: Neugarten BL, Havinghurst RJ, Tobin SS: The measurement of life satisfaction. J Geront 16:134-143, 1961.

Mental Status Evaluation
Found in: Perlin S, Butler RN: Psychiatric aspects of adaption to the aging

process. In Birren JE, et al: Human aging, a biological and behavioral study. Washington DC, US Government Printing Office, 1963.

Mental Status Questionnaire.
Found in: Kahn RL, Goldfarb AI, Pollack M, Peck A: Brief objective measures for the determination of mental status of the aged. Am J Psychiat 117:326-328, 1960.

Mini-Mental State
Found in: Folstein MF, Folstein SE, McHugh PR: Mini-Mental State: a practical method for grading the cognitive state of patients for the clinician. J Psychiat Research 12:189-198, 1975.

Parachek Geriatric Rating Scale (Parachek JF) and Treatment Manual (King LJ)
Available from:
Greenroom Publications
8512 East Virginia Avenue
Scottsdale, AZ 85257

Personal Mental Health Data Form for Older People
Butler RN, Lewis MI: Aging and Mental Health: Positive Psychological Approaches. St Louis, CV Mosby Co, 1973, pp 149-163.

Philadelphia Geriatric Center Minimal Social Behavior Scale
Adapted by: Lawton MP: from Farina A, Arenberg D, Guskin S: A scale for measuring minimal social behavior. J Consulting Psychol, 1957, p 121.

Philadelphia Geriatric Center Role Maintenance Scale
Found in: Lawton MP: Assessing the competence of older people. In Kent DP, Kastenbaum R, Sherwood S (eds): Research Planning and Action for the Elderly. New York, Behavioral Pub Inc, 1972, p 135.

Physical Self-Maintenance
Adapted by: Lawton MP, Brody E: From Langly-Porter Scale.
Found in: Brody EM: Long-Term Care of Older People: A Practical Guide. New York, Human Science Press, 1977, p 347.

Sensory Training; Reality Orientation; Remotivation; Geriatric Rating Scale (Self Care Behaviors); Generation of Leisure Activities; Activity Gains; Ecology Format; and Radius of Activities
Found in: Weiner MB, Brok AJ, Snadowsky AM: Working with the Aged. Englewood Cliffs, NJ, Prentice-Hall, Inc, 1978, pp 206-233.

Structured Learning Therapy (SLT) Skill Survey
Found in: Goldstein AP, Sprafkin RP, Gershaw NJ: Skill Training for Community Living: Applying Structured Learning Therapy. New York, Pergamon Press, 1976.

Treatment Plans and Progress Notes

After the client has been evaluated for his current functioning level, appropriate treatment should be planned and implemented. Currently, the problem-oriented approach to documenting treatment is the method most often used by the majority of hospitals and agencies in the United States.

Besides determining a client's functioning level, other pertinent information, such as past and current interests, usual daily routine, educational level, employment history, retirement history, strengths, and problems that are currently troubling the client needs to be explored.

Together, the client and the treatment team determine the goals, both short and long term, as well as the method by which these goals are expected to be achieved. The person who will be administering the method is identified, and a specific time is set as to when a definite short term goal should be accomplished. Thus, goals are developed in an objective and measurable manner.

Consumer Organizations

The following list includes a number of associations and organizations that are involved with the concerns of the older adult.

Administration on Aging (AOA)
330 Independence Avenue SW
Washington, DC 20201

Adult Education Association of the USA
810 18th Street NW
Washington, DC 20006
   Publishes *Lifelong Learning: The Adult Years*

American Art Therapy Association
One Cedar Boulevard
Pittsburg, PA 15228

American Association for Music Therapy
35 West Fourth Street
New York, NY 10003

American Association for Rehabilitation Therapy, Inc.
Box 93
North Little Rock, AR 72116

American Association of Homes for the Aging (AAHA)
Suite 770
1050 17th Street NW
Washington, DC 20036
   Represents non-profit nursing homes

American Association of Marriage and Family Counselors
225 Yale Avenue
Claremont, CA 91711

American Association of Physician Assistants
488 Madison Avenue
New York, NY 10022

American Association of Sex Educators and Counselors
5010 Wisconsin Avenue NW
Washington, DC 20016

American Association of Retired Persons (AARP)
1909 K Street NW
Washington, DC 20006
   Sponsors workshops, volunteer programs, health insurance plans, drug
   discounts
   Publishes *Modern Maturity*

American College of Nursing Home Administrators
Suite 409
8641 Colesville Road
Silver Spring, MD 20910

American College of Hospital Administrators
840 North Lake Shore Drive
Chicago, IL 60611

American Dance Therapy Association
2000 Century Plaza
Suite 230
Columbia, MD 21044

American Dental Association
21 East Chicago Avenue
Chicago, IL 60611

American Dietetic Association
430 North Michigan Avenue
Chicago, IL 60611

American Geriatrics Society, Inc.
10 Columbus Circle, NW
Washington, DC 20006
   Publishes *Journal of the American Geriatrics Society*

American Health Care Association
1200 15th Street NW
Washington, DC 20005
   Represents the profit-making nursing homes

American Library Association
50 East Huron Street
Chicago, IL 60611

American Medical Association
535 North Dearborn Street
Chicago, IL 60605

American Medical Technologists
710 Higgins Road
Park Ridge, IL 60068

American Nurses Association
2420 Pershing Road
Kansas City, MO 64108

American Occupational Therapy Association
1383 Piccard Avenue
Rockville, MD 20850

American Optometric Association
7000 Chippewa Street
St Louis, MO 63119

American Orthotic and Prosthetic Association
1440 N Street NW
Washington, DC 20005

American Osteopathic Association
212 East Ohio Street
Chicago, IL 60611

American Personnel and Guidance Association
Two Skyline Place, Suite 400
5203 Leesburg Pike
Falls Church, VA 22041

American Pharmaceutical Association
2215 Constitution Avenue NW
Washington, DC 20037

American Physical Therapy Association
Suite 500
1156 15th Street NW
Washington, DC 20005

American Podiatric Association
20 Chevy Chase Circle NW
Washington, DC 20015

American Psychological Association
Clinical Psychology Division of Adult Development and Aging
1200 17th Street NW
Washington, DC 20036

American Social Health Association
1740 Broadway
New York, NY 10019

American Speech-Language-Hearing Association
10801 Rockville Pike
Rockville, MD 20852

Center for Studies of the Mental Health of the Aging
National Institute of Mental Health
Alcohol, Drug Abuse, and Mental Health Administration

Parklawn Building
5600 Fishers Lane
Rockville, MD 20857

Continental Association of Funeral and Memorial Societies
1828 L Street NW
Washington, DC 20036

Family Service Association of America
44 East 23rd Street
New York, NY 10010

Gerontological Society
1835 K Street NW
Washington, DC 20006

Supports scientific activities in four professional sectors: biological sciences; clinical medicine; behavioral and social sciences; and social research, planning, and practice.

Supports summer institutes for scientists and educators in the field of aging; supports professional growth programs.

Publishes special papers and monographs in addition to two professional journals, *The Gerontologist,* and *The Journal of Gerontology.*

Supports special research projects, and holds scientific meetings.

Gray Panthers
37th & Chestnut Streets
Philadelphia, PA 19104
   A political activist group

Medical Engineering and Electronics
2 East 63rd Street
New York, NY 10016

National Association for Mental Health
1800 North Kent Street
Rosslyn Station
Arlington, VA 22209

National Association for Music Therapy
901 Kentucky Avenue
Suite 206
P.O. Box 6010
Lawrence, KS 66044

National Association of Social Workers
Suite 600
1425 H Street NW
Washington, DC 20005

National Caucus on the Black Aged
Suite 811

1730 M Street NW
Washington, DC 20036
   Interested in elderly black concerns

National Citizen Coalition for Nursing Home Reform
c/o Ms. Elma Griesal
National Paralegal Institute
2000 P Street NW
Washington, DC 20036

National Council of Health Care Services
Suite 402
1200 15th Street NW
Washington, DC 20005

National Council of Senior Citizens
1511 K Street NW
Washington, DC 20006
   Lobbies for the needs of the elderly

National Council on the Aging, Inc.
600 Maryland Avenue SW
West Wing 1000
Washington, DC 20024

   Maintains a comprehensive library of materials on aging; supports
the National Institute on Age, Work, and Retirement; undertakes original research and conducts employment projects; through the National
Institute of Senior Centers, it creates program materials and provides
training and assistance to a nationwide network of senior centers and
clubs.
   Publishes *Perspective on Aging, Aging and Work,* and *Senior Center
Reports.*
   Through the Public Policy Center it monitors legislation, presents
testimony, and disseminates information about the elderly to political
bodies and the general public; its Center of Arts and Aging offers
technical assistance, consultation, and acts as a clearing house for ideas
and information concerning the arts and aging.
   Through the National Voluntary Organizations for Independent
Living for the Vulnerable Aged it provides assistance in promoting and
maintaining independent living for the elderly.
   Its National Media Resource Center on Aging provides information,
publications, and assistance to the multimedia field to change
stereotypes of and by older adults.

National Institute on Aging (NIA)
9000 Rockville Pike
Building 31
Bethesda, MD 20014

National League for Nursing
10 Columbus Circle
New York, NY 10019

National Recreation and Park Association
3101 Park Center Drive
Alexandria, VA 22302

National Rehabilitation Association
1522 K Street NW
Washington, DC 20005

National Senior Citizens Law Center
Paul Nathanson, Director
Sally Hart Wilson, Nursing Home Specialist
1709 West 8th Street
Los Angeles, CA 90017

Opticians Association of America
1250 Connecticut Avenue NW
Washington, DC 20036

The following books, pamphlets, and periodicals provide information which is useful to the geriatric consumer:

Adult Children and Older Parents

Otten J, Shelly FD: When Your Parents Grow Old. New York, Funk and Wagnalls, 1976.
Information and resources to help adult children cope with the problems of aging parents.
Silverstone B, Hyman HK: You and Your Aging Parent: The Modern Family Guide to Emotional and Financial Problems. New York, Pantheon Books, 1976.

Advocacy

American Association of Retired Persons
1909 K Street NW
Washington, DC 20049
Publications:
Modern Maturity (bi-monthly)
Articles about health, food, travel, sports, books, humor, legislation, and personalities
AARP News Bulletin (monthly)
Reports news of national developments and local association activities
AARP Retirement Guides
Topics on choosing a retirement locale, financial planning, second careers, and nutrition.

Gray Panther Books and Materials
Gray Panthers

3635 Chestnut Street
Philadelphia, PA 19104
Publications:
Economic Study Guide
Horn L, Griesal E: *Nursing Homes: A Citizens Action Guide: How to Organize, Plan, and Achieve Nuring Home Reform in Your Community.* Boston, Beacon Press, 1977.
Kuhn M: *On Aging—A Dialogue*
Perretz H: *Gray Panther Manual*
Gray Panther Bibliography
Gray Panther History
Gray Panther Network—Newsletter

Community Resources

Contact your local area agency on aging for specific information. Many county area agencies on aging, as well as smaller community areas, print resource booklets that list current community programs. These often include the times and days of the week programs meet, as well as a listing of addresses and phone numbers.

Consumer Information

Consumer Information Catalogue
Consumer Information Center
Pueblo, CO 81009
Quarterly
Available at most free public libraries, the catalogue lists booklets from almost 30 agencies of the federal government and covers such topics as how to fix a car, and how to save money on food, health care, and energy.

Health Information

There are a large number of booklets, printed by the NIH, the NIMH, and the NIA, that pertain to older adults. These may be obtained by writing to:
Superintendent of Documents
US Government Printing Office
Washington, DC 20402
The information contained in these publications range from: *A Guide to Medical Self-Care and Self-Help Groups for the Elderly* (NIH Publication 80-1687), to *Using Biofeedback with the Elderly* (NIH Publication 79-1401).

Legal Assistance

Martindale-Hubbell Legal Directory
1 Prospect Street
Summit, NJ 17901
This directory consists of a set of volumes that lists lawyers by city, state, age, education, experience, years in practice, and area of specialization. It may be found in a local public library.

Nursing Homes

Berger SG, D'erasmo M: Living in a Nursing Home: A Complete Guide for Residents, Their Families, and Friends. New York, Seabury Press, 1976.

Periodicals and Newsletters

Accent on Living Magazine
P.O. Box 7000
Bloomington, IL 61701

Aged Care and Services Review
Havorth Press
149 Fifth Avenue
New York, NY 10010

Alzheimer's Disease and Related Disorders Association, Inc. Newsletter
292 Madison Avenue
Eighth Floor
New York, NY 10017

Geriatrics
Lancet Press
4015 West 65th Street
Minneapolis, MN 55435

Nursing Homes
Heldref Publications
4000 Albemarle Street, NW
Washington, DC 20016.

Prime Time
Prime Time Publications
1700 Broadway
New York, NY 10019

Reading for the Older Adult

Interage: Older Adult Resources
Interage
P.O. Box 60728
Sacramento, CA 95828
This 25-page booklet tells how to get needed or wanted services for the older adult.

Knopf O: Successful Aging. Boston, GK Hall and Co, 1977.
This book, written by an 85-year-old active physician, includes topics such as legal considerations, physical and emotional changes brought on by aging, self acceptance, retirement, and the use of leisure time.

Vinning EG: Being 70: The Measure of a Year. Boston, GK Hall and Co, 1978.
Ms. Vinning, tutor to Crown Prince Akihto of Japan after World War II, offers her interpretation and an answer of the meaning of growing old, in the form of a year's journal.

What to Talk About

Brody EM: Visiting your relative at the Philadelphia Geriatric Center: A note to family and friends of our residents. In Brody EM: Long-Term Care of Older People: A Practical Guide. New York, Human Science Press, Inc, 1977, pp 323-332.

Work/Life Counseling

Ganikos ML (ed): Journal of Employment Counseling—A Special Issue. March, 1980.
This is a special issue for work/life counseling for older people.
Order from:
American Personnel and Guidance Association
Two Skyline Place
Suite 400
5203 Leesburg Pike
Falls Church, VA 22041

References

1. Richman L: Sensory training for geriatric patients. A J Occu Ther 23: 244-245, 1969.
2. Weiner MB, Brok AJ, Snadowsky AM: Working with the Aged. Englewood Cliffs, Prentice-Hall, Inc, 1978, p 69.
3. Barnes EK, Sack A, Shore H: Guidelines to treatment approaches: Modalities and methods for use with the aged. Geront 13:515-518, 1974.
4. Nursing Service, Guide for Reality Orientation. VA Hospital, rev ed. Tuscaloosa, AL, Feb, 1970, pp 8-12.
5. Schwenk MA: Reality orientation for the institutionalized aged: Does it help? Geront 19:373-377, 1979.
6. Goldstein AP: Structured Learning Therapy: Toward a Psychotherapy for the Poor. New York, Academic Press, 1973.
7. Goldstein AP Sprafkin RP, Gershaw NJ: Skill Training for Community Living: Applying Structured Learning Therapy. New York, Pergamon Press, 1976.
8. Lopez, et al: Effects of overlearning and incentive on the acquisition and transfer of interpersonal skills with institutionalized elderly. J Geront 35:403-407, 1980.
9. **Lewis SC: The Mature Years: A Geriatric Occupational Therapy Text.** Thorofare, NJ, Charles B Slack, Inc, 1979, pp 65-67, 84, 134-136, 152, 153.
10. Schembri W: Renewing old talents. In Youry M (ed): Perspective on Aging 9:11, 12, 1980.
11. Butler RN: The life review: An interpretation of reminiscence in the aged. In Kastenbaum R (ed): New Thoughts On Old Age. New York, Springer Pub Co Inc, 1964, p 266.
12. Butler RN, Lewis MI: Aging and Mental Health: Positive Psychological Approaches. St Louis, CV Mosby Co, 1973, pp 43-44.
13. Synder LH: Environmental changes for socialization J Nurs Admin Jan: 44-48, 1978.
14. Shore H: Designing a training program for understanding sensory losses in aging. Geront 16:159-161, 1976.
15. Battle D: A speech therapist considers speech and hearing problems for the elderly. In Deichman ES, O'Kane CP (ed): Working with the Elderly: A Training Manual. Buffalo, DOK Pub, Inc, 1975, pp 51-58.
16. Colavita FB: Sensory Changes in the Elderly. Springfield, IL, Charles C Thomas, 1978, p 128.
17. **Bloom M: Evaluation instruments, tests, and measurements in long-term care.** In Sherwood S: Long-Term Care: A Handbook for Researchers, Planners, and Providers. New York, Spectrum Pub Inc, 1975, pp 504, 575-577.

Bibliography

Berger RM: Training the institutionalized elderly in interpersonal skills. Social Work 24:420-423, 1979.

Chomsky N: Language and Mind (Enlarged Edition). New York, Harcourt Brace and Jovanovich, Inc, 1972.

Cornbleth T, Cornbleth C: Evaluation of the effectiveness of reality orientation classes in a nursing home unit. J A Geriatric Soc 27:522-524, 1979.

Emlet CA: Reminiscence: A psychosocial approach to the institutionalized aged. Am Health Care Assoc Journal 5 (September):19-22, 1979.

George LK, Bearon L: Quality of Life in Older Persons: Meaning and Measurement. New York, Human Science Press, 1980.

Hamill CM, Oliver RC: Therapeutic Activities for the Handicapped Elderly. Gaithersburg, MD, Aspen Systems Corp, 1980.

Karney RJ, Edmunds EP, et al: A comparison of treatment approaches for improving conversational skills among psychogeriatric residents. Presentation at Research and Aging practice Seminar II, Philadelphia, January 23, 1981.

Kiernat JM: The use of the life review activity with confused nursing home residents. Am J Occup Ther 33:306-310, 1979.

Linder EC, Harpaz L, Samber S: Therapeutic Dance/Movement: Expressive Activities for Older Adults. New York, Human Science Press, 1979.

Paire J: Sensory stimulation helps. Presentation at Research and Aging Practice Seminar II, Philadelphia, January 23, 1981.

Sargent SS (ed): Nontraditional Therapy and Counseling with the Aging. New York, Springer Pub Co, 1980.

9
Informative Experiences for Providers and Consumers

A care provider's working knowledge of gerontology can be expanded by reading pertinent books and journals, attending courses, workshops, and lectures focused on geriatrics, talking with other health care professionals who work with the elderly, and talking with the elderly themselves. Another way is to be part of a consciousness-raising session. Probably one of the best ways to learn about specific aspects of gerontology, however, is to pick a topic relating to the elderly, and present a program on it.

This chapter looks into several different ways of educating both the elderly, and those who care for them, through workshops, fairs, programs, tests, sensitivity sessions, and conversation.

There are many topics in gerontology which deserve in-depth exploration. They can be as broad as the approaches to continuum of care, or as narrow as the uses and abuses of the geriatric wheelchair. Topics such as these could be used as a program in themselves, or as one issue in a broader context. For an idea of how to present broad or specific subjects, see Appendix B for Continuum of Care Approaches, and Appendix C for information on the problems with unintentional misuses of the gerichair.

Workshops, Seminars, and Conferences

The most important aspect to be concerned with is understanding the special needs of the target audience, and designing a project to satisfy those needs. In order to insure success, the project must contain meaningful and useful subject matter.

A major step is to organize an interested, hardworking committee, headed by a coordinator who will oversee the project and distribute the workload. Once the committee has established a purpose and goal, each member can assume specific responsibilities. First, a specific topic must be chosen. Then, the committee should find a suitable speaker or group of panelists. It should be noted that by enlisting the presence of well-known personalities, good audience attendance is often guaranteed. People are anxious to hear them and will usually encourage friends to come as well. Next, specific committee members must design the program and prepare flyers; contact the media and arrange to advertise the project; obtain a locale that is convenient for the target audience (eg, accessible to public transportation, having adequate parking); acquire any needed audio-visual equipment such as a public address system, a slide projector, and screen; provide food and beverage if the project extends over many hours; plan how to cover the cost of the affair (eg, admission charge, sponsorship by an institution or organization, or receive funds from a grant); and develop a means to evaluate the project's worth based on audience reaction.[1]

What types of information do consumers seek? A review of the numerous brochures dealing with gerontological education programs reveal certain aspects they all have in common. Emphasis is placed on current achievements, programs, methodology, and theories involving aging; information on institutions, halfway houses, home care; discussions on appropriate care for elderly parents, as well as respite services for adult children; and improving attitudes towards aging, especially the attitudes of those who routinely care for the elderly.

The *Highlights by Older Adults* program held at a shopping mall in Montgomery County, Pennsylvania, is an example of the type of project laid out above. This event was sponsored by the Montgomery County Task Force on Older Adults, a voluntary citizen consumer and professional organization interested in improving the quality of life for the older residents of the county. The goals for this project were to inform people of existing human and health services in the local community and to provide elders with an arena in which they could display their skills and achievements.

Because the budget was very limited (no more than $35.00 was available), all costs had to be kept to a minimum. The coordination methods involved establishing a locale that was cost-free and accessible to public transportation (a local shopping center) and contacting participating agencies and interested individuals by public service news media. Cost-free news spots are allocated in most local newspapers and on radio stations if the project is non-profit and open to the community. Mail, telephone, and group meetings were also used to spread the word.

Tables displaying the hobby exhibits, artwork, handcrafts, and agency information demonstrated the elder person's skills, and served to inform consumers of the types of services available to them in their local community. The agencies, organizations, and groups that exhibited included homemaker's home health aids, a bank with information on specialized services for older persons, visiting nurse associations, a private craft group that only sells merchandise made by elders, numerous senior adult activities centers, a retired senior volunteer program, the county Geriatric and Rehabilitation Center/nutrition programs, the county Public Library home bound program, the geriatric services of a state hospital, an employment agency that councils older people, and the County Department of Consumer Affairs. The discussion and entertainment portion of this project featured three County Commissioners, the director of the County Area of Aging Agency, a panel of three elderly Retired Senior Volunteer Program participants, the Syncopated Seniors (a band composed of older people who had earlier represented the United States as goodwill ambassadors to Rumania), and a speaker from the Gray Panthers.

There were 20 exhibits and a total of 370 people involved. This type of program created an awareness on the part of the community that agencies working cooperatively can produce a minimum cost program that involves consumers and providers.[2]

Personal Experiences

Professional speakers can discuss different aspects of gerontological care with great effect, but sometimes hearing the personal experiences of a layman can be just as enlightening. For one thing, they can provide individual examples, and for another, they can give a professional health care provider a sometimes sobering view of how they appear to the consumer.

The following dialogue describes the experiences of a woman who had to cope with the problems of two ill elderly parents.

Dialogue with Mrs. Z, a married, 59-year-old career woman, who was the only child of two dying parents whose ages were 74 and 79 at the onset of their decline.

Question: Would you please share some of your insights into the kinds of things you found were necessary to do in order to preserve your parents' privacy and independence during the difficult days when both of them were weak and generally incapacitated?

Answer: *My parents lived 100 miles away from me. When they could no longer care for themselves without some form of assistance, it became necessary to find a way to shorten this geographic distance. As both my husband and I worked, the most realistic answer was to move my parents close to us. This meant uprooting them, which of course, was not without its problems. However, it was the only way that I could find so that I would be able to be with them daily and still be with my husband too.*

Previous to this move my parents had received weekday help. My husband and I had been driving the 200 mile round trip to their home in order to provide weekend coverage. At this point they had become even more dependent, and evening assistance was added to their list of needs.

My husband and I helped them move into their own apartment that was **within a 15-minute drive from my home and work. The move was not** *traumatic for my mother. But my father went into a severe depression* **which lasted close to six months. By this time, he was incontinent and had very little memory left. He called me by my mother's name, and** *it was impossible for him to learn anything new. He went into a severe depression which lasted about six months. Then he began to be able to locate himself, and to understand that he was in an apartment with my mother. He also became reassured to the fact that he wasn't going to be abandoned.*

In the meantime, my father's condition began to deteriorate even more. He could no longer remember what he had eaten. My mother was very responsive to him, but she also was in great need of support and relief. In their new condominium she had been able to form friendships. It became important for her own welfare to be able to attend social activities that were sponsored by the condominium complex. In order for her to go, my husband and I provided the companionship and supervision my father needed.

There were also a number of personal things that I did to help my mother's morale and in general to assist her. In terms of morale, I drove her to the beauty shop weekly. She suffered from myelo-fibrosis, a fibrosis of the bone marrow in which the body does not produce enough red blood corpuscles. As a consequence, she fatigued and bruised easily, and was in general, extremely fragile. Her medication, prednisone, protected her from infection, but as a side effect, she was too weak to travel by public transportation. Therefore, transportation to the dentist, the doctor, the food market and drug store, the bank, and the department store was provided by me.

In addition to physical needs and wants, my mother also needed intellectual stimulation. I brought her at least six or seven books a week from the library. I stopped by at least once a day, including weekends, and took care of them on the days the housekeeper who came four days a week was not there.

My father was in a nursing home the last two months of his life. I went with my mother to visit him, at least three or four times a week—a 20 mile round trip. This, frankly, was the worst time of all—because it was as if we had failed. We could no longer take care of him. He always knew who my mother was but during this time he turned his face to the wall when she approached him. He was in need of 24-hour professional care in the home. It meant that every available dollar would have had to have been utilized in his care. However, my mother needed some of these dollars, as she, too, was quite ill. We searched for, and after two tries, found an excellent home where the care was personal and very professional.

Question: What was your husband's role in all this?

Answer: *He assumed many of my responsibilities in our house. For instance, he would prepare supper so that I could be with my parents on the way home from work. He also was willing to give up a great deal of his time with me. He sacrificed a considerable amount of our social life so I could be with my parents.*

Question: Did the grandchildren assume a positive role?

Answer: *Yes, most definitely! Our two daughters were extremely supportive.*

They visited frequently and would relieve me when they could. One daughter lived with my parents for two months before they moved to their new condominium.

Question: What were your most difficult problems, and how were you able to resolve some of them?

Answer: *Getting reliable help was the most pressing problem. You really need excellent financial resources to provide the dignified and comfortable life that an elderly parent deserves. The private commercial services had rigid restrictions on what could be done by a companion, and the public agencies who were usually willing to help, never seemed to have enough personnel to go around.*

Individual caretakers usually find these jobs boring, as they are restricted to a limited environment. Often they have to deal daily with irritable, troublesome clients with no outlets for their own frustrations. It was not unusual for us to provide support to the housekeeper in order to prevent her from imposing her will upon my parents. In reality, I assumed the total health care of my parents at the sacrifice of my own time. Once, when I had arranged to go for a short vacation, the woman who was supposed to care for my parents never showed up.

Even though I assumed this complete care of my parents, I had to allow my mother to feel that she was in control, and was capable of making her own decisions. Even though physically, she was totally dependent on me, mentally, she was a totally functioning being. Preserving her personal dignity and identity were prime cosiderations.

When my father was in the nursing home, my mother was very ill herself. We were able to arrange for a housekeeper for her four days a week, and I filled in on the other three days. Neighbors also can be a warm and very wonderful resource. One of the neighbors across the hall was a nurse. My mother called on her many times.

My mother lived one year less two days after my father died. During that year, she came to our house and spent weekends with us. She also, unfortunately, spent a lot of time in the hospital.

Question: What advice would you give to other adult children with sick elderly parents?

Answer: *Whenever possible, let them live in their own surroundings with whatever supports you can provide for them. Caretakers in a parents' home with you providing additional support, until the situation becomes impossible, seems a good solution. A child cannot force a decision upon a parent. No one should feel guilty if it becomes necessary to place a parent in a nursing home. You have to weigh your own needs —marriage, children—with that of your parents.*

I received a lot of help from my mother's doctor, who encouraged me to vacation while she was in the hospital. While away, I arranged for both her and my friends to visit with her each day. When he knew that her condition was absolutely irreversible, he suggested to me that it was time for her to be placed in a nursing home, and I agreed.

Question: Do you have any regrets?

Answer: *No, because of the way I cared for my parents there are no regrets. However, being sick and experiencing the loss of abilities in the final years can make one angry and anguished. The lack of dignity in which a human being ends his life can be distressing. For example, my father couldn't even evacuate his bowels. Instead, he required a daily enema. Every moment of my father's last years pained him. He had been a virile man who suddenly became helpless and dependent.*

Question: Do you have any suggestions you could offer that would make caring for sick elderly parents easier?

Answer: *The greatest need for caretaking children is relief. I am certain more families would be willing to care for their ailing parents, if they knew they could get relief, such as day-care or weekend care, vacations, co-op sitting arrangements, and evening coverage.*

In this respect, more public and private agencies should arrange for or be responsible for providing these much-needed services.

Training Programs

There are a number of programs and exercises, known as empathetic enhancement, that are designed to help those who work with the older adult to more fully understand how that person feels. One of the major goals of these programs is to improve the quality of care that is rendered to the elderly. The following is a list of resources that include a variety of different types of sensitizing experiences:

1. Epstein C: Learning to Care for the Aged. Reston, VA, Reston Pub Co, 1977, pp 173-183, "Exercises in Awareness and Skill Development."

2. Ernst M, Shore H: Sensitizing People to the Process of Aging: The Inservice Educator's Guide. Denton, TX, University Center for Community Services—Center for Studies in Aging, North Texas University.

3. Robichaud MP, Brown ML: A Simulation Experience to Sensitize Persons to the Sensory Losses of the Elderly. Presented in Washington DC, at the Annual Scientific Meeting of the Gerontological Society, November 26, 1979.

   The four-hour program consists of a true-false quiz, application of inhibitors to limit vision, hearing, touch dexterity, and mobility, assignments of 12 tasks to be performed with inhibitors in place, and a discussion period.

   Further information may be obtained by writing to:

   M. Phyllis Robichaud and Miner L. Brown
   Jewish Center for the Aged
   Chesterfield, MO 63017

4. Shore H: Designing a training program for understanding sensory losses in aging. Gerontologist 16:157-165, 1976.

5. University of Michigan—Wayne State University
   Institute of Gerontology
   Ann Arbor, MI 48108

The Institute has developed a number of educational programs designed to improve attitudes about and understanding of the elderly.

6. Lewis S: A Consciousness-Raising Training Program Concerning Aging. This program is reproduced in Appendix D.
7. Palmore E: Facts on Aging: A Short Quiz. Gerontologist 17:315-320, 1977.
8. Menks, F: The Road of Life: A simulation board game designed to facilitate affective learning.

> For information, contact:
> Louisa Scott
> Health Center Communications
> University of Florida
> 904-392-2621

9. Hoffman TL, Reif SD: Into Aging: A Simulation Game. Thorofare, NJ, Charles B Slack, Inc, 1978.

The Service Provider's Role

Anyone who is working with the elderly has a commitment to learn as much as they can about their field. Interest in gerontology has dramatically increased over the past few years, as people are living longer, and the population as a whole is growing older. To be able to provide the most up-to-date service to the elderly, providers must constantly read new books and journals, attend workshops and seminars, and most of all, *listen* to those they serve. After all, how else can they find out what elderly consumers want?

References

1. Lewis SC: The Mature Years: A Geriatric Occupational Therapy Text. Thorofare, NJ, Charles B Slack, Inc, 1979, pp 133, 134.
2. Lewis S: Community program unites OT and the consumer. Rockville, MD, OT Newsletter, July, 1976.

Bibliography

Davis LJ: Service Provision and The Elderly: Attitudes of three generations of urban women. Occup Ther J Reas 1(April):32-52, 1981.

Hasselkus BR: Commentary: Service Provision and the Elderly: Attitudes of three generations of urban women. Occup Ther J Reas. 1(April):53-55, 1981.

Lewis S: A geriatric program fair: The state hospital as an agent for community interaction. Hospital and Community Psychiatry 27:154-159, 1976.

Miller DB, Barry JT: Nursing Home Organization and Operation. Boston, CBI Pub Co, 1979.

Moos RH, Lemke S: Assessing the physical and architectural features of sheltered care settings. J Gerontology 35: 571-582, 1980.

Segal SP: Community care and deinstitutionalization: a review. Social Work 24:521-527, 1979.

10
Working with
Older Adults

W e are challenged as never before to provide the older adult with substantive, therapeutic, and educational programs that are targeted at improving the elderly person's ability to function independently as long as possible.

With the present decline in the birthrate and a projection of longer life, it is possible to estimate that each new decade will continue to bring with it an increase of people over 65. Some researchers believe that babies born within the next 35 years will have an opportunity to achieve a life expectancy of over 125 years. These same investigators also feel confident that by the year 2100 it will be possible to attain a life expectancy of 600 to 1,000 years.* These startling revelations make one realize that the human service provider's obligations to older citizens will continue to grow and flourish.

Who works with the elderly? Older adults, as consumers, need to know just what types of service and care they can expect. Service providers need to be aware of the job opportunities that exist in gerontology as well as the specific responsibilities and challenges that any given profession offers.

The list of those who work with the elderly is endless. The following is a partial list of some of the professions, trades, and allied professions that offer service to the older adult in the course of their business:

Building industry: Architects; builders; and tradesmen such as carpenters, plumbers, and electricians. Involvement may include nursing homes, senior

Living to age 1,000. The Philadelphia Bulletin, *June 6, 1977, p 1.*

housing projects, retirement villages, sheltered apartment complexes, and geriatric rehabilitation centers.

Travel: For pleasure—travel agents, transportation personnel such as flight attendants, bus drivers, porters, pursers, activities directors, train attendants, conductors, tour guides, and hotel management and support services.

For daily needs—taxi drivers, bus drivers, subway attendants, train attendants, and conductors.

Communication and electronics industry: Television sales and service personnel, electronic alerting systems personnel, hearing aid sales and service personnel, and telephone sales and service personnel.

Drug industry: Administrative personnel, scientists, laboratory assistants, detail personnel, pharmaceutical salesmen, and pharmacists.

Food industry: Food scientists, farmers, sales personnel, food processors, grocery store personnel, restaurant management and support services.

Medical industry: Medical physicians, osteopathic physicians, social workers, registered nurses, licensed practical nurses, hospital administrators, dieticians, nursing home administrators, physical therapists, occupational therapists, x-ray technicians, emergency medical technicians, paramedics, medical records administrators, respiratory therapists, assistants to primary care physicians, laboratory technicians, histologic technicians, medical assistants, speech and hearing therapists, thanatologists, therapeutic recreation specialists, art and music therapists, therapy assistants, dentists, podiatrists, dental assistants, dental hygienists, rehabilitation counselors, orthotists, opticians, mobility specialists, hospice administrators, and psychologists.

Mortuary services: Funeral management and support services, florists, cemetary management, and support services.

Theology: Chaplains, ministers, priests, nuns, and rabbis are some of the people who perform religious services.

There is hardly a profession or trade that does not touch, in some way, the concerns of an older person. This list, representing just a sample of the vocations that have some type of relationship to elderly people, reminds us that almost all businesses and careers, either directly or indirectly, are involved in gerontology.

There are many ways in which an individual can acquire knowledge about jobs which directly relate to gerontology. Books, journals, conferences, and interviews are some examples. Several methods of inquiry will be examined in more detail below.

Literary Inquiry

Books are one of the best ways to obtain detailed information on a specific profession. Journals, newsletters, leaflets, and booklets may not be able to provide the detail of a textbook, but will probably have more up-to-date information on gerontology or related professions. Most of this type of literature is available in local libraries, and therefore, provides an inexpensive resource for both the lay and the professional reader.

The Occupational Outlook Quarterly (US Department of Labor) is an excellent source for discovering what jobs are currently available and how a specific profession serves its clients. An in-depth summary of the profession is presented by an individual with intimate knowledge of the field. This quarterly includes a variety of job options.

Another resource, somewhat related to the *Occupational Outlook Quarterly*, is the *Occupational Outlook Handbook* (annually printed by the US Department of Labor). This handbook describes what workers do on the job, the training and education that is required, advancement possibilities, employment projections for the future, wages, and working conditions.

Textbooks that discuss a specific field are another source for acquiring information regarding professional specialization. These may be found in the library under "Gerontology", or the specific field of interest. College or university libraries are the best place to look for books on specific professions. Or, if looking for up-to-date information, check the topical index of a local bookstore's copy of *Books In Print*. Remember that many reference books not directly related to the field of interest may still contain a section on it.

Newsletters, either from professional or lay organizations, represent another way in which information can be obtained concerning professional caregiving responsibilities. Again, these may be found at a local public library. If not, check the library of a local retirement home, or write directly to the organization. Some addresses are provided in Chapter 8, pp 116-124.

Written Inquiry

Another way of obtaining knowledge about a particular profession is to seek it in writing from someone who is currently engaged within it. Unlike a verbal inquiry, written questions must be to the point, comprehensive, yet contain an element of elasticity to allow the writer room to expand, if it is necessary to clarify a point. The following are a basic set of questions which can be utilized for this purpose:

1) Would you please highlight your educational and work experiences? Which have been the most influential and helpful in your work with the elderly?

2) What kinds of programs do your profession offer that can be helpful to the older person? In what types of settings do people in your profession work?

3) Would you cite how your professional intervention was helpful to older people?

Verbal Inquiry

The verbal transmission of past experiences is an old, yet meaningful and successful way to learn. The following interviews of professionals working in gerontology detail their experiences, thoughts and concerns for older adults.

It is impossible, in one chapter, to interview all those persons who are involved in gerontologically-related careers. Instead, the following interviews are intended to be viewed in terms of providing a sampling of the responsibilities, methods, and approaches that different professionals use in order to help their older clients. The ideas of the people interviewed are individual, and not necessarily reflective of the agencies and institutions they serve.

Interview with Deborah W. Frazer, PhD,* Director of Geriatric Programs for a community mental health center.

Question: Would you please highlight some of your educational and professional work experiences?

Answer: *In 1969 I graduated from a small coeducational college with a BA in Psychology. At that time I perceived that people's problems were more economically and socially determined than psychologically determined.*

For five years I worked with political and religious organizations that were concerned with social change. At the end of that time I began to have a more complex appreciation for any given problem being multiply determined—including a psychological aspect. I felt that I did, indeed, have some skill in psychological intervention and decided to go back into that field, but taking with me the whole picture—including the economical and political factors in a supposedly personal problem.

I was one of 12 people who began a clinical psychology program within a large urban university. Over the course of my first two years there, I realized that this multi-faceted approach to individual problems was somewhat different than my fellow students. Where they were directed toward ultimately being in private practice, I would be working with people who suffered from a range of social, economic, and personal problems. These are people who are typically underserved by mental health professionals.

With that orientation, I chose an internship in a large state mental hospital where I stayed on to take a job in a geriatric unit. I often thought that the patients in our unit were the exact opposite of what we, in graduate school, had learned were good patients. We were taught that the people who respond well to treatment exhibit the Yavris syndrome: young, attractive, verbal, rich, intelligent, and successful—people who could afford to pay the private practitioner the requisite $75.00. Our state hospital patients, on the other hand, were in many ways society's outcasts—old, unattractive, nonverbal, poor, often of low intelligence, and certainly unsuccessful.

Question: While working at this facility, how did you use your professional skills?

Answer: *When I finished my internship and began to work as an employee at the state hospital, my boss gave me only one instruction—go over to the geriatric unit, see what needs to be done, and do it!*

This was a flexible job with less stress on a defined professional role than on trying to use all my faculties for problem solving. There was a certain amount of traditional clinical psychology work that involved assessments, individual and group psychotherapy, supervision of students and interns, and research. Other things I attempted were program development, helping with staff development, developing linkages with other agencies; and in many

Printed by permission of Deborah W. Frazer, PhD.

ways one of the most valuable roles I played was an advocate—for patients, for aides, for housekeeping staff, and for our building, vis a' vis the rest of the hospital.

In response to my boss' instructions, the first thing that clearly needed attention was the physical environment of our patients. When I walked into the building, I got depressed, and I assumed that it had the same affect on our patients and the staff. So one of the most interesting projects which I tried, and with which I was most identified was the therapeutic environment project.

We attempted to involve all the staff and as many patients as possible in bringing some warmth, color and life to a barren and deprived environment. The importance of this project was not so much in the actual physical changes that occurred, but in bringing to staff and patients a sense that things could change and that they could have some control over these changes.

Question: What are your present job responsibilities?

Answer: *After four years I felt for my own growth I needed to leave the state hospital system—to try applying some of my skills and knowledge to a community setting. I was aware of the limitations of my job with the state system where I felt a great deal of responsibility but had no formal authority.*

So I left to take a job as Director of Geriatric Programs for a community mental health center where I am responsible for two-day treatment programs with a total census of just under 200 clients, an average daily attendance of 30 to 35 at each center, and a staff of 12.

The goals of our program are similar to any partial hospitalization program—in that we try to prevent hospitalization or institutionalization, and we try to ease transition back to the community when someone is leaving an inpatient facility. We are an intensive service open five days a week from 9:00 am to 3:00 pm, providing individual and group psychotherapy and a full range of therapeutic activities. Although each client's goals are different, you might say that in general we try to maximize each person's potential.

Question: Were there any specific problems that needed solving in relationship to your new role as administrator?

Answer: *Yes. Part of the problem with our center is that it began on a grant as a senior center, not as a mental health center. For funding reasons it had to become a mental health program. During the transition there was a great deal of confusion about the difference between a senior center and a geriatric day treatment center. I was hired specifically because I came from a clinical background and, because of my background, I could clarify this difference for our staff and for the community.*

Consequently, a big part of my job is spent in clarifying our niche in the geriatric continuum of care. This involves a great deal of staff development work in terms of sharpening their clinical skills, and also involves communication and interaction with other community agencies serving the aging to better define the distinction between our services. One of the great satisfactions of this job, of dealing in the community, is that I see played out in our clients' lives much of the economic and political theory I developed in earlier years.

I encourage my staff to understand the client's problems, not only in a clinical sense, but also in a systematic sense, and to take account of people's lives when problem solving with the client. An example of this is that we encourage political activism among our clients through senior organizations.

Question: What type of changes in your new job were the most notable in comparison with your first job's responsibilities?

Answer: *The major job change for me was going from a primarily clinical role to a primarily administrative role. In an administrative capacity I now have authority as well as responsibility. The dues I pay for that is the inordinate amount of paper which crosses my desk every day.*

The one major use of my clinical skills which I retain in my current job is that I do the initial interviews of every person who comes to the center. I spend approximately one to two hours with each person, doing a detailed assessment and clinical interview, working with them to develop treatment goals. I value this as the only way I have of keeping personal and direct contact with our clients. I think this is necessary to keep my humanity as an administrator.

Some of my other responsibilities include representing our program in the aging and mental health network; working with a grant writer to develop proposals; running team meetings and staffing conferences at each center; hiring new staff; staff development; keeping abreast of regulations; and generally acting as the communication link between the geriatric program and the larger community mental health center.

Question: Would you please describe how your intervention was helpful to an elderly person?

Answer: *I wish I could tell you some glorious tale of how six years of a PhD program in clinical psychology led to some sophisticated intervention which changed someone's life. But the only things that I can think of that seem to have made a difference to people are very simple gestures.*

A person who comes to my mind is one of my state hospital patients, Mrs. B, who was 84 years old at the time. She had a sister, 86 years old, who had visited Mrs. B in the hospital once a month for the past 50 years. By reading her chart, I discovered that these visits had ceased, due to the 86-year-old's inability to make the trip. Arranging transportation for Mrs. B to be taken on visits to her sister was only a small gesture towards someone who had endured a lifetime of institutionalization. And, yet because it means so much to Mrs. B, in the gesture I probably felt more satisfaction than in any psychological test I had administered, or report I had written.

In general, the things that seem to make a difference for the people I work with are small concrete acts or just being there for them, with warmth and interest. My most moving experience so far was an interview with an older woman, who after denying all problems for 45 minutes, was then able to admit, for the first time to anyone, including herself, that she was dying of cancer.

140

This wasn't the result of a clinical technique or a specific skill. It was a matter of just being interested in her and caring about her. Where we take it from here will require professional intervention. But even then, techniques are useless without a basic caring attitude.

Interview with Mr. James G. Dailey, MHA, NHA,* Administrator of a home for the aged.

Question: Please describe your facility.

Answer: *It is a 156-bed residential care, church-owned facility. People are first admitted into the home in the residential section. As they grow older the intermediate care and skilled nursing care wings are available if the need for remediative and restorative service arises. Residents may come from all walks of economic life. No one is turned away for financial reasons. In terms of the spiritual needs of the residents, we maintain a chapel on the grounds, and a priest is always available.*

Question: Would you highlight your educational and work experience?

Answer: *I have a master's degree in hospital and health services administration and I have participated in post graduate course work. I have one year of experience as a resident in hospital administration at a 500-bed general hospital, and six years of experience in administration of a geriatric residential home.*

Question: Primarily, how do you see your role?

Answer: *I see myself as the oil in the motor—a facilitator. My primary function is to keep the residential care system moving in the direction that is most beneficial for the resident. Often I find myself in the role of intervener or advocate for the older person. We are interested in the psychological, spiritual, and social well-being of our residents, and try to help the family and the resident resolve family problems. My role is that of a generalist enlisting the support and resources of staff specialists such as nursing, dietary, laundry, accounting, physicians, speech therapy, and so on, for the benefit of the resident. Not only are staff members a resource to the resident but they can well serve as a resource to each other.*

Question: Could you cite a specific example in which an older person was helped by your intervention?

Answer: *A number of older people are ambivalent about giving up their homes or apartments to come and live in a home for the aged. For some this can be a trying experience. For instance, one older women who had been brought to look at our facility by her family was in tears. I asked to speak with her alone and told her that we wanted people to come who really wished to be here. We talked about the fact that she had a major decision to make—where she would spend the remaining days of her life—and I suggested that she delay an immediate decision. As an alternate option, I suggested that she visit the facility many times over a two month period. While visiting, she could talk to*

Printed by permission of Mr. James G. Dailey, MHA, NHA.

the other residents and attend the activities, as well as church services. The choice should be hers. Six months later she decided to come to our facility, and she has been with us for four years—an active participant in our residential community.

This interview originally appeared in *The Mature Years: A Geriatric Occupational Therapy Text.* Its focus is not only upon how an elderly individual was helped, but it also offers suggestions for those planning to enter the field.

Interview with Ruth Levine,* EdD, OTR, Director of a Community Occupational Therapy Consultants group; Program Planning Consultant, Department of Occupational Therapy at a large urban state-related university.

Question: What first made you decide to become involved in community occupational therapy programs and services?

Answer: *Originally I wanted to work with a drug addiction population, but my clinical field work coordinator teacher, Clare Spackman, suggested that I look into a job at the Community Nursing Service of Philadelphia. When I graduated from college in 1969, occupational therapists were rarely involved in community service; therefore, I was not aware that this was a viable alternative to inpatient clinical work. The person who interviewed me at Community Nursing Service was eager to hire an occupational therapist and supported some of the ideas that I discussed with her.*

Question: What do you consider to be the most important personality traits for therapists who do home care work?

Answer: *Basically, there is a need for a pragmatic individual who is flexible and can problem solve in a variety of different social structures. He or she must be a generalist with good group dynamic skills. The goal of the home care agency team is to teach other family members or caretakers to carry out treatment programs and care for the client. Thus, technical programs must be simplified so that family members can render daily treatment.*

Question: Would you discuss a specific case history in which an elderly individual was helped by your service?

Answer: *Mr. M was a black, 67-year-old lower bilateral amputee with a right hemiplegia on his dominant side. He was aphasic and diabetic also. He lived with his wife in a public housing project. Mr. M was referred to occupational therapy by a Public Health nurse who wanted to promote his dressing skills. Mr. M. was visited by the occupational therapist who found that his goal was not in the area of ADL, but rather to increase the functioning of his right upper extremity. The occupational therapist introduced exercises and a bilateral activity—a turkish knotted rug. Mr. M worked religiously at his exercises and his rug which gradually became a total investment for him. Even on days when he felt very ill, Mr. M reported that he was compelled to do a minimal amount of work on his rug. Treatment continued for six months. During this period he almost died twice, but he always managed to struggle through. Also during this time he and his wife shared mementos of their life together. The occupational therapist supported this interaction*

*Printed by permission of Ruth Levine, EdD, OTR.

142

between husband and wife and assumed the role of active listener. One week after the rug was completed, Mr. M died. On the last occupational therapy visit, Mrs. M proudly displayed Mr. M's rug. This was the last activity that they had shared. Although saddened by Mr. M's death, she seemed able to accept this fact peacefully.

Question: Even though a client may be dying, should all attempts be made to continue treatment?

Answer: *I personally believe they should. No therapist is skilled enough to determine the exact date of any person's death.*

Question: What advice would you offer a novice occupational therapist coming into the field of home health care services?

Answer: *Basically, the person needs skills in both psychosocial and physical dysfunction occupational therapy. Primarily, one needs to know how to relate to the joys and tragedies of daily life and still love people. A final point is that the therapist must lead a balanced life so that he or she can develop an individual philosophy toward all aspects of life, including illness and dying as well as health and living.*

Interview with Mrs. Agnes Ferrara, RN, MA,* Executive Director of a Visiting Nurse Association serving an urban/suburban community of 140,000.

Question: Would you please highlight the types of services that your agency offers to older adults?

Answer: *We are a multi-faceted, Medicare-certified home health agency serving people of all ages, races, religions, ethnic, and economic backgrounds. We are a public health agency promoting wellness. That means we strive to focus upon early detection and prevention of illness whenever possible, and that we also focus on current concepts relating to the general promotion of overall health and well-being. Our goal is to help the client achieve as much independence as he is able to develop and maintain. Supportive 24-hour, seven-day-a-week care is always available. Our answering service responds to phone calls around the clock; and they plug into our Professional Staff if anything arises which needs immediate attention. Through the agency the services of many varied disciplines are provided to our clients, usuall on an hourly basis. In our service area the older adult has a comprehensive health service program available to him. This includes Medicare coverage in the home, consultation to local hospitals and nursing homes to evaluate patients on admission in preparation for discharge; health care and supportive services to boarding and rooming houses; daily health counseling and screening services at senior adult activity centers; referral to anyone on a free basis at 12 mini-health centers; daily blood pressure checks to detect hypertension at 41 different community sites including the Agency's Headquarters; essential medical, dental, screening, counseling, and teaching services at two primary health care centers; and a full gamut of supportive and complimentary in-home health services in addition to the above are provided by our allied health services program.*

Printed by permission of Mrs. Agnes Ferrara, RN, MA.

Working with Older Adults 143

These additional in home services include long- and short-term care; private duty services by RNs, LPNs, Home Health Aids, Homemakers, Housekeepers, Housecleaners, Companions, and the recruitment and training of such personnel. Some examples of the type of care offered by this particular program are laundry, chore, and transportation service, also nursing, bathing, respite or relief for family members, and hospice service to the terminally ill and their families.

Question: Would you please cite an example of how your agency was able to help an older person?

Answer: *We are currently serving an older woman, Ms. Y, who is 65+ years old and separated from her husband, and who came to us with multiple problems. She had a cardiac condition, and most recently underwent abdominal surgery for a growth in her intestinal tract. This client is quite obese and had also fractured her arm. Ms. Y lives with a male companion, Mr. G, also 65+, in a first-floor apartment. He had a severe drinking problem, and had also suffered a heart attack. On Ms. Y's return from the hospital, we provided her with skilled nursing care and physical therapy. She was placed on a special diet, with low salt content, to prevent further colon complications and to help her with her obesity and heart condition. Housecleaning, shopping, cooking, and personal care services were also provided through our allied health services program. Mr. G, a veteran, was encouraged and supported by our agency to seek help with his drinking problem at a nearby veteran's hospital. Currently, he is undergoing treatment. Through VNA intervention, both these older adults are now living more functional, productive, and meaningful lives.*

Interview with: Patricia Reed, MA,* Counselor, and member of the counseling service of an urban community college of 12,000.

Question: What is your educational and work experience background?

Answer: *My degrees include a BS in Education and an MA in Counseling and Guidance. I have worked as a counselor in a large public school system and in the community college setting.*

Question: Could you please relate how professional counseling intervention is helpful to older adults? Would you specifically cite how you were able to help an older person?

Answer: *The counselor's role varies as to the individual needs of the client. For example, some people might need skills development; others might require structured intensive support and opportunities to build self-confidence; while still others might need advice in curriculum planning and career development. Specifically, I would like to tell you about a very interesting woman who just turned 70. She is twice widowed and has a wide variety of work experience, including electronics, bookkeeping, singing—she toured the country during the depression years—factory work, and professional sewing for women's specialty dress shops. She came to the counseling center seeking advice as to what course work she should take. She had enrolled in an advanced*

*Printed by permission of Patricia Reed, MA.

144

psychology course without realizing she should have taken the introductory course first. Although she had done quite well in the course, she felt she needed guidance in planning her future. For many years she had wanted to write books about her philosophy, which is concerned with the interrelationship between religion, technology, and science. However, she thought few people would take her seriously unless she could acquire a doctorate. So at age 68 she decided to go to college. Armed with little in the way of financial resources—a small pension, social security, a parttime job as a seamstress, and some student financial aid—she began her college career. She graduated from the community college with a 3.5 average and was elected to membership in Phi Theta Kappa, the honor society of junior and community colleges. Currently, she is enrolled as a junior in a four-year liberal arts college. Her goal as author and doctoral candidate is well on its way. My role in helping this highly motivated older woman was threefold; that of active listener and supporter; that of advisor to which courses to pursue; and that of facilitator of the transfer process to a baccalaureate degree institution.

Interview with: Shirley Keisler, MA,* currently working in a 200-bed alcohol and drug rehabilitation center.

Question: Would you please highlight your educational and professional experiences?

Answer: *I graduated from a large state related university with a BA in Fine Arts and pursued my graduate degree in Art Therapy from a medically related educational institution. During my internship I was assigned to a variety of settings, including a learning disabled children's day facility; a county psychiatric chronic care facility of 400 beds; and a partial psychiatric day hospital serving 100 patients.*

Question: How were you able to help an older person professionally?

Answer: *Miss K, a single woman of 65 years who had a history of psychotic episodes, had been in and out of mental hospitals for over 15 years. She had no friends or family and had become dependent upon institutions as a way of life. When I first had contact with Miss K, she appeared to be mute and had been so for many years; had poor motor skills; possessed few self care skills; and minimal socialization skills. I initially questioned the ability of my therapeutic intervention to make positive changes in Miss K's ability to function. However, this was based on her incapacitating mental illness. I did not consider her age as a handicap in treatment.*

She came to individual art therapy sessions of one hour each twice a week. I chose to have simple art materials available for Miss K to use—in this case, crayons and a 12 x 18 inch piece of drawing paper. At first, she was unable to reach independently into the box to take out a crayon. I had to place it in her hand. Miss K would begin to scribble on the paper, but would continue to draw off the paper and on to the table.

Printed by permission of Shirley Keisler, MA.

An evaluation of the first few sessions revealed that Miss K's drawings were at the lowest level of development. She was completely unable to draw or recognize what she saw. She could only produce unrecognizable scribbles which she spread beyond the paper's border. This demonstrated that Miss K had difficulty with reality testing, as she could not tell where the paper ended and the table began.

I began working with Miss K by giving her extremely large pieces of paper so she could learn to contain her picture, and I provided her with positive reinforcement for staying within the borders. By giving her an opportunity to understand where the end of the paper was and where the table began, she slowly began to participate in a form of reality testing.

Later, I put an object in front of her, and she was able to respond with short answers such as, "flower," or "vase." For the first time that anyone at the institution could remember, Miss K began to speak. We had established some form of trust relationship that had enabled her to respond in a socially acceptable way.

Miss K had also shown symptoms of anxiety. The drawings provided her with an opportunity to release some of her anxious feelings. During our sessions, Miss K began to use more words instead of gestures. She was able to tell me what she needed, liked, or wanted and showed less symptoms of hallucinations.

My treatment of Miss K was terminated when I left the facility. Because she had responded so well in the art therapy sessions, arrangements were made for her to continue treatment with another art therapist on staff.

By my last meeting with her, Miss K had progressed from using only one color in her drawings to using four or five. She had become conscious of the border and even reinforced it by making a frame for her pictures. Her subject matter was usually recognizable. For instance, she was able to draw flowers in the center of the picture with a distinct ground line. She was experiencing reality testing by being able to recognize and translate into concrete form what she was seeing. Miss K had become quite prolific and drew at least five or six pictures in a session. She could take her own papers and crayons and initiate the drawing process without being told what to do by the therapist. Miss K readily came to all sessions.

The art therapy program accomplished several goals. Miss K began to speak again, she was able to relate to people and things around her, her overwhelming anxiety began to diminish, and there was a lessening in the amount and severity of her hallucinations. In addition, the art therapy sessions had provided her with an opportunity for productive and meaningful activity.

Interview with Mary Stadler Palumbo, PhD,* Lecturer and Instructor in Food Science and Nutrition.

*Printed by permission of Mary Stadler Palumbo, PhD.

Question: Would you please highlight your educational and career experiences?

Answer: *My professional degrees include a BS and MS in Food and Nutrition and a PhD in Food Science. Some of the subjects that are required to complete this program involve coursework in chemistry, nutrition, microbiology, and engineering as applied to foods and food processing.*

My work experience in this field began in my graduate student days when I was teaching an experimental food lab to college juniors. In this course we experimented with food rather than just cooking. We would alter the amount of eggs or baking powder in a cake to understand the results—essentially it was the study of the effects of different formulations on a finished product. Later I became involved in research through the aid of a number of grants and a fellowship. During the time I was completing my master's degree, I investigated the interaction between starch and milk proteins. My doctoral studies included research into the experimental methods that can be utilized to determine the amount of fat in a lipo-protein. Later, after receiving my PhD we moved, and I taught a course at a large state university in food enzymes—both the enzymes that occur naturally in food and those that are added in processing methods. Currently I am teaching nutrition to both a class consisting of a variety of students such as those majoring in dietary science, recreation, administration of health facilities, and administrative justice, and a freshman nursing class in the continuing education division. Some of the topics we study include digestion, absorption, metabolism of food, and how a lack of certain nutrients affect a person's metabolism. We also examine the utilization of the assessment of nutritional status. This assessment is useful in determining if any subclinical deficiencies are present. The growth patterns of a person as related to nutrition may affect his health in a subtle way, as opposed to out-and-out nutritional diseases such as scurvy. Irregular growth patterns may give clues as to an individual's nutritional condition.

Question: Are students being taught about nutrition and the older person? What are the major concerns of nutrition and aging?

Answer: *The nutritional needs of elderly people are now included in most nutritional courses. Older people are at high risk for malnutrition. There are a number of reasons for this: 1) a good number of elderly people do not enjoy eating as much as they once did. As they get older, they find that certain foods give them gastric distress; 2) because of poor dental condition, some foods are more difficult to eat than others; 3) as one ages, less saliva is secreted, and consequently, more moist food is sought with the result that the diet becomes more limiting; 4) with the passage of time there is a decrease in the amount of digestive juices that are secreted. It becomes increasingly difficult to digest fat; 5) even if an older person had an adequate diet in earlier years, he can no longer eat it. Most older people find it difficult to substitute food, due to set eating habits; 6) there is also a social/psychological factor—loneliness. It is difficult for some people to motivate themselves to cook for one person. Therefore, a number of these people may depend on snack foods; 7) economics is another cause for malnutrition. There may not be enough money, and a good number of poor elderly do not have proper cooking facilities; 8) due to physiological changes in taste and smell there is less pleasure in eating. Food does not taste as good as it once did; 9) an elderly parent may use poor eating habits as a way of getting attention from an adult child; and 10) finally, there are a number of misconceptions and old wives' tales about nutrition that may interfere with a healthy diet.*

Question: What is an appropriate diet for someone 65 or over?

Answer: *A person over 65 needs the same kinds of foods as a younger person—just fewer calories. Because one's basal metabolism usually decreases with aging, fewer calories are needed.*

A proper diet consists of daily partaking of the basic four foods, which include:

1) *Two servings of meat, fish, poultry, or substitutes such as eggs, dry beans, peas, or peanut butter. These contain protein, B vitamins, iron, and a trace of zinc. Proteins are involved in the replacement of body tissues and serve as a source of energy.*

2) *Two servings from the milk group, such as milk or cheese. We need milk throughout our lives. Without long range calcium intake older women in particular, develop a greater risk of osteoporosis. If the blood levels of calcium are not maintained, the body will compensate, and consequently, they will be maintained at the expense of bone calcium.*

3) *Four helpings from the fruit and vegetable category. Dark green vegetables such as spinach and green beans, and dark yellow vegetables, such as carrots and winter squash, provide the body with a rich source of vitamin A. Citrus fruit such as oranges, grapefruit, tangerines, and tomatoes, melon, potatoes, strawberries, and pears supply the body with ample amounts of vitamin C.*

4) *Four helpings of wheat products or rice, provide an inexpensive source of energy. The fiber is helpful in elimination, too.*

Question: Would you please give some advice as how to help an older person improve his nutritional habits?

Answer: *In working with an older person who is on a fixed diet, start by trying to broaden it a little at a time. It is difficult to change eating habits of a lifetime. If a person has been immobile, there is usually a loss of protein and calcium. Therefore, these people should be provided with more calcium and protein to make up for that loss.*

There are some older people who eat well sporadically. They may eat very well when others are around, but when they are alone, they will resort to tea and crackers. This can create a problem known as an alternation between a negative and positive protein balance. These people should be encouraged to eat properly on a steady basis—good nutrition all through the week.

Interview with: Donna Fey-Greger, BS, BA,* Coordinator of a family planning service for a 1,300-bed state psychiatric facility.

Question: Would you please highlight some of your educational and work experiences?

Answer: *I have a BS in Psychology and a BA in Communications. Currently, I am pursuing graduate course work in psychology. During my undergraduate years I became involved in a number of projects involving human sexuality. I was responsible for helping to start a family planning unit at the university I attended. In my senior year I became a teaching assistant for a human sexuality course. While I was a sophomore I had attended an honor students' seminar. Our chosen project was the aged. As a result of this project, I had the opportunity to become involved in a sexuality survey of nursing homes.*

I had a lot of preconceived ideas of the answers that I might get from my clients. All of the interviewers were college-aged. We thought that the majority of the older people in the nursing home would refuse to talk to us. We thought it would be unlikely for a woman over 70 to know what an orgasm was. We felt that we were the sex discoverers! A good number of us held the assumption that these old people would have little concrete knowledge of sex and little pleasure in sex.

Question: Were you suprised?

Answer: *Yes, from the first interview! First of all, 80% of the people that we surveyed were glad to talk with us. Perhaps the most rewarding thing to happen was that we became teachers instead of interviewers. We had a prepared list of questions to ask each patient and that served as a springboard for patients to ask us questions—even if it was only to clarify a word we had used. I found that they were less likely to use medical terms, or what is considered to be polite terms, or even to know what the words were. Clitoris, uterus, and vagina were the least-known terms. In general, there was much ignorance about a woman's reproductive system. However, Biblical terms, such as womb, were known.*

When they asked questions, that gave us the opportunity to discuss the answers. Many times it was something they had wondered about for a long time. Usually, they were not aware of how to find the answers. Frankly, they exhibited a strong curiosity about sex which I had not expected. Apparently, during adolescence and even during adulthood, there had been little opportunity for access to this type of information concerning human sexuality.

Question: Did anyone feel ashamed of their body?

Answer: *Absolutely. For instance, I interviewed a woman who in 37 years of marriage had never seen her husband naked. They dressed and undressed in the bathroom and only made love in night clothes under the covers, with the lights out. She said she had always been curious but that "nice girls" didn't express these kinds of desires. In a sense, many of these interviews served as a liberating experience.*

*Printed by permission of Donna Fey-Greger, BS, BA.

For the patients, this time provided an opportunity to dispel some myths and misconceptions that many of them had carried their whole lives. For us, it provided an opportunity to learn that we did not discover sex, and that many people aged 60+ still have sexual thoughts, feelings, and desires. A large number of patients stated that they had stopped having sex earlier than they would have wanted because of societal pressures and a lack of information about mid-life changes in their bodies. For example, we know that by the time a man is 55, he will probably need some form of direct tactile stimulation to obtain an erection, and that a woman of the same age may not lubricate as easily as she did before menopause.

When these changes take place without people understanding why, they may begin to feel as though they shouldn't be having sex anymore. Some of the patients thought this was nature's way of telling them to stop being sexually active—so they stopped. Others stopped because our society says that if you are not young, attractive, and healthy, you have no right to be sexual. There is a general, sometimes unspoken, disapproval of sexual activity in older people. Consequently, society has coined the term, "dirty old man," which is used as a negative stereotype. In the same vein society assumes that an older woman who takes a younger man on by supporting him in return for sexual favors, could not attract him any other way. Then, too, one also finds that many adult children take the role of protector as far as their parents' sexuality is concerned.

Question: How did the staff in these nursing homes regard sex among the patients?

Answer: It is unfortunate that staff also see themselves as the protector. They often regard sex between the elderly as distasteful, or cute—but not serious. Therefore, we find in a good many nursing homes that couples are either separated or that privacy is unavailable. Nursing homes that do try to provide some kind of privacy frequently come up against the opposition of adult children who regard the availability of sexual expression as abusive or unwanted by their parent.

Question: Were there any other discoveries that were made in the course of this survey?

Answer: One of the saddest things we discovered was the lack of available male companionship for elderly women. With the ratio of men to women over 65 about one to three, there is little opportunity for women who desire a romantic or sexual involvement to have one.

Question: Would you please cite an example of how your intervention was helpful to an older adult?

Answer: At my present facility I was referred to a gentleman of 77 who was depressed, and frequently made sexual remarks to staff and other patients. The referral said that he was not sexually active but that staff was increasingly distressed by his sexual comments.

I met with him and discovered in our talks that he thought he had been committed to a psychiatric facility because he was crazy and that the root of that craziness was the fact that he had masturbated as a child. When he was 15, *he had been taught by his mother that he would end up being crazy (among other horrible things) if he masturbated. To him, his sexual comments to staff were merely filling a gap of continuing to act out his craziness in a sexual way. I explained to him that masturbation is normal and that most people, at some time in their life masturbated—and that, indeed, many people masturbated after adolescence.*

Afterwards, the staff noted a marked decrease in his need to make inappropriate sexual remarks, and in fact, he appeared to be more comfortable and less depressed in general—especially in the areas of socialization and sexuality. He no longer felt the guilt that he had carried with him for over 60 years. It was as though a burden was lifted from him, and he was free of the worry that he had created his illness by a pleasurable act in adolescence.

Interview with Doris T. Freudenberg, MD,* Board Certified Physiatrist, Chief of Service of Physical Medicine.

Question: Would you please highlight some of your career experiences and responsibilities?

Answer: *For 13 years I have served as Chief of Service of Physical Medicine and Rehabilitation of a 400-bed acute care suburban community hospital and an 88-bed physical rehabilitation hospital. My responsibilities include helping to determine the diagnosis and prescribing the appropriate treatment for patients who are referred to physical medicine. This involves the coordination and utilization of a number of disciplines and services to improve the patient's functional level.*

Question: Would you please cite an example in which your professional caregiving and administrative talents were utilized in helping the rehabilitation of an elderly person?

Answer: *Mrs. N, a 71+ widow who lived alone in her own apartment, was admitted to the acute care hospital with a stroke which left her paralyzed in her left arm and leg. She showed symptons of disarthria (slurred speech) due to weakness of the facial muscles. Previous to this incident she had been in good health and had not experienced any significant medical problems. After a complete medical examination, she was referred to Physical Medicine.*

At that time I administered a complete evaluation of her physical and neuromuscular status and prescribed an appropriate program. Her Physical Medicine program consisted of physical therapy, occupational therapy, speech therapy, nursing care, and the services of a social worker. In all therapies an effort is made to treat and strengthen the affected extremities as well as those unaffected. All treatment is carried out with the input and consent of the patient.

Physical therapy concentrated on strengthening the leg muscles and ambulation, starting on parallel bars. At this point an early evaluation regarding bracing need and assistive devices was made. It was decided to delay

*Printed by permission of Doris T. Freudenberg, MD.

this decision to allow time for recovery to occur and keep a current record of the patient's needs.

Occupational therapy determined that while she had weakness in her left arm and leg, she had no visual or sensory problem. The occupational therapist planned a program aimed at: 1) strengthening the left upper extremity; 2) training in ADL; and 3) improving standing and sitting balance.

Mrs. N was also trained both in her room and in the department how to turn in bed, change position, get on and off the bed, and eventually transfer in and out of the tub, and on and off the toilet.

Speech therapy focused upon strengthening the facial muscles and alleviating the disarthria. The program included specific exercises designed to strengthen the facial muscles and a concentration upon techniques to improve speech production.

Nursing's role included the intake of appropriate nutrition, bowel and bladder training and appropriate skin care to prevent the formation of decubiti, and all of the more traditional nursing functions.

Social service's function involved contacting the family—there were two children who did not live near Mrs. N—and helping them to decide how much they could help and what their wishes were. Social service also evaluated the patient's funds to determine the extent of resources avialable with or without Medicare, Medicaid, or private insurance. The social service worker was also responsible for initiating the transfer process to another facility.

Mrs. N progressed nicely. Ten days later it was determined by all involved that she needed the services of a rehabilitation hospital, and transfer was accomplished thereafter.

Question: Would you please explain the rehabilitation process that then took place?

Answer: *When she arrived at the rehabilitation hospital, another intensive physical medicine and rehabilitation evaluation was administered by all the rehabilitation team members. It was decided that Mrs. N should continue a similar program, but that the emphasis be more on doing things for herself, and gaining independence.*

Eventually, a short-leg plastic brace and cane were prescribed. With regard to her home setting, Mrs. N informed us that there was no tub stool or toilet rails in her apartment. Because she would need these devices in order to function independently, they were purchased and installed. The patient's functioning ability was evaluated in a simulated setting in terms of independence in self-care (using the toilet, taking a bath, using the kitchen, making her bed), and mobility.

Mrs. N continued to make good progress. She was reviewed weekly by the entire team. Mrs. N, the team, and her family felt the time had come for a six-hour visit to her home setting. One of Mrs. N's daughters agreed to accompany her mother. During that time Mrs. N was able to carry out a number of household tasks. The visit was quite successful, and both Mrs. N and her daughter were pleased.

Before discharge, a comprehensive evaluation in home independence (eg, ability to plan menus, make meals, use a washer/dryer, make the bed, use the telephone) was administered. Mrs. N was able to successfully complete all the tasks.

Twenty-six days after her arrival at the rehabilitation center, Mrs. N was discharged to her home with homebound services. The home care program consisted of: 1) providing continued physical and occupational therapy; 2) checking regularly on her medical needs through the services of the visiting nurse; 3) providing weekly services by homemakers; and 4) providing one hot meal a day through Meals-on-Wheels.

One week after Mrs. N was discharged, the social service worker contacted her to see how things were progressing. Four weeks later, Mrs. N came to the rehabilitation hospital for an outpatient follow-up visit. She was seen by the physiatrist and evaluated regarding her progress and the need for continuing supportive home services. Mrs. N's children had also been consulted. It was determined that she no longer needed physical or occupational therapy or visiting nurse services as she was functioning well at home and could perform her own exercises.

Several other outpatient visits were made and eventually the patient was discharged from our care. Through a well-planned coordinated effort started in the acute hospital and continued in a rehabilitation hospital and then the community, Mrs. N was able to return to her own home and meet our true rehabilitation goal, the achievement of her highest possible potential.

Interview with Harriet Treatman, MSW,* member of the Academy of Certified Social Workers (ACSW).

Question: Would you please discuss some of your professional and civic work experiences?

Answer: *My professional background has included social work with a family service agency where we saw individuals, couples, and families. The population, in general, consisted of white middle-class people. Fees were paid by means of a sliding scale. I also worked in the patient services division in the psychiatric clinic of a large teaching hospital where individuals, families, and couples were seen. The hospital was located in the heart of a large metropolitan area. Fees were met by means of a sliding scale also. The population consisted of clients from varied ethnic and racial backgrounds. I later worked for a community mental health center with inpatient and outpatient services. This center, like many others, was funded as a result of the 1967 Mental Health Act. The caseload consisted of individuals, families, and couples. The center, located in a large city, was situated in a specific neighborhood setting. The population was mixed racially and ethnically. Fees were paid by means of a sliding scale and third party payers.*

Question: How do you view the social worker's role in helping the older adult?

Answer: *The social worker's role can range from helping an individual connect with appropriate community resources to doing intensive family therapy as a*

Printed by permission of Harriet Treatman, MSW.

life enabling strategy. Social workers are involved in helping people choose to use themselves, or available services, in a more aware and constructive manner.

Question: Would you give me an example of how you helped an older person professionally?

Answer: *Mr. M, an 87-year-old hard-drinking man, was hospitalized because of an acute psychotic episode. He had been living at a home which he and his wife maintained. His 74-year-old wife, a severe diabetic, was currently being hospitalized to control her diabetes.*

The couple was irascible, and both were more interested in arguing with each other then in paying attention to recommended vital health procedures. An important consideration to both of them, while they were hospitalized, was the continued care and maintenance of their three large German Shepherds. A large part of their financial resources had been devoted to these dogs.

It was apparent to medical personnel that Mr. M's continued drinking would precipitate another episode and that his nutritional needs would have to be more satisfactorily met to avoid further hospitalizations.

When it became time for Mr. M to be discharged from the hospital, it was obvious that intervention was necessary. The Ms clung to the idea of maintaining their own home. But they had been physically and psychologically unsuccessful in taking care of themselves. Although they had many children—four who were middle-aged, and two about 20 years younger—few of them had the psychic resources to live with and care for their parents.

Prior to Mr. M's discharge from the hospital, I contacted all of his children and arranged a meeting in the hospital with them, Mr. M, the physician, and myself. At this time, due to her diabetic distress, Mrs. M was not at the meeting. My purpose in structuring it this way was to help Mr. M acknowledge responsibility for himself and to help his children in realizing that they were responsible for him as well. I also utilized the authority of the physician to underline the necessity for Mr. M to control his drinking.

Preliminary results of this meeting developed the reluctant consensus that all parties would need to continue to plan together, and that Mr. M's release from the hospital would be contingent on their doing so. In reality, the Medical Assistance was running out and Mr. M's psychiatric condition had improved to the point where he was ready for discharge.

Subsequent sessions enabled some old family issues to be resolved. For example, the oldest son's long-festering hurt as the father's apparent need for a second family brought him to finally face his pain and ask, "Why did you need them? Weren't we enough?" This son, who had previously been supplying his father with liquor, was able to discontinue these destructive actions and support the father's staying with the youngest son and wife, while Mrs. M was hospitalized.

In terms of the totality of the plan, all family members were drawn into the scheme (for instance, the youngest daughter helped with hygiene procedures for Mrs. M on a scheduled basis). It was important to find a balance between what the elderly couple needed and what each child could supply without damage to his or her own life.

Through a constructive experience each person took away a better sense of self.

Interview with Virginia T. Sherr, MD,* Board Certified Psychiatrist, Fellow of the American Psychiatric Association, currently in private practice.

Question: Would you please highlight some of your career experiences in the area of service to the elderly?

Answer: *For ten years I was director of a 300-bed inpatient geriatric unit of a large state psychiatric facility. During that time my major involvement was the development and directorship of a geriatric community evaluation and treatment service team.*

Question: Would you tell me more about this program? What led you to initiate it?

Answer: *We were receiving referrals for psychiatric hospitalization for patients who had never had a thorough evaluation. Most were not candidates for long-term psychiatric evaluation. Often, these people were misunderstood, as they had many communication deficits—hearing, speech, vision. Nursing homes and community agencies seldom performed in-depth health and social evaluations. Consequently, there was little appreciation of the real problems. The slogan seemed to be: There is nothing left but to get rid of the patient. We wanted to define and get rid of the problem. I also was concerned that once a person was uprooted, the vaccuum which was created in the community would soon be filled by another person. The individual in question became dissociated with his environment.*

The attitude at home was that this person was gone forever. Often the family felt that a final solution had arrived. The ranks were closed. The option of returning home was psychologically discounted. If the source of community referral to us had been a nursing home, a bed might not be available once the patient had been removed from the treatment setting.

Question: Once the Geriatric Community Evaluation and Treatment Service had begun to provide services, did you find that families and community agencies were willing to receive information concerning helping their relatives or clients remain in the community?

Answer: *Yes. Prior to admission, any help offered was readily received. People did not know what to do and were very accepting in most cases. People were glad to know what the problem was, and how we, they, and the patient could deal with it.*

Question: Would you tell me about the operational aspects of the service?

Answer: *Our program offered personalized and preventive psychiatric, social, and medical attention to distressed older adults.[1] The mobile team, consisting of three geropsychiatrists, one liason visiting nurse, three social workers, one*

*Printed by permission of Virginia T. Sherr, MD.

occupational therapy consultant, one therapeutic recreational consultant, and two secretaries, handled referrals of disturbed older adults to the state psychiatric facility.

The approach was one of immediate and flexible interaction which permitted problem solving at the older person's place of residence. The three basic tenets of the service included: the diagnosis and treatment of the presenting problem; prevention and/or resolution of the impending residential staff or family crisis which had led to the original referral; and introduction of social and psychiatric safeguards to ensure the client's long-term success in the community.

Question: Would you give some indication of how many older adults you were able to evaluate and how many of these people required long-term institutional care?

Answer: *In 8½ years of service the team evaluated at least 1,438 troubled elderly people and consulted with 77 nursing or retirement homes. During that time, only 222 clients required admission into the hospital.*

Question: Would you please cite an example of how your professional intervention was helpful to an older person?

Answer: *Mr. J, a gentleman in his late 70s, had suffered cardiac arrest while dancing. The rescue squad had administered CPR, and he was sent unconscious but alive to the local emergency room. Upon physical recovery and return to consciousness, Mr. J had the appearance of severe brain damage. He was totally disoriented, possessed emotional and mental instability, had marked loss of recent and remote recall, suffered severe loss of judgment and intellect, and he was mostly incoherent. Several months after his cardiac arrest I was called to see him by a nursing home where he had been transferred. He was at that time, extremely belligerent uncooperative, and combative—shaking his fist at staff, fighting restraints, and threatening to strike others.*

I treated the situation in terms of a crisis. There were two perspectives: one was that the man was totally out of touch with reality and that he had a very poor prognosis. It appeared he might spend the rest of his life heavily tranquilized in a nursing home. The second perspective was quite the opposite. Experience had taught me that there is no way to predict for certain if a situation could just be assisted, could be cured, or some combination in between. This perspective, of not being able to be sure of the outcome, allowed me to approach him with an open mind.

Innovation and hopefulness were two key concepts. Formerly, the staff had reason to be afraid of this patient. If the staff could pick up the hopefulness, there might be an opportunity for a continuity of the hopeful approach from all sectors.

Mr. J's treatment consisted of chemotherapy to calm his belligerent mood, and reeducation to improve his orientation status. In terms of chemotherapy it was necessary to titrate slowly up to a maximum of 20 ml of Haldol a day. Ordinarily, one can hope for a good resolution with a much smaller dose, such as only .05 ml 2—3 times a day. However, this gentleman was a large man and so combative that he required a much larger dose for a very brief period of time.

Reeducation consisted of gently teaching Mr. J that he was not a prisoner of war in a military hospital. His delusions were based on a lack of information. Since his cardiac arrest, Mr. J had not understood accurately what had happened to him, so he was extremely mistrustful. He needed to be reeducated to a whole new way of life. I talked with him, without directly confronting his false beliefs, about what had happened to him and where he was. Mr. J needed to hear this many times, over several months, before he could put the missing pieces together for himself. He had been an energetic man and had been unable to understand the role of instant invalid, interpreting it in the light of his past military experiences.

Once Mr. J truly understood what had happened he became easier to manage. When he finally began to realize that he was in a neutral medical facility, he demanded that he play an active and helpful role there. He was given a daily schedule of purposeful tasks, such as assisting other patients to the dining room.

In summary, treatment for this man was a fusion between hope and psychiatric skill. Without hope on the part of the staff, he might have remained in the nursing home for the rest of his life.

Mr. J's self-image had been badly shaken. He had always been a competent and independent person. This was the basis for his self-esteem. When his usual in-charge image was no longer operational, he could not comprehend what had happened.

Eventually, Mr. J's dosage of Haldol was brought down to 0.25 ml a day. He has now returned to his home where he lives with his wife.

Endnote

There is much that service providers are doing, and with the dawning of advanced scientific inquiry and technology there will be more that can be done. In all our undertakings we need to couple two interests: love, compassion, enthusiasm, and respect for the human spirit, with an investment in learning the most current geriatric developmental theories. Without question, each provider is responsible for keeping abreast of the latest developments within his own field of specialization. Together, providers, consumers, and the society at large can help to make life in the later years meaningful and relevant.

Reference

1. Sherr VT, Eskridge OC, Lewis S: A mobile, mental hospital based team for geropsychiatric services in the community. J Am Geriatr Soc 24: 363-365, 1976.

Appendix A

Communication and Elders

Communication is described as an interchange or sharing of thoughts, feelings, or information. Synonymous with communication are words such as divulge, announce, disclose, and reveal.[1]

Most important in the process of communication is being able to think. "In its loosest sense thinking signifies everything that is in our heads or that goes through our minds...." However, "reflective thought involves not simply a sequence of ideas, but a consequence—a consecutive ordering in such a way that each determines the next as its proper outcome...Technically speaking, it is a term of thought. Each term leaves a deposit which is utilized in the next term. The stream or flow becomes a train, chain, or thread."[2] So, we see that in order to communicate we must think first. We need to order our thoughts and present them in a logical way so that others will understand what we are trying to say.

The focus of this section will be upon social communication involving speaking (including voice inflection), gesturing, listening, touch, body positioning, and silence. It should be remembered that literature, music, and art are also avenues of transferring meaning and giving expression to the human condition.

Culturally Determined Factors Affecting Communication

Social mores and the indigenous culture play a vital role in understanding why people might choose a certain style or manner of communicating. In our culture, time is quantified by dividing it into years, seasons, months, weeks, days, hours, minutes, seconds. However, not every culture values time in such a precise manner. Individuals, too, possess different time scales. In working with the older person one needs to understand that these differences exist in each individual.

Personal distancing with others is definitely influenced by culture and custom. For example, the culturally proper and comfortable space for distance between Americans and British is quite different than that of Latins.[3] When one is caring for an elderly individual, it is important to know what that person's preference is in terms of comfortable distancing.

Each one of us has a space or an area that we feel is our own. This is known as territoriality. A favorite chair or a special area in a certain restaurant demonstrates this concept. So too, the older adult may often enjoy congregating with others in a special area of a park. An elderly resident of a nursing home may claim a specific area in the lobby as his territory. Spacial rights are even further enforced in our culture by the conception of individual ownership of land and property. Our entire legal system is designed to protect these rights. The concept of life-space for each individual even extends beyond death when the deceased person is accorded a coffin, a cemetery plot or a mausoleum.[4]

The house in which a person has lived for years has special significance. In order to ease the transition period when an older individual is planning to move from his territory, it is important for him to bring a number of familiar items that have been acquired through the years—in essence, bringing his territory with him.

Culture is a powerful and complex part of the communication process. Therefore, in order to assure that one understands another individual, he must make certain that he is knowledgeable of the other person's culture and cultural habits. It is within this context that rapport can be achieved.

Transactions

The communication process relies upon sharing. The type of sharing involved includes linguistics, body mechanics, and the bioelectric integration of the central nervous system. In terms of understanding the bioelectric intricacies of communication, Fabun utilizes a transaction chain that includes the following scheme:

(1) Sensations are *taken in* → (2) *transformed* into electrical codes → (3) information is *retained* (memory patterns stored in the nervous system as electro-chemical codes) → (4) codes are changed into muscular *reactions* → (5) reactions are *received* by others.[3]

There are many patterns of communication. The simplest pattern involves a sender, a message, and a receiver. Other patterns may include a sender, a message, a receiver, and the receiver's response. Obviously, including more persons or extending the conversation will lead to a more complicated transaction process. Because communication has so many parts and sub-parts, care providers should be aware of just how complicated this process is. For the older person who is depressed or who suffers from a confusional disorder, a number of the parts of this process may be altered. Patience and understanding of the situation are essential elements in providing appropriate and meaningful care.

If one wishes to establish a communicative relationship with an older client, it is important to be aware of and make use of the following recommendations:

1) Do not assume that the client knows what you are talking about.

2) Do not assume that you know what the client is talking about without asking questions to validate your assumptions.

3) Individual experiences are never identical. What happens inside one person did not necessarily happen in the same way inside someone else.

4) We establish communication best by discovering what is common in the succession of our experiences.[3]

Rules of Address

All communities employ a particular set of rules when one person addresses another. This is especially true when the person is a stranger. The speaker may use a form of address to indicate rank, age (eg, Mister, Sonny) or professional identity (eg, Father, Doctor). Sometimes there may be an insulting tone—such as addressing someone on the basis of a visible deformity (eg, gimpy), or derogatory slurs about their race, religion, or national origin.[5] For a person in his seventies it may be insulting, indeed, to be referred to as "Pops", or by his first name only. It is always wise to consult the older person to find out what he or she prefers.

Elements of Conversation

In any type of conversation, not only are the techniques of communication important, but the quality and depth of the transaction are an essential part of a meaningful dialogue.

A person who discloses his deepest feelings is always vulnerable. The discloser is usually faced with the immediate and explicit consequences of his disclosure. A great deal of trust must be engendered in a communication of this type.

Once the information has been disclosed, the receiver's role becomes all-important. The quality of the receiver's response has a direct bearing upon the quality of the interaction and ongoing relationship. For instance, one can imagine how upsetting an older individual might feel if the care giver he was talking to became distracted with the needs of another client and suddenly got up and walked away in the middle of a conversation, without giving any clue or understanding as to why he left. Would that older individual be likely to trust that particular care giver again? Too often service providers, burdened with a multitude of responsibilities, become so involved with tending to immediate needs, that they may easily forget to fully inform their clients as to what exactly is taking place. This is a particularly disturbing problem if the older person was in the process of disclosing his innermost thoughts and feelings.

In order to understand the significance of the self-disclosure process, one first must understand what self-disclosure is. In reviewing the characteristics of self-disclosure, one should keep in mind that building a trust relationship usually rests on the tenets of a person being able to discuss his feelings without fear or reprimand. Once a person has revealed very personal information about himself to another, he becomes exceedingly vulnerable. No service provider should ever take a self-disclosure encounter lightly—for it is the building block upon which a meaningful relatioñship can be secured.

Characteristics of Intrapersonal Disclosure

1) *Intensity*—This is subjective importance that is attributed to the self-disclosure. It includes the level of intimacy and answers the questions, "How many others know?" and "What is the relationship of the discloser to those others who know?" The degree of emotional charging and the risk entailed in making the disclosure known are also important factors;

2) *Modality*—This involves the method by which the revelation is made—verbal, behavioral, or gesticulative;

3) *Type*—Different kinds of self-information (eg, thoughts, sensations, feelings, perceptions, judgment, institutions, fantasies, actions, desires) are included within this category;

4) *Availability*—This refers to differences in self-information that a person might readily have available for disclosure;

5) *Content*—Content categories could be in the area of personal values, political ideologies, religious beliefs, finances, and sexual practices. It is the topic or subject matter that is being discussed.

Characteristics of Interpersonal Disclosure

1) *The appropriateness of the disclosure*—Disclosure which changes the topic mood without a reason that is understandable to the intended receivers is not likely to be considered appropriate;

2) *Motivation*—The reasons or needs which prompt a person to disclose personal information contribute to the overall meaning that the disclosure has for others;

3) *Timing*—This factor is linked closely to appropriateness and motivation and is the *when* in which something is stated;

4) *Tense*—This dimension lets the receiver know when a given piece of information took place. Past, present and future tenses are related to this factor;

5) *Intention*—Intentional self-disclosure implies the discloser's willingness to be known either by revealed self-data or by the specific receivers to whom he has revealed it; and

6) *Curvilinear relation*—This factor relates the amount or degree of self-disclosure with the quality of interpersonal relationships formed. Obviously, the disclosure of personal information is essential to a qualitatively rich and meaningful interpersonal relationship.[6]

Techniques of Communication

Knowing *how to* and *in which manner* one should communicate is essential if rapport is to be established with clients. When appropriate, elderly people can also improve their socialization skills through instruction in these techniques. This includes developing mastery of active listening and responding with understanding.

Active Listening

Physical Attending: The use of the body to communicate.

1) *Face the person squarely*—Let him know that you want to be involved in his conversation;

2) *Adopt a posture of openness*—Crossed arms can be a sign of lessened involvement with others;

3) *Lean toward the other person*—This is another way of indicating availability and involvement;

4) *Maintain good eye contact*—When talking to another person, spend much of the time looking directly at him and;

5) *Try to feel comfortable*—Remain relatively relaxed but interested while listening to another person.

Psychological Attending: This includes the utilization of active listening, which means the person attending needs to listen to all of the messages that the sender is giving. Total listening involves awareness of the other person's nonverbal behavior, voice, words, and silence.

1) *Nonverbal behavior*—Facial expressions, body movement, and silence convey messages of communication. Nonverbal behavior can be considered similar to punctuation in written language and may be used in much the same manner as question marks, exclamation points, periods, and italics. Nonverbal behavior can confirm what the sender is saying. It can deny or confuse what is being said (eg, if a person is angry with someone and smiles while she is telling him this, then the message is totally confused). It may also strengthen, emphasize, or add emotional color to what is being said.

2) *The quality of the speaker's voice*—The way in which a person uses his voice can punctuate or modify verbal behavior. Voice quality, the way in which words are said, like nonverbal behavior, can confirm, deny, confuse, strengthen, or emphasize what is being said. It can also add emotional color to one's statements (eg, if someone says he likes a particular piece of music, with a tone of voice emitting enthusiasm, then not only does he confirm with his voice what he is saying, but he also adds an emotional dimension as well).

3) *Silence*—This is a powerful tool; without saying a word, a person can convey a number of feelings (eg, anger, annoyance, disinterest, distrust); and

4) *Verbalization*—The language that one uses—the actual choice of words—can convey very clearly how he feels.

Responding With Understanding

This includes total listening (ie, words, nonverbal messages, voice-related cues), trying to identify the feelings a person is expressing and the behaviors and experiences that give rise to these feelings, trying to communicate to the person and understanding what he seems to be feeling and the sources of these feelings, and responding by not evaluating what the person has to say, but by showing one's understanding of the other person's point of view. Good responding depends upon good listening.

One pitfall to avoid is that of hollow listening. In this situation, little attention is paid to what another person has said, and the listener's response reflects this. Specific techniques that enhance good response skills include:

1) *Use plain language*—Communication and understanding will be enhanced if the speaker's language is in tune with the other person's language;

2) *Make your manner and tone of speaking communicate;*

3) *Give yourself time to reflect*—By allowing time to think, it is easier to digest and get to the core of what the other person has said;

4) *Respond frequently*—By responding relatively frequently, the conversation can be maintained as mutual and spontaneous;

5) *Respond to the other person's feeling and/or content.*[7]

Problem Solving

Being able to communicate and help others often requires skill development in problem solving and decision making. Many geriatric care providers are faced with crisis situations. During these periods of time it is especially important to have some knowledge of problem-solving procedures. Timmins offers a six-point plan that can serve as a guide to this process. It includes:

1) *Defining the problem;*

2) *Analyzing one's self* in relationship to the problem;

3) *Collecting all the facts* that relate to the problem;

4) *Developing a wide range of alternative solutions,* including no action;

5) *Examining each alternative solution* in the light of a number of different factors (eg, risks, effort, timing, resources, values, feelings); and

6) *Selecting a composite course of action* that incorporates the most viable part of each alternative and that eliminates the least successful part of each alternative.[4]

The basics of communication and problem solving have been explored. The more that the service provider is able to learn in these areas, the more he will be able to help his client. Active listening and responding with understanding are essential to the welfare of the older person. Imagine the frustration that an elderly individual must feel when he realizes that the service provider he was talking to was actually involved in another task the entire time. Communication opportunities await the care giver at every turn. Whether one is involved in helping to bathe an older adult or assisting him in feeding tasks, the service provider can utilize that moment to communicate and establish deeper bonds of rapport.

References

1. Stein J (ed): The Random House Dictionary of the English Language: The Unabridged Edition. New York, Random House, 1973, p 298.
2. Dewey J: Industrial Operation: How we think. In Cathcart RS, Samovar LA: Small group communication: A Reader, Dubque, IA, WMC Brown, 1970, pp 117, 118.
3. Fabun D: Communications: The Transfer of Meaning. Beverly Hills, CA Glencoe Press, 1965, pp 21, 22, 23-25, 32-35.
4. Timmins LE: Understanding through communications: Structured experiments in self exploration. Springfield IL, Charles C Thomas, 1972, pp 111, 196.
5. Farb P: Word Play: What Happens When People Talk. New York, Alfred A Knopf, 1974, p 5, 17.
6. Culbert SA: The interpersonal process of self-disclosure: It takes two to see one. In Hart JT, Tomlinson TM: New Directions in a Client-Centered Therapy. Boston, Houghton Mifflin Co, 1968, pp 1-31.
7. Egan E: You and Me: The Skills of Communicating and Relating to Others. Monterey CA, Brooks/Cole Pub Co, 1977, 114-122, 135, 139, 168.

Appendix B

Continuum of Care Approaches

What does continuum of care mean? If we think of care options in terms of a continuum that has at one end total independence and at the other end complete skilled institutional care, a wide variety of care levels and arrangements may be included within these two extremes.

The following types of options are representative of some of the care programs that are currently available.

Nursing Homes

Since 1964 there has been a 67% increase in the number of people residing in nursing homes. Between the years of 1960 and 1970 the number of nursing facilities increased by 140%. The government responded to this need for long-term care by passing Medicare-Medicaid Titles 18 and 19 of the Social Security Act. Legislation (eg, Hospital Medical Facilities Construction, Hill-Burton Act, and Nursing Home Mortgage Insurance) was developed to aid and encourage the nursing home industry.[1]

Perhaps one of the most emotional and controversial issues of our time, in terms of service for the frail, at-risk elderly, is the quality of care found in nursing homes. Numerous articles and books have exposed some of the scandalous conditions that a number of older residents have experienced while living in a nursing home. *Unloving Care: The Nursing Home Tragedy* by Bruce C. Vladeck is a prime example of a thoughtful and penetrating book that analyzes this subject.[2]

The following types of options are representative of some of the care programs that are currently available.

Continuum of Care Approaches

	•TOTAL INDEPENDENCE
Community/home care programs within the household	socialization centers; clubs housekeepers companions homemakers friendly visitors telephone check-up programs nutrition programs Meals-on-Wheels visiting nurses mental health center programs adult day-care programs hospice home care
Shared or group related households	shared age-integrated living—families-of-choice intermediate housing boarding/domiciliary/foster care sheltered housing halfway houses
Institutional care	general acute care hospital rehabilitation hospital/center home for the aged with infirmary county hospital state mental hospital hospice care in a center nursing care (personal care home, extended care facility, intermediate care facility, skilled nursing care facility) **•COMPLETE SKILLED INSTITUTIONAL CARE**

Because of the interest and need for care excellence in nursing homes, workshops, conferences, and health fairs should allot time to explore this subject. Topics could include: a discussion of the different types of nursing homes and the kind of care given; resident rights, including advocacy; what to look for in selecting a home, and characteristics of quality care in nursing homes.

Categories of nuring homes include:

— *Proprietary Facility*—refers to private profit-making nursing homes.
— *Non-Proprietary Facility*—these are often administered by religious, fraternal, or ethnic organizations, and are non-profit institutions.
— *Personal Care Home*—licensed to accept four or fewer persons who need custodial/intermediate nursing care. Medicaid will pay for care that has fulfilled licensure requirements.
— *Intermediate Care Facility (ICF)*—designed to provide personal care, simple medical procedures such as special diets, or uncomplicated dressing changes, and intermittent nursing care. They are funded through Medicaid.
— *Extended Care Facility*—receives Medicare/Medicaid funds. These homes are often doubly certified as Intermediate Care Facilities and Skilled Nursing Care Facilities. Extended Care Facilities are an extension of hospital care, with a probability of discharge.
— *Skilled Nursing Care Facility (SNF)*—provides **long-term,** unlimited nursing care with no requirement of previous hospitalization. This type of facility is funded by a federal/state cost sharing program. There are fundamental standards which must be met under Medicare regulations (20 Code of Federal Regulations S405 et seq). These include: 1) there must be related medical services. This includes one or more physicians or registered nurses. Twenty-four hour nursing service with one fulltime RN must be provided; 2) clinical records of each patient must be maintained; 3) there must be an appropriate plan for dispensing and administering drugs and medicines; 4) a proper utilization review plan must be maintained; 5) all state licensing requirements must be met; 6) there must be a fulltime qualified administrator; 7) physicians must be available for emergency care; 8) the dietary service must be supervised by a qualified dietitian; 9) when appropriate, a full range of therapeutic programs are to be provided. These programs must be administered and maintained by qualified personnel; 10) a restorative nursing care program designed to maintain and improve a patient's ability to carry out activities of daily living (ADL) is to be provided; and 11) no resident is to be excluded from any of the facility's benefits on the grounds of race or national origin.

Skilled nursing care facilities are also required to administer and maintain a *Patient's Bill of Rights,* conferred by 20 Code Federal Regulations S405.1121 (K). This bill grants the following rights to each and every resident of a nursing home. The client:

must be informed prior to or at time of admission of the rights, rules, and regulations governing client conduct and responsibilities (through written acknowledgment by the client);

must be fully informed, at time of admission and during his stay, of all the services that are available in the facility as well as related charges;

is to be fully informed by a physician of his medical condition unless this is medically contraindicated. This must be documented by the physician in the medical record. The client has the right to refuse to participate in experimental research;

must be afforded the opportunity to be a participant in his treatment plan;

must be given reasonable advance notice of any intended transfer or discharge;

is to be encouraged and assisted in his rights as a citizen;

may manage his own financial affairs and must be permitted to receive at least a quarterly accounting of his financial transactions;

must be free from mental and physical abuse (eg, chemical or physical restraints, except when necessary to protect the client from self-injury or injury to others). This must be authorized in writing by a physician for a specific and limited amount of time;

must be assured confidentiality of his personal medical records;

must be afforded respect (eg, privacy in treatment, and care for his personal needs);

is not required to perform any service for the facility that is not included in his therapeutic care plan;

may communicate and associate privately with persons of his own choosing, and may send and receive unopened personal mail, unless medically contraindicated. This must be documented by the physician in the medical record;

may meet with and participate in the activities of social, religious, or community groups of his own choice unless medically contraindicated as documented by the physician in the medical record;

may retain and use his personal clothing and possessions as space permits; and

if married, is assured privacy for visits by the spouse. If both are inpatients and wish to share a room, they are to be permitted to do so (unless medically contraindicated. This must be documented by the attending physician in the medical record).[1]

In terms of advocacy, Horn and Griesal have prepared an excellent resource book, *Nursing Homes: A Citizen's Action Guide: How to Organize, Plan, and Achieve Nursing Home Reform in Your Community,* that can be used by groups of citizens who are interested in nursing home reform.[3]

What does one look for in determining the adequacy of a nursing home? The following represent some questions that can be used to analyze and consider when visiting a prospective nursing home:

1. Do the residents look well cared for—satisfied, happy, distraught, apathetic?

2. Are the residents treated with respect and dignity?
3. Is the atmosphere custodial or rehabilitative and supportive?
4. Is the facility well-run—organized, clean, and free from urine odor?
5. Are there activities going on, and if so, are they dignified and meaningful? Do the residents participate in these activities?
6. Is there a volunteer program?
7. What are the meals like—is there variety and quality? Is the food hot?
8. Is the facility cold and sterile or warm and pleasant?
9. Do the staff interact meaningfully with the residents?
10. Would *you* like to spend the rest of your life in this facility?[3]
11. Is there transportation available for visitors to reach the resident?
12. What is the licensure status of the facility?
13. What are the safety factors—fire escapes, fire drills, handrails, stairwells protected and marked?
14. What types of rooms are available—single, double, bath facilities?
15. What are the hidden costs—hand feeding, special diets, other therapeutic services such as physical or occupational therapy?
16. What kind of noise level exists—high, soft, pleasant?
17. What are the provisions for religious services?[1]

What are the characteristics that constitute quality care in nursing homes? During 22 hearings conducted from 1969 until 1973 the United States Sub-Committee on Long Term Care put on a search for positive programs that distinguished the finest homes in the nation. Its *Supporting Paper Number 6— What Can Be Done In Nursing Homes: Positive Aspects in Long-Term Care* (Washington DC, US Government Printing Office, Stock Number 052-070-03084, September, 1975) describes these findings.

There are two major factors that were at the foundation of all programs: one was an attitude of positive hope—a belief that the older adult's physical and mental problems could, in most instances, be prevented, and that even when these problems were present they could be reversed through therapeutic programs. The other was a basic belief in human dignity and self-worth.

The committee identified four major categories of innovation and excellence in nursing home care. These are:

1) A positive approach to rehabilitation and therapy through techniques such as sensory training, reality orientation, and remotivation, enhances care.

2) Environmental improvements to nursing homes promote better patient care and greater comfort to the residents (eg, colors, arrangement of the furniture).

3) Innovative and positive approaches in the education and utilization of employees leads to improved care of the geriatric resident (eg, employee sensitivity training in which an employee assumes a client's role, as in patient-for-a-day programs).

4) Comprehensive and integrated patient care activities and services that replace television viewing and weekly bingo games—activities with a special focus upon self-government, such as resident councils, provide meaningful approaches to improving the quality of life within the long-term care setting.

Community Care Options

Ninety-five percent of this country's elders live in their community.[4] Of this group, it is estimated that one out of every seven requires some type of supportive service in order to maintain independent living.[5] As our population grows older, it can be assumed that there will be an ever-increasing need to provide programs that enable older adults to live in their neighborhoods as long as possible.

What are the alternatives for the frail elderly besides nursing homes? There are a number of care programs or alternative living arrangements that offer support within the community setting, such as adult day care, adult hospital centers, community mental health center programs, programs to prevent institutionalization, visiting nurse associations, and home health care agencies. Another concept, shared age-integrated living, or families-of-choice, provides the well elderly or slightly impaired older adult with a new option for community living. The British warden plan for sheltered housing and the State of Illinois' comprehensive program of home care services will be considered. Other varieties of community living accommodations have been discussed in Chapter 7.

Because of the human consequence of institutionalization, there has been a growing interest in finding ways of caring for the infirm elderly in their own communities. Adult day-care, a concept borrowed from Scandinavia and England, is being developed to increase the options that are available to older people who no longer live independently. Adult day-care centers and day hospitals are attached to hospitals or nursing homes. The programs are targeted at preventing institutional placement, or shortening a hospital or nursing home stay. Goals for these programs are aimed at: 1) preventing mental and physical decline; and 2) teaching self-care skills to promote continued independent functioning. These centers provide one-stop medical and nursing care, social services, rehabilitation, activities, hot meals, and round-trip transportation. Depending on individual needs, participants can attend anywhere from three to six hours per day, one to five days a week.

One of the problems with adult day-care is funding. Medicaid provides the greatest source. Medicare limits payment for specific treatments that the day-care center may provide. Commercial insurance companies may also reimburse certain outpatient medical services rendered by adult day-care hospital centers. At present, there are attempts in the Senate to remedy this situation. A proposal, known as the Community-Based Long-Term Care Act, targeted at combining all noninstitutional care into one comprehensive system that could eliminate existing financial barriers, including those that limit expansion of adult day-care and inhome services, is expected to be considered in the United States Senate.[6]

In September of 1979, the Illinois Department on Aging began a unique program of home care services to a large population of citizens—all those who are 60 and over and who are in danger of institutionalization—on a statewide basis. No means test (ie, test of indigency) was imposed. Consequently, assessment is based on the level of actual self-care. This is a flexible approach to family support and disability level. This program represents one of the few attempts in the United States at providing a universally available program that is oriented to social functioning rather than legal, professional, or fiscal categories of eligibility.

The community care bill was signed into law in August, 1979, by the 81st General Assembly of the State of Illinois. The statute authorized a wide variety of services from which the Department of Aging selected four that were to be implemented the first year: 1) chore/housekeeping; 2) homemaker; 3) home health; and 4) adult day-care.

Although it is still too early to examine the full impact of this program, it is possible to briefly review some of the implications. From the viewpoint of developing in state government a capability to serve the older adult, the community care program is a success. In terms of cost-effectiveness, no judgment can be made as yet. The uncovering of a large backlog of need, the problems of 3,400 transfer cases, the prevalence of over-eligible cases, and the difficulty in determining if regular home-delivered services really delay the individual's institutionalization all make it difficult to assess the true issues of risk, prevalence, and cost.[7]

Home health care, such as that provided by a visiting nurse association or a private agency, permits citizens to receive health care in the privacy of their own home. Statistics show that within a nine year period, home health agencies in the United States have grown from 1,163 to approximately 2,300 agencies.[*]

Home health agencies can offer a multi-faceted array of services designed to help the client to achieve as much independence as he or she is able to develop or maintain. A complete discussion of this type of care, in the form of an interview with an executive director of a visiting nurse association agency, can be found in Chapter 10, pp 143-144.

Mental health center and hospital day programs offer therapeutic help to troubled elders in the community. An examination of one such center's program is also discussed by its director in Chapter 10, pp 138-141.

Institutions themselves may develop intervention programs that are designed to prevent institutional placement. Such a program is discussed in Chapter 10, pp 154-157, with the psychiatrist who designed and implemented it.

Besides home care and day-care programs, there are a number of alternative living arrangements that offer support to elders in the community. On June 4, 1980, Maggie Kuhn, National Convener and Founder of the Gray Panthers, told members of the House Select Committee on Aging that she believed that families built by choice may be the answer to the changing family patterns that have occurred in recent times. She is one of nine members of an age-integrated household, where the participants range in age from 22 to 75. Kuhn stressed that

*Day-Care Services. Washington DC, Office of Policy, Planning and Evaluation, Medical Services Administration, Social and Rehabilitation Service, US DHEW, 1972.

the young and the old have to be integrated to provide some immunization against gerontophobia—unreasonable fear and hatred of aging. The members of the age-integrated household she belongs to share resources, goals, values, and life styles. In this way a network of mutual responsibility is developed. The family-of-choice lives together cooperatively, but not communally. Thus, in a sense, the traditional extended family has been recreated while still maintaining the needs of mobility and privacy.

The presence of non-related people can provide stability to a household, and can aid in mediating stress on relationships. Kuhn presented a number of resolutions that were related to enhancing the family-of-choice approach. Some of these included: 1) there is a great need to recognize the value and viability of intergenerational living and association; 2) there should be federal initiatives to provide alternatives to age-segregated housing; and 3) federal initiatives should be promoted that aid community groups in the private sector to begin day-care centers that combine programs for old people and children.[8] Certainly, these suggestions could prove to be a viable alternative to institutional segregation.

The concept of the British warden system of minimal service sheltered housing with resident wardens to aid functionally impaired and socially deprived older adults in maintaining privacy and independence has strong implications for utilization in the United States.

How does this system work? The typical sheltered housing arrangement provides separate apartments that are designed to be barrier-free and easy to maintain. Each apartment is connected by either an intercom or alarm system, so that nearby help is readily available. There are at least two communal spaces—a lounge and a laundry room. Support services are provided as needed to help clients maintain their units as they become increasingly more disabled. The resident warden helps to assure that the residents will receive a "proper and consistent flow of peripatetic social services." This is the crux of the program. It is believed that this type of care can provide the same level of support as service-abundant sheltered housing at less cost and less risk of evolving institution-like environments run by and for the convenience of support staff.

The warden, usually a housewife who lives in one of the units with her family, is often defined as a friendly neighbor who is available 24 hours a day. Usually, the warden and the elderly residents come from the same neighborhood and same life style. Wardens have described their role as being somewhere between neighborly and the intimate support that might be expected of a relative. The warden, who is not required to have any special training in nursing or social service at the beginning of the job may: 1) make critical decisions about when or when not to involve family or support services; 2) provide direct support care; 3) organize social activities; 4) provide social counseling; and 5) most importantly, develop an engaging, supportive, and friendly atmosphere in which to live.

The implications for utilization of warden-maintained minimal service sheltered housing programs in the United States are considerable. It appears to be a humane and at the same time a low-cost method for helping to maintain older adults in their neighborhoods. The feasibility of transferring this role model to the United States deserves consideration. Although there are a number of obstacles to overcome (eg, willingness in the United States to build smaller communities—no more than 40 units; a need for a better-developed visiting service system; the heterogeneous population of most American communities as opposed to the traditional British homogeneous population), utilization of a program of this nature may prove fruitful to aging Americans.[9]

References

1. Burger SG, D'Erasno M: Living in a Nursing Home: A Complete Guide for Residents, Their Families, and Friends. New York, Seabury Press, 1976, pp 24, 25, 28, 81-84.
2. Vladeck BC: Unloving Care: The Nursing Home Tragedy . New York, Basic Books, 1980.
3. Horn L, Griesal E: Nursing Homes: A Citizen's Action Guide: How to Organize, Plan, and Achieve Nursing Home Reform in Your Community. Boston, Beacon Press, 1977, pp 33, 114-115.
4. What Do You Want to Be When You Grow Old? New York, Roering Pfizer, May, 1976, p ii.
5. Brody E: High risk groups among the elderly, their families and their communities. In Serving High Risk Groups Among the Elderly, Families, and their Community. Madison, WI, Univ Wisconsin Extension Department of Social Work, 1972, pp 3-19.
6. Kodner LD: Day care offers options for elderly. New York Times, May 15, 1980, pp C1, C8.
7. Taker MA, Anderson S, Rogers JC: Implementing community care in Illinois: Issues of cost and targeting in a statewide program. Gerontologist 20:380-387, 1980.
8. Steele L (ed): Choice for the old: Kuhn. Guidepost 23:1, 6, 1980.
9. Heuman LF: Sheltered housing for the elderly: The role of the British warden. Gerontologist 20:318-329, 1980.

Appendix C

Improving Attitudes Towards Aging

The most significant thing about quality care is the attitude with which it is rendered. Sometimes, something that was intended for a caring and thoughtful purpose can be utilized, often unintentionally, in such a way that degradation is the result. For those who are concerned with retaining the dignity of the older person, there is a need to be able to recognize when this occurs. A positive approach, including an attitude of hopeful rehabilitation, can often help to dispel this problem. Constant alertness for attitudes that foster dependency and paternalism is the key.

L.H. Snyder aptly gives an example of how a device, the geriatric wheelchair, which was created solely for the betterment of the frail elderly individual, has come to be used to restrict that person's independence and individuality. The geri-chair, with wheels of three- to five-inches in diameter, cannot be moved by the occupant. Designed to provide additional physical support for the frail person, this chair has had a number of negative spin-off effects that have created social barriers. Some of these are that its higher seat and elongated backrest restricts peripheral and rear vision; its height from the floor makes footrests necessary, and in turn creates obstacles, as they are unwieldy, plus they have to be moved whenever the person gets in and out; due to its size, it can only be placed in areas with a great deal of room; and the table-tray which can be attached across the front of the chair can be used to restrain the activity of the elder. In fact, some institutions refer to this type of equipment as a restraining chair. In actuality, the geri-chair has been used to compensate for the side-effects of psychotropic drugs, which cause poor balance, shortages in staffing and volunteer resources, and for putting off working effectively with a person who exhibits wandering behavior.

Psychologically and socially there are, unfortunately, a number of other negative results. Staff members, other residents, and visitors often assume that persons in the geriatric wheelchair are sicker than other people. Investigators have commented that many of the aged infirm who use these chairs experience a loss of self-esteem. "Perhaps the geriatric wheelchair which looks much like a baby's highchair, adds to this aura of dependence."[1]

Despite the problems associated with this piece of equipment, Snyder presents a number of suggestions that can be helpful in overcoming a number of the previously mentioned negative outcomes. These include the following recommendations:

1) Use the chair without the tray-table; wheel the individual up to a standard table.

2) Learn to see the chair as for transportational use only. Once in the desired area, change the person into a more traditional seat.

3) Check to make certain that elders in the geri-chair have access to television, windows, and other types of visual options.

4) Arrange congregate seating in such a way that the person in this type of chair can have an increased access to joining the group.[1]

Reference

1. Snyder LH: Living environments, geriatric wheelchairs and the older person's rehabilitation. J Gerontological Nurs 1:18, 19, 1975.

Appendix D

A Consciousness-Raising
Training Program Concerning Aging*

Objectives

Specific objectives are to:

— become aware of the role of advocacy in rendering service to the older
person;

— identify a number of social concerns that affect the older person;

— compare society's views on aging with personal views;

— identify and discuss some of the primary diseases that affect the older adult;

— describe and discuss specific physical changes that occur during the aging
process;

— describe and discuss contributions made by elders; and

— identify and discuss the effect of institutionalization upon the older person.

*© 1980. Sandra Cutler Lewis, MFA, OTR. All rights reserved.

Part One

Time: 20 minutes
Equipment needed: A blackboard, chalk, eraser, paper, and pencils.
Group size: Recommended range four to 40 participants.

The trainer states the following: "Within the next two minutes, write down all the characteristics or thoughts that come to your mind when you hear the words 'old person'. Begin writing."

At the end of the two minutes the trainer says, "Stop writing. I am now going to ask each one of you what you have written." The trainer proceeds to ask each participant what he has written, and records this on the blackboard. However, a specific characteristic need only be written once. The characteristics are then compared and discussed in terms of what is commonly considered by today's society as having positive or negative attributes.

This exercise explores attitudes towards the older person that most people hold. It offers a time for reflection, expression, and understanding of long-held beliefs in terms of society's values. For instance, a discussion concerning a comparison of a young face (smooth skin and full hair color) to an old face (wrinkled skin and gray hair) reveals that our society, based upon youth orientation, often regards the aging process as undesirable. The cosmetic industry has developed a number of options (ie, hair dye, lotions to smooth the skin) for those people who wish to camouflage the signs of aging.

Part Two

Time: 50 minutes for the test; 75 minutes for discussion
Equipment needed: Question sheets, separate answer sheets, and pencils.

The trainer hands out the question sheets and states, "I will give you question sheets that can be answered by circling either true or false. Please write the rationale for your answer in the space provided after the questions. This is an ungraded test that is designed to be a vehicle for information and discussion in promoting awareness of the problems, needs, and achievements of the elderly. You will have 50 minutes to complete this form. At the end of the test there will be time for comparison and discussion. Correct fact sheets with appropriate references will be given for you to use as a resource."

The trainer hands out the question sheets and pencils and says, "You may begin."

Questions

1. There is very little evidence that parent abuse/neglect exists in this country.
   True   False
   Comments:

2. Humor directed towards the elderly often depicts them as being unable to function sexually, ultra-conservative, mentally incompetent, and possessing many physical infirmities.

   True   False

   Comments:

3. Few older adults feel the need to use cosmetics to alter their image and look young.

   True   False

   Comments:

4. Privacy in an institutional or nursing home setting can be an important component in helping the resident maintain a sense of self.

   True   False

   Comments:

5. Listening to older people tell stories about the "good old days" is harmful, as they should learn to live in the present and forget the past.

   True   False

   Comments:

6. Work provides a number of satisfactions. When a person retires, new activities should be sought that offer similar satisfactions.

   True   False

   Comments:

7. Increasing numbers of older adults (65 to 75) are now attending to their very old (85+) parents.

   True   False

   Comments:

8. Although the Older Americans Act was designed to develop a number of programs that help the elderly, some critics point out that new problems have emerged that affect service.

   True   False

   Comments:

9. Today's older person does not seek career changes or possess an interest in lifelong learning.

   True   False

   Comments:

10. It is unlikely to assume that older people past 60 years of age have an active interest in sex.

    True   False

    Comments:

11. Glare and loss of ability to adapt to sudden changes of light intensity are two major problems that confront the older adult.

    True   False

    Comments:

12. Sensorineural hearing loss is not characteristic of the type of degeneration that takes place during the aging process.

    True   False

    Comments:

13. A younger person's capacity to increase production of body heat in a cold environment and to dissipate body heat in a warm environment is greater than an older person's capacity.

    True   False

    Comments:

14. By the age of 60 most persons have lost 50% of their taste buds.
    True   False
    Comments:

15. Older women outlive older men and outnumber them by a ratio of 3:1.
    True   False
    Comments:

16. One's ability to perceive changes in body orientation and body positioning in space decrease little during the aging process.
    True   False
    Comments:

17. Approximately one half of elderly men and women with severe intellectual impairment suffer from Alzheimer's disease.
    True   False
    Comments:

18. Eighty-six percent of older people have at least one form of chronic health problem.
    True   False
    Comments:

19. The incidence of depressive illness has a tendency to remain the same as one ages.
    True   False
    Comments:

20. In terms of chronic disease, the following conditions are ranked respectively in order of their prevalence—cerebral vascular disease, arthritis, and Parkinson's disease.

   True   False

   Comments:

21. Ninety-five percent of the elderly do not live in institutional settings.

   True   False

   Comments:

22. Only 5% of older adults' income comes from public assistance programs.

   True   False

   Comments:

23. Because of negative attitudes toward aging, large companies continue to refuse to hire the older executive.

   True   False

   Comments:

24. Marc Chagall, Arthur Rubenstein, Benjamin Franklin, Imogen Cunningham, George Burns, Grandma Moses, Pablo Picasso, Joan Miro', and I.B. Singer have one thing in common—because of the aging process they were not able to continue to be active past the age of 65.

   True   False

   Comments:

25. There is no new incentive for the advertising media to become interested in the older consumer.

   True   False

   Comments:

Answers

1. **False.** Parent abuse/neglect problems are beginning to surface as a real and deeply serious condition besetting the American family. The abuse can range from verbal threats to physical assault.

   Source: Langway L, Zabarsk M, Hager M, Huch J: Unveiling a family secret. Newsweek, February 18, 1980, pp 104-105.

2. **True.** In a recent study of 2,217 cartoons that appeared in a variety of American magazines, the following negative themes regarding the elderly recurred frequently: sexual dysfunction, ultra-conservative attitudes, mental incompetency, and physical infirmities.

   Source: Smith MD: The portrayal of elders in magazine cartoons. Gerontologist 19, 408-412, 1979.

3. **False.** Many cosmetic firms spend millions of dollars in developing rinses and dyes that will hide the "tell-tale gray". This is supported by numerous advertisements.

   Source: Lewis SC: The Mature Years: A Geriatric Occupational Therapy Text. Thorofare, NJ, Charles B Slack, Inc, 1979, p 4.

4. **True.** A person's privacy is important and can be reflected in terms of sexual modesty and individuality. Too often in a number of nursing homes, privacy is ignored because they are "just old people."

   Source: Broderick C: Sexuality and aging: An overview. In Solnick R (ed): Sexuality and Aging. Los Angeles, University of California Press, The Ethel Percy Andrus Gerontology Center, 1978, p 6.

5. **False.** According to Butler, "The life review is conceived of as a naturally occurring universal mental process characterized by the progressive return to consciousness of past experiences, and particularly, the resurgence of unresolved conflicts; simultaneously and normally, these revived experiences and conflicts are surveyed and reintegrated."

   Source: Butler RN: The life review: An interpretation of reminiscence in the aged. In Kastenbaum R (ed): New Thoughts on Old Age. New York, Springer Pub Co Inc, 1964, p 266.

6. **True.** According to the theories of Friedman and Havighurst, work provides the following five universal functions: income; regulates life activity; offers identification and status; provides opportunities to associate with others; and makes available opportunities for a meaningful life experience. Upon retirement, it is important that the retiree find new activities that offer similar satisfactions to what the worker had experienced during the employment years.

   Source: Barron ML: The Aging American: An Introduction to Social Gerontology and Geriatrics. New York, Thomas Y Crowell Co, 1961, pp 78, 189.

7. **True.** Increasing numbers of older adults (65 to 75) are now attending their very old (85+) parents. The phenomena of a population that was once considered older in its own right, has produced a group of care givers to even older parents.

Source: Bennett A: Aging Americans: Caring for the elderly greatly changes lives of many US families. Wall Street Journal, November 16, 1979, pp 1, 4.

8. **True.** Caroll Estes warns that it is the aging enterprise and not older Americans that have become the focus of government policy.

Source: Estes C: The Aging Enterprise. San Francisco, Jossy-Bass, Inc, 1979.

9. **False.** Many older adults are now actively seeking instruction in areas that will promote second career changes. Thousands of older persons are taking advantage of lifelong learning.

Source: Hechinger FM: Education's new majority. Saturday Review. September 20, 1975, pp 14-19.

10. **False.** There are many reasons why adults over 60 participate in an active sex life. Some of these are: an opportunity for expression of passion, loyalty, affection, and admiration; an affirmation of one's body and its functioning; the pleasure of being caressed; or an affirmation of life. Sayings such as: "There may be snow on the roof, but there's still fire in the furnace," are an affirmation of the older person's determination to denounce the stereotype of grandma and grandpa sitting in their rockers on the porch watching life go by.

Source: Butler RN, Lewis MI: Sex After Sixty: A Guide for Men and Women in Later Years. New York, Harper and Row, 1976, p 136.

11. **True.** During a person's lifetime the size of the lens increases gradually. By age 80 it is 50% larger than at age 20. Consequently, less light is able to reach the retina. This results in the older person being unable to adapt to sudden light changes and glare.

Source: Shore H: Designing a training program for understanding sensory loss in aging. Gerontologist 16:15, 1976, p 165.

12. **False.** Sensorineural hearing loss is characteristic of the type of degenerative loss that most elderly people experience. In this condition there is damage to some of the nerve endings in the cochlea. Consequently, the ear responds to sounds in an uneven manner, and there is loss of the ability to discriminate high frequency sounds, such as the consonants s, t, p, and k.

Source: Battle D: A speech therapist considers speech and hearing problems for the elderly. In Deichman ES, O'Kane CP (eds): Working with the Elderly: A Training Manual. Buffalo, DOK Pub, Inc, pp 51-53.

13. **True.** It has been established that older adults are less able than younger ones to maintain a constant body temperature when exposed to a cold or hot environment.

Source: Colavita FB: Sensory Changes in the Elderly. Springfield, IL, Charles C Thomas, 1978, p 82.

14. **True.** By the age of 60 most persons have lost 50% of their taste buds. Research demonstrates that the taste buds in the front of the tongue where salt and sweet are located, atrophy first. As a result, many older persons complain that their food may have a bitter or sour taste.

Source: Shore H: Designing a training program for understanding sensory losses in aging. Gerontologist 16:157-165, 1976.

15. **True.** Older women outlive older men and outnumber them by a ratio of 3:1.
    Source: Butler RN, Lewis M: Aging and Mental Health: Positive Psychosocial Approaches. St Louis, CV Mosby Co, 1973, pp 29-30.

16. **False.** There is a decrease of the kinesthetic sense as one ages. These changes may be due to neurological and neuromuscular dysfunction. There is a decline in muscular strength and tone, and disturbance of body mechanisms. To compensate, many older adults may change their gait pattern: greater time is needed in ground contact.
    Source: Shore H: Designing a training program for understanding sensory losses in aging. Gerontologist 16:157-165, 1976.

17. **True.** Alzheimer's disease, once thought to occur mostly in people under age 65, is now recognized as the most common cause of severe intellectual impairment in older people. Approximately one half of elderly people with severe cognitive deficits are thought to have Alzheimer's disease.
    Source: Alzheimer's Disease. Washington, DC, US DHEW, NIH Publication No 79-1646, September, 1979.

18. **True.** Eighty-six percent of older adults have at least one form of chronic health problem. Many elderly people experience two, three, or even four diseases or areas of dysfunction at the same time.
    Source: Butler RN, Lewis MI: Aging and Mental Health: Positive Psychosocial Approaches. St Louis, CV Mosby Co, 1973, pp 34, 50-60, 69, 74-80.

19. **False.** The incidence of depressive illness tends to increase with age, especially in the 75 to 85 age bracket where suicides account for 27.9 deaths per 100,000 population.
    Source: Kastenbaum R, Aisenberg R: The Psychology of Death. New York, Springer Pub Co, Inc, 1972, p 252.

20. **True.** Cerebral vascular disease, arthritis, and Parkinson's disease are ranked in order of their prevalence.
    Source: Davis JC: Team management of Parkinson's disease. J Am Occup Ther 31: 300-303, 1977.

21. **True.** Approximately 5% of the elderly live in institutions.
    Source: Rabushka A, Jacobs B: Are old folks really poor? Here with a look at some common views. New York Times, February 15, 1980, p A29.

22. **True.** Only 5% of an elderly person's income is derived from public assistance programs.
    Source: What Do You Want to Be When You Grow Old? New York, Roering-Pfizer Pharmaceuticals, May, 1976, p 11.

23. **False.** As economic and marketing uncertainties continue, a number of larger companies are hiring the more seasoned executive. For instance, William M. Batten, 67, former chairman of the J.C. Penney Co., was called out of retirement to become Chairman of the New York Stock Exchange. John L. Hanigan, 65, was hired as Chief Executive of Genesco, Inc.
    Source: Barmash I: New jobs for old hands. New York Times, May 29, 1977, pp C1-C7.

24. **False.** Each one of the outstanding world contributors mentioned continued to work well past the age of 65.

   Source: The local library—look under biography.
25. **False.** Older persons have become a lucrative market. Several magazines, such as *Prime Time, 50+,* and *Modern Maturity* cater to the mature reader. *Cineamerica,* a new cable TV station, is scheduled to begin programming for those over 50.

   Source: A magazine for the over 45 set. Newsweek, December 31, 1979, p 50.

Part Three

Time: Approximately 100 minutes (seven minutes per cartoon).

Materials needed: A copy of the set of 14 cartoons for each participant.

The trainer states the following: "The use of the cartoon, or the caricature, has been helpful in stimulating people to think about political and social conditions. The lithographs of the great French artist, Honore' Daumier, are constant reminders of the use of professional power over the lay person. Although they are over 100 years old, many of these works, depicting injustice, are as fresh and vital today as the day they were first created.

"American culture has utilized the cartoon as a way of poking fun at current life styles and attitudes. Today, we are going to view 14 cartoons that were especially created to help us think about some of the problems that older people encounter in the community and in institutional living. These cartoons in no way reflect upon a single institution, agency, center, or profession. Rather, their purpose is to shock us into an in-depth examination of current attitudes and practices that relate to the older adult. Care givers, in particular, have a vital role to play, and need to think of themselves not only in terms of rendering services, but also in terms of assuming an advocate role.

"Each cartoon will be viewed separately and a brief discussion will follow."

1. **Compliment?** (Read statement as participants view cartoon.)

In our culture, youth and beauty are considered to be synonymous. If someone wants to pay a compliment to an older adult, he will often say how young that person looks. If one could learn to say, "Gee, Mrs. Y, you look great," and eliminate any reference to young or old, then perhaps ageism would wane.
Discussion:

COMPLIMENT?

2. 20th Century America

Here again, we see the effects of a culture that worships the youthful body. Constant advertisements on television and in other communication media remind us that gray is ugly—something that needs to be camouflaged. Is it a crime to be old? Why does our society make people feel ashamed of wrinkled bodies and graying hair?

Discussion:

20th Century America

3. Taking Advantage

Street crime has become a constant fear of many elderly. The slow gait and bent frame that is often associated with aging makes many older adults easy targets for purse or wallet snatching. Because of this fear, a growing number of older people have become afraid to venture out at night or to use public parks.

Discussion:

4. **Easy Prey**

Swindling old people out of their savings by promising them great returns on their investments, "full" retirement programs, and full health coverage through a multitude of health insurance policies has become the practice of many people who believe that the elderly are vulnerable to such action.

Discussion:

5. Boarding House Blues

For financial reasons many older adults end their days in retirement hotels or boarding homes. Often they are limited as to what they can bring with them, and cherished mementos of a lifetime may have to be discarded.

Discussion:

6. Never Taken Seriously

For many younger people, sex and the elderly seem to be an unrealistic concern. Instead, older adult relationships are often thought of in terms of a young boy and girl—sort of sexless and "cute."

Discussion:

7. End of the Line

With the decline of the extended family and the rise of the nuclear, increasing numbers of at-risk older adults are being cared for in institutions. A large number of these facilities use names that evoke thoughts of a paradise-like lifestyle. Many older people who need the services of a medical facility feel that they are being abandoned by their family, friends, and society, and fear the very thought of institutional living.

Discussion:

8. The New Case

A new arrival to a care facility may feel shy, disoriented, angry, or frightened. Even when well-intended questions to discover the extent of a disability are asked, the new resident may not be able to respond appropriately.

Discussion:

THE NEW CASE

9. A Question of Taste and Expectation

The elderly resident is not often thought of in terms of being able to react sexually. Therefore, many staff members may not be aware that their manners or clothing style might sexually arouse their clients.
Discussion:

10. Quiet Isn't Deaf

There are times when well-meaning staff may talk about a resident—who appears to be unresponsive—in his presence. Often, staff personnel may not realize that although this person does not act responsively, he may be perfectly capable of understanding all that is being said.

Discussion:

Quiet Isn't Deaf

11. Activities?

Activities for older adults should not be an echo of childhood. Instead, they should be thought of in terms of stimulation and challenge. Staff should ask the question, "Would I like this for myself?" Activities should concur with the resident's ability and ethnic background, and should have some prestigious value to the client.

Discussion:

12. The Trouble Maker

Living in institutions usually means following the rules of the facility. Sometimes it is difficult to individualize and respond to each resident's request. Behavior that is interpreted as disoriented may be a reflection upon the resident's inability to cope with the restrictions of institutional living. The geri-chair is often used to help restrain confused, disoriented, wandering residents, particularly those who have a history of falls.

Discussion:

THE TROUBLE MAKER

13. Patient Input

When talking to older people with multiple problems, staff needs to speak slowly and clearly, and wait for the older person's response so that they may have a true opportunity to participate in their own treatment plan.

Discussion:

14. Paper, Paper, Paper

Paperwork involving both documentation of progress notes and the completion of private and public health forms has increasingly cut in on staff/client time.

Discussion:

PAPER - PAPER - PAPER

Index

A

Accidental Hypothermia, 71
Accommodation (visual), 46
Action and Advocacy groups for older adults, 91
Adult children and older parents (literature), 121
Adult day-care centers, 168, 172
Adult day hospitals, 172
Advocacy, 8, 170
Aging,
  biological, 27
  chronological, 27
  primary, 37
  psychological, 27
  secondary, 38
  sociological, 27
Aging Americans, 5
Albee, E, 3
Alzheimer, A, 61
Alzheimer's disease, 61, 123
American Association of Retired Persons (AARP), 91, 117
Amine, 56

B

Burns, G, 8
Butler, RN, 5, 63, 115
Butyrophenones, 57

C

Camacho, H, 14, 15
Cancer, 70
Cardiovascular system, 42, 43
Cataracts, 46
Cerebral infarctions, 67
Cerebral vascular accident (stroke), 67, 68
Chagall, M, 8
Changing roles, 88
Ciliary muscle, 46
Clark, MA, 85, 86
Clergy (Theology), 136
Climacteric, 41
Cochlea, 44-45
Communication process, 159-163
    body positioning, (movement), 163
    conveying understanding, (responding with understanding), 164
    cultural determinants (attire, color, distancing), 159-160
    gesturing, 159
    listening, 163
    non-verbal behavior, 163
    physical attending, 163
    psychological attending, 163
    responding skills, 164
    rules of address, 161
    self-disclosure, 161, 162
    silence, 163
    speaking (voice quality) 163
    touch, 159
    transaction chain, 160

Communication programs, 99-112
    attitude therapy, 102
    communicating with the hearing impaired, 108
    communicating with the visually impaired, 110-112
    communication with the aphasic, 109
    life review, 106, 107
    opportunities for increased learning, 104
    reality orientation, 101-102
    remotivation, 103
    senior center humanities program, 105

unilateral visual/perceptual neglect, 69
uremia, 74
Dopamine, 57
Dynamic Spatial Reconstructor (DSR), 62

E

Egnal, A, 16-18
Egnal, L, 18
Eisenhower, DD, 96
Electron microscope, 61
Elum, B, 20
Embolism, 68
Emphysema, 70
Endorphines, 57
Enkephalins, 57
Epstein, C, 132
Evaluations/assessments, 63, 113-115
Exercise, 49-52
    exercise resources, 52
    program, 50, 51
    therapeutic goals, 50, 51

F

Fabun, D, 160
Fallica, A, 52
Families-of-choice living arrangement, 174
Farina, A, 115
Federal Register, 96
Ferrara, A, 143-144
Fey-Greger, D, 149-151
Fink, M, 114
Flextime, 6
Folsom, J, 101
Folstein, MF, 115
Folstein, SE, 115
Food Scientist/Food Science and nutrition, 146-148
Fraud (and the elderly), 6
Frazer, DW, 138-141
Freakany, GA, 51
Freudenberg, DT, 151-153
Friedman, EA, 86

G

Gallbladder disease, 73
Garfunkel, A, 3

Human sexuality, 41, 42, 149-151
Hyperthermia, 72
Hypochondriacal neuroses, 58
Hypothermia, Accidental, 71, 72
Hypotonia, 41
Hysterical neuroses, 58

I

Immobilization, 72
Intermediate care facility, 169
Intervention programs (alternatives to institutionalization), 172, 173
Interview with an adult child caretaker, 129-132
Interviews with older adults, 12-25
    Camacho, H, 14-16
    Egnal, A, 16-18
    Egnal, L, 18
    Elum, B, 20-21
    Korr, M, 12-13
    Niebuhr, KD, 24-25
    retired high school teacher, 18-20
    retired motel owner and manager, 21-22
    retired university professor, professor emeritus, 13-14
    Thoenebe, HS, 22-24
Interviews with professionals who serve the elderly, 138-157
    Dailey, JG, nursing home administrator, 141-142
    Ferrara, A, executive director of a visiting nurse association, 143-144
    Fey-Greger, D, human sexuality counselor, 149-151
    Frazer, DW, psychologist, 138-141
    Freudenberg, DT, physiatrist, 151-153
    Keisler, S, art therapist, 145-146
    Levine, R, occupational therapist, 142-143
    Palumbo, MS, food scientist, 146-148
    Reed, P, college counselor, 144-145
    Sherr, VT, psychiatrist, 155-157
    Treatman, H, social worker, 153-155
Intraocular lens implant, 46
Intrinsicality, 37
Involutional melancholia, 56
Ischemia, 67

J

Jeffers, FC, 79

K

Kahn, RL, 115

Murphy, E, 114
Muscular system, 41
Myocardial infarction, 67

N

National Cancer Institute, 81
National Citizen Coalition for Nursing Home Reform, 120
National Institute of Aging, 5, 62, 81, 82, 94, 121, 122
National Institute of Health, 49, 122
National Institute of Mental Health, 122, 94
Nervous system, 41
Neugarten, BL, 34, 115
Newsletters and periodicals, 123
Niebuhr, KD, 24-25
Nixon, RM, 96
Norepinephrine, 56, 57
Nursing, interview with an executive director of a visiting nurse association, 143-144
Nursing home administrator/administration (interview), 141-142
Nursing homes, 169, 170, 171, 172
    extended care facility, 169
    intermediate care facility, 169
    non-proprietary, 169
    nursing home reform, 170, 171, 172
    personal care home, 169
    proprietary, 169
    skilled nursing care facility, 169
Nutrition (interview with a food scientist), 146-148

O

Obsessive-compulsive neurosis, 58
Occlusion, 68
Occupational Outlook Handbook, 137
Occupational Outlook Quarterly, 136
Occupational therapist (interview of), 142, 143
Older Americans Act, 5, 92
    Title I, 92
    Title II, 92
    Title III, 92
    Title IV, 92
    Title V, 92
    Title VI, 93
    Title VII, 93
    Title VIII, 93
    Title IX, 93

Title X, 93, 94
Olfactory epithelium, 47
O'Keefe, G, 8
Omnibus Budget Reconciliation Act of 1981, 95
Organic brain syndrome, 59, 60
Organizations associated with elderly concerns, 116-121
Osteoarthritis, 64, 65
Osteoporosis, 66
Osteosclerosis, 45

P

Pacinian corpuscles, 48
Palmore, E, 133
Palumbo, MS, 146-148
Parachek, JF, 115
Paranoid states, 58
Paraphasia, 69
Parent abuse, 4
Parkinson's disease, 63, 64
Patient's Bill of Rights, 169
Peck, A, 63, 115
Periodicals and Newsletters, 123
Perlen, S, 63, 115
Personality disorders, 58
Pfeiffer, E, 63
Phenothiazines, 57
Phobic neuroses, 58
Physical conditioning, 49-52
    exercise program, 51
    exercise resources, 52
    safe exercising pulse rate, 49, 50
    therapeutic exercise goals, 50, 51
Physiatrist, interview with, 151-153
Piaget, J, 28-30
Picasso, P, 8
Pick's disease, 60
Plantinectomy, 45
Plutchik, R, 114
Pollack, M, 63
Polyuria, 43
Position Emission Tomography (PET), 63, 68
Presbycusis, 45
Presbyopia, 46
Presenile dementia, 60
Problem solving, 164

Third party payers, 96
Thoenebe, H, 22-24
Thrombosis, 68
Timmins, LE, 164
Tinnitus, 45
Tobin, SS, 34
Training Programs, 132-133
Transaction chain, 160
Treatman, H, social worker, 153-155
Treatment plans, 116
Truman, HS, 96

U

Unilateral visual/perceptual neglect, 69
United States Sub-Committee on Long Term Care, 171
Universality, 37
University of Michigan-Wayne State University, 132
Uremia, 74
Urinary tract, 43

V

Verwoerdt, A, 79
Vladeck, BC, 167

W

Wall, P, 49
Wall Street Journal, 5
Warden living arrangement (British minimal service sheltered housing), 174,
    175
Weiner, MB, 115
Weisman, AD, 79
White House Conferences on Aging, 96
Work, the five universal functions, 86
Workshops, preparation and presentation of, 127-133

Y

Yavris syndrome, 138